This visual diary is dedicated to my husband, C. William Crain, who first took me to China in 1977 and has given me a lifetime of support and encouragement to follow my dreams.

谨将此书献给我的丈夫——威廉·柯雷,是他1977年第一次将我带到中国,并在我的追梦途中给了我毕生的支持和鼓励。

Sharon Crain　雪莲

亲历巨变
Witness to Change
一位美国女性眼中的当代中国
After Mao to Now

Sharon Crain （美）雪莲 著

吴进 译

陕西师范大学出版社
Shaanxi Normal University Press

图书代号　SK9N0903

图书在版编目(CIP)数据

亲历巨变——一位美国女性眼中的当代中国／（美）雪莲著；
吴进译.—西安：陕西师范大学出版社，2009.9
ISBN 978-7-5613-4845-1

Ⅰ.亲…　Ⅱ.①雪…②吴…　Ⅲ.改革开放-成就-中国
Ⅳ.D61

中国版本图书馆CIP数据核字（2009）第155704号

书　　　名	亲历巨变——一位美国女性眼中的当代中国
图书作者	Sharon Crain　（美）雪　莲
译　　者	吴　进
出 版 人	高经纬
统筹策划	孙冰红　雷永利　李卫东
责任编辑	雷永利　曾学民
责任校对	安　雄　王　岚
书籍装帧	陕西吉人广告设计有限公司

出版发行	陕西师范大学出版社
社　　址	西安市长安南路199号
邮政编码	710062
网　　址	http：//www.snupg.com
经　　销	新华书店
印　　刷	西安煤航信息产业有限公司

开　　本	787mm×1092mm　1/16
印　　张	17
字　　数	200千字
图　　片	209幅
版　　次	2009年9月第1版
印　　次	2010年1月第2次印刷
印　　数	1501～4500
书　　号	ISBN 978-7-5613-4845-1
定　　价	98.00元

读者购书、书店添货或发现印刷装订问题，请与本社印务中心联系、调换。
联系电话：(029) 85255630　85303890

I would like to congratulate Sharon Crain on the publication of her pictorial album *Witness to Change* in China.

Sharon is one of my best friends. As a scholar and a social activist, she started to get involved in China studies four decades ago and became a good friend of Helen Foster Snow who is my beloved friend.

I have known Sharon for about thirty years. Sharon's sincere efforts in promoting the friendship and mutual understanding between the people of China and the United States are much appreciated and admired. This book reflects vividly the progress and development of China in the latest 30 years and also shows Sharon's passion and warm feelings towards the Chinese people. I am sure that it will appeal to those who are interested in knowing more about China and I am convinced that people will love this book.

衷心祝贺雪莲女士的图片集《亲历巨变》的出版。

雪莲是我最好的朋友之一。作为学者和社会活动家，她在40年前就开始涉足中国研究，后来又成为我的挚友海伦·福斯特·斯诺的好友。

我认识雪莲已经30年了，她在增进中美人民的友谊和相互了解方面所作的真诚努力让我深感钦佩。这本书生动地反映了过去30年中国的进步和发展，也展示了雪莲对中国人民的深厚情谊。我相信这本书对那些希望更多地了解中国的人们是有感染力的，也确信人们将喜欢它。

Huang Hua 黄华

I am deeply impressed after reading the photo collection book done by Sharon Crain. I have known her for more than two decades. Her book vividly shows part of the great changes that have taken place since China adopted the policy of opening up and reform thirty years ago. Sharon is one of the bridge builders of friendship between peoples of China and the United States. I hope that many more Chinese and American readers of this book will join her rank in promoting mutual understanding and friendship between our two great nations.

雪莲的图片集给我留下了深刻印象。我认识雪莲已经20多年了。她的书生动地反映了改革开放30年来中国发生的巨大变化。雪莲是中美两国人民之间友谊之桥的建设者。我希望她的书会使更多的中美读者加入到她的行列中，推动我们两个伟大国家间的相互理解和友谊。

Ling Qing

Foreword 1　　序

  2007年9月，我在"三秦友谊奖"颁奖会上初见雪莲女士。在此之前，我是通过有关媒体对雪莲女士有所了解，知道她是西安——堪萨斯友好城市的主要发起人，陕西师范大学的名誉教授，陕西人民的老朋友。

  多年来，雪莲女士致力于推进中美友好交流与合作事业，为中美友好事业做了许多有益的事情。比如，她促进了更多的美国公民来访，加强了更多的中美地方团体、非政府组织之间的交流，特别是在美国民间与陕西民间的交流取得了突出成就。在她的积极努力下，我省户县农民画走出国门，在美国堪萨斯市展出并获得成功。当然，雪莲女士的努力也赢得了陕西人民的尊敬，2007年，她获得了陕西省人民政府授予的"三秦友谊奖"。

  雪莲女士是美国著名的学者型作家，她致力于研究中国历史，广泛传播中国文化，有效促进了美国民众对中国的了解。难能可贵的是，雪莲女士十分关注中国的教育事业，尤其是陕西的教育事业。作为陕西师范大学名誉教授，她推进了陕西师大与美国高校教师的交流与交换；她组织向陕西师大图书馆捐赠了近2000册图书。此外，她还在陕西师大发起成立了雪莲英语俱乐部，设立个人捐资的"追梦奖学金"等等。雪莲女士情系陕西、情系教育的行为，体现了她的高尚情操和炽热情怀，她的行为是师德的一种广播与弘扬。

  从1977年算起，雪莲女士深入中国已有三十余载，在其教学、工作之余，她以陕西为驻足地，足迹遍及中国大江南北，用相机与文字记录了一位国际友人眼中发展的中国，奋进的中国。如今，这份饱含深情的图片集就要出版了，而且，雪莲女士的这本图片集被中国新闻出版总署列为"庆祝新中国成立60周年百种重点图书"选题。这真是一件可喜可贺的事情，相信它的问世能够让更多的海外朋友了解中国和中国改革开放的伟大成就，也相信朋友们会喜欢这本书。

  是为序。

陕西省省长　袁纯清

二〇〇九年八月九日

Foreword 2 序 2

三十年，六株玉兰
——序雪莲女士《亲历巨变——一位美国女性眼中的当代中国》

2007年11月，一位关注中国、热爱师大的美国女性——雪莲女士在长安校区文渊楼边植下一株玉兰，纪念自己访华三十周年；她说，这是她在陕西师大栽下的第六株玉兰。三十年，六株玉兰，见证着陕西师大与一位文化交流使者之间的深厚感情。因此可以说，雪莲女士是陕西师大的老朋友了。

1982年，她第一次来到陕西师大任教，之后，她多次到陕西师大访问和讲学。1997年，在她的直接帮助下，陕西师大成立了雪莲英语俱乐部，并陆续收到来自雪莲女士本人及海外人士的现金和图书捐赠。为鼓励学生对理想的追求，她捐资设立了"追梦奖学金"。从1997年至今，雪莲女士共捐赠图书近2000册，价值人民币10000余元。目前，俱乐部已经在新老校区拥有了两个机构，而且成为学校最具活力的学生社团之一。1999年雪莲女士被陕西师大聘为客座教授。二十七年来，雪莲女士先后与陕西师大五位校长友好往来，与师生建立了亲密的关系，为学校的建设与发展作出了卓越贡献。

作为文化使者，1977年雪莲女士首次来到中国。此后的三十年间，她访华十余次，不遗余力地奔走于中美两国之间，致力于中华文化在美国的交流与传播。她使得越来越多的美国人走进中国、认识中国、热爱中国，她是新时期中美友好关系的架桥人。雪莲女士担任着美国威灵基金会主席，对中国的心理健康服务事业也作出了很大的贡献。她还是华美协进社理事，1979年中美建交后，为第一批赴美留学生制定了"中国学者培养计划"。

1989年春，雪莲女士作为堪萨斯—西安姊妹城市协会主席，亲随堪萨斯市市长来到西安，正式签订了堪萨斯—西安"姊妹城市"协议。此后，为推动两个城市的友好交流，她发起并推动了多项意义深远的活动，如促成了中国户县农民画在美国的展出，参与推进中国农村地区教育工程的建设等等。她还同电影纪录片制作人Vladimir Bibic出品了两部关于中国的教育影片《中国乡村的变化》和《历史视阈下的现代中国》，后者曾荣获美国电影金鹰奖。

她的这种无私奉献的精神，赢得了中国人民和美国人民的尊重与赞誉。2002年，她被授予"户县荣誉农民"的称号。2007年，又被授予陕西省"安上村荣誉村民"称号。2007年，雪莲女士获得由袁纯清省长颁发的"三秦友谊奖"。需要说明的是，该奖项是陕西省人民政府向国外友人颁发的最高奖项。

雪莲女士与陕西师大、与西安、与陕西省、与中国交往的三十年，也是中国改革开放，经济社会飞速发展的三十年。三十年来，她与中国人民一起见证了共和国改革开放的艰辛与喜悦，并以特别的方式参与和推进着中国的发展，以独特的视角和镜头记录着中国的改革画卷。2007年10月，雪莲女士在陕西师大长安校区图书馆举办个人摄影展，展示了一个外国人眼中中国三十年的历史变迁。

时逢共和国六十华诞之际，陕西师大支持雪莲女士将摄影展的作品汇集成《亲历巨变——一位美国女性眼中的当代中国》，并由陕西师范大学出版社安排出版。这一方面是对改革开放三十年来中国和陕西师大发展的回顾与展望，另一方面也是为感念雪莲女士为陕西师大、为西安、为陕西省、为中国三十年来所作的贡献。书中绝大多数照片都是由雪莲女士亲自拍摄、收集并整理，内容包括中国的变迁、影响中国变化的重要人物、中美关系的改变、陕西师大等。雪莲女士从感性的视角记录了从她第一次访华至今中国巨大的变化，用热切的情怀见证了中国三十年来的迅速变化，展示了自改革开放以来中国社会的迅速发展和中美关系的巨大变迁。这些照片可以说是她在中国的一本影像日记，是她三十多年在中国美好记忆的缩影，也反映了雪莲女士对中国人民和中国文化的理解。

三十多年来，雪莲女士长期在中国从事大学教学工作，致力推进中美教育事业和文化的交流。她把大半生的爱播撒在中国的土地上，用人生扛起了中美文化交流的使命，其超越国界的高尚品格和奉献精神，感人至深。依我看来，雪莲女士被称为社会活动家、摄影家和饱含爱心的慈善家都是当之无愧的。

"不在天堂，却感到天堂的幸福"，"西安是我的第二故乡，我爱西安，我爱陕西师大。我们是一家人，四海之内皆兄弟"，与雪莲女士见面时，她常常用这些话语表达自己对中国、对西安的热爱以及对陕西师大的深厚情感，让我倍感亲切与感动。雪莲女士以及华美协进社的桥梁作用，使更多的美国教育家、教师和学生来到中国，来到陕西师大，促进了中美人民之间的相互了解与文化交流，加快了陕西师大开放办学和国际化发展的步伐。

七十年前，中国人民的伟大领袖毛泽东讲到：一个外国人，不远万里，来到中国，毫无利己的动机，把中国人民的解放事业当做他自己的事业，这是什么精神？这是国际主义的精神，这是共产主义的精神，每一个中国共产党员都要学习这种精神。今天，我们在沿着雪莲女士走遍中国的履痕回望中国三十年的发展，在饱览一位美国女性镜头中变化的中国的同时，还应该学习她在促进文化交流方面所表现出的崇高品质和精神，像她一样不断拓展我们的国际视野和胸襟，为我国的发展、为世界的发展作出我们的贡献。简言之，对于雪莲女士，我们应该了解她、学习她，还要感谢她；对于她眼中的发展变化，我们应该认识之、推动之，还要努力继续之。

是为序。

陕西师范大学校长 房喻

二〇〇九年九月

Contents 目录

I ← Preface 1　前言1
Balancing the Changes while Moving Forward
在变化和前进中寻求平衡

IV ← Preface 2　前言2
Witness to Change
亲历巨变

VI ← Preface 3　前言3
A Visual Diary
视觉日记

VIII ← Calligraphic Inscription
书法家题词

Section One 第一章 → 001

001 ← Inside China: Constant Change
持续变化的中国

002 ← Introduction
导言

010 ← Change in the Social Structure
社会结构的变化

041 ← Change in the Economic Structure
经济结构的变化

057 ← Coping with Change
应对变革

Section Two 第二章 → 069

069 ← Heroes: Then and Now
今昔英雄

070 ← Introduction
导言

070 ← People Who Influenced Change
影响巨变的人们

096 ← Influential Writers Documenting Change
记录变化的知名作家

101 ← Ordinary Citizens Affected by Change: Shopkeepers, Peasants and Minorities
被巨变影响的普通人：店主、农民和少数民族

127 ← **Section Three　第三章**

　　Beyond Borders: Change in International Relations → 127
　　国界之外：国际关系的变化

　　Introduction → 128
　　导言

　　Historic Landmark Events: Changing China's Interaction with the World → 129
　　标志性的历史事件：中国与世界关系的改变

　　Sister-State and Sister-City Relationships Reap Benefits → 138
　　省际和城际的国际交流

　　Student and School Exchanges: Open Minds and Expand Learning → 145
　　学生交换和学校互访：打开心灵、学习新知

　　Personal Reflections: Looking Back and Looking Forward → 154
　　个人的反思：回顾与展望

161 ← **Section Four　第四章**

　　Shaanxi Normal University: A Microcosm of Change in Chinese Education → 161
　　陕西师范大学：中国教育变化的缩影

　　Introduction → 163
　　导言

　　Observations while Teaching and Learning during Five Presidents at ShiDa → 176
　　教书学习之余的观察：历经陕西师范大学的五位校长

　　Physical Changes Reflect the Reshaping of University Life → 188
　　天翻地覆的大学生活：硬件变化

　　Restructuring Education: Old Methods Merge with New Approaches → 214
　　教育改革：新旧方法的融合

　　Beyond the Classroom, Learning from Other Countries → 237
　　走出教室：向国外学习

　　Witness to Change, after Mao to Now → 246
　　亲历巨变：改革开放至今

　　Acknowledgments → 251
　　致谢

Preface 1 前言1

Balancing the Changes while Moving Forward
在变化和前进中寻求平衡

From a train window on my way to Xi'an in 1982 I watched this peasant balancing his two baskets. He was walking forward but looking back. The wall behind him was crumbling. He left an imprint on my mind as I wondered: How will he balance the radical changes sweeping across China and manage the difficult challenges he must face? What benefits or burdens will be added to his life? How will individuals like this man throughout China and government leaders in Beijing maintain the careful balance necessary to move forward?

1982年,在开往西安的列车上,我捕捉到窗外一个普通农民的形象。他挑着担子,一边走一边回头看,身后是破败的颓墙——一幅让我充满好奇的图画:他将怎样面对席卷中国的急剧变化以及伴随而来的艰难挑战?等待他的是欢喜还是悲愁?这样的普通人在中国成千上万,他们和北京的领导人将怎样在迈向未来时保持一种谨慎的平衡?

For centuries Chinese peasants have planted their seeds and hoped for a plentiful harvest to fill their bowls and feed their families. They have toiled and suffered under imperial rule and often endured foreign humiliation. For generations they have waited patiently for change. "We listen to the thunder, but count on the rain." It is an aged peasant expression. They have listened to political rhetoric but counted on action to follow.

数百年来,中国农民播撒着希望的种子——希望有一个好收成,养家糊口,艰难度日。他们辛勤劳作,却遭受着封建剥削和帝国主义的欺凌。一代又一代,他们耐心地期待着变革。"我们听到的是雷,但期盼的是雨。"这是一个上了年纪的农民的话。他们听到的一直是政治家的许诺,但他们期待的是行动。

On my first trip to China in 1977 my plane was delayed for a day and a half. They said it was due to thunder and volatile weather conditions. I later learned it was due to political turbulence in Beijing at that time. No one knew what would happen but people throughout China were listening for what might follow in the years to come: China was on the verge of monumental change.

1977年,当我第一次前往中国旅行的时候,乘坐的飞机延误了一天半。我被告知延误是由于天气原因,但后来我了解到是因为那时北京的政治形势比较混乱。没人知道将要发生什么,但是全国人民都在等,看接下来会有什么变化——中国正处在一个巨变的关口。

1982，陕西、挑担的农民
Peasant with baskets, Shaanxi Province, 1982

Nineteen seventy-seven was a pivotal year in China's transformation after the tumultuous years of the Cultural Revolution, just after the death of Mao Zedong with 27 years of central control.

1977年是中国转型的关键一年，那时"文化大革命"的混乱岁月刚刚过去不久，毛泽东也刚刚去世，他对国家长达27年的领导遂告终结。

No one then realized it would mark the beginning of experimental reforms, which would move China from an underdeveloped country to a leading economic power in the 21st century with a speed and magnitude unprecedented in the world.

那时没人认识到一种实验性的改革开始了，它将导致中国以世界上前所未有的速度和规模从一个发展中国家成长为21世纪的经济强国。

Furthermore, no one was aware that the re-establishment in 1977 of the National University Entrance Examination (gao kao) would lead to educational reforms that could prove to be as revolutionary as the economic reforms.

另外，也没人认识到1977年高考的恢复意味着一场像经济改革一样深刻的教育变革。

From my first year in 1977, and then as I returned repeatedly for over thirty years, spanning four decades, I became a witness to one of the most dramatic periods of change in China's 5,000-year history. Seeds were planted during these transformative years, which would yield an exceptionally bountiful harvest.

从那一年开始，在接下来的30年——跨越四个年代——里，我多次访问中国，见证了中国五千年历史上最富戏剧性变化的这一段历史。在这些年播下的种子会带来巨大而丰硕的成果。

Sharon Crain　雪莲

Preface 2

前言 2

Witness to Change
亲历巨变

What does it mean to be a witness to change? It means to record with words, memories and photographs what happened and to reveal that information as accurately as possible. For me it was seeing the changes up close and learning from the people who brought about the changes, as well as from the people whose lives were being changed.

亲历巨变意味着什么？它意味着用文字、记忆和图片尽可能准确地记录下这些年来发生的事情。对我来说，它也意味着近距离地观察这些变化，并了解那些造成和经历了这些变化的人们。

I embarked on a long personal journey inside Chinese homes, lives and minds, traversing China's vast expanse: from the Foreign Minister in Beijing to an Uzbek woman in Xinjiang, from a special peasant family in Huxian to my PhD students at Shaanxi Normal University in Xi'an, from the egg seller in the market to a Buddhist monk in Tibet. By developing meaningful friendships with people in different areas and diverse positions, and by becoming actively involved I began to gain a clearer understanding of the enormous complexity within China and the extreme difficulty for ordinary citizens and government leaders to balance the changes while moving forward.

我踏上了自己的漫长旅途，深入到中国人的家庭、生活和内心世界。这些中国人相差极其悬殊：从北京的外交部长到新疆的乌孜别克族妇女，从陕西户县的特殊农民家庭到我陕西师大的博士生，从市场上卖鸡蛋的小贩到西藏的喇嘛。他们虽然分布在不同的地区和岗位上，但我和他们都建立了令人难忘的友谊。从他们那里，我开始认识到中国国情的复杂性，了解到个人和政府都面临的在变革发展中求得平衡的极其困难的局面。

Many of my friendships would span three or four generations as I returned and learned from their children and grandchildren and witnessed the continuous alterations in their housing, food, jobs and thinking. For me it was the openness and intimate friendships with these people that drew me back each time to learn more. Their individual stories became the threads connecting one generation to the next, one decade to the next, as the changes in their lives reflected the changes in China, right before my eyes.

我和许多中国朋友的友谊跨越了三到四代人。从他们的儿辈和孙辈那里我看到了这几代人在住房、饮食、工作和思想方面发生的变化。正是这种坦诚和亲密的友谊吸引我回到中国，并从他们那里了解更多。他们的故事成为联结不同年代人们间的线索，而他们的变迁成为发生在中国的巨大变化的缩影。这一切就发生在我的眼前。

In Chinese, the word xian (线) literally means "a thread" that connects and hold the fabric together. But in the hearts of the Chinese people it symbolically reflects an ancient belief that there is a thread connecting us to others. The spelling of this word for "connections" in Chinese Pinyin and the word for the ancient city of Xi'an (西安) in Chinese Pinyin are the same. For me, the two words became closely interwoven as I sank my roots in the city of Xi'an(西安) and began an intricate web of connections with the people.

在中文里，"线"的功能就是"将织物连缀在一起"。但在中国人的心里，它也象征性地反映了一种古老的观念，即有一根线将我们和他人联系在一起。而且"线"的拼写与"西安"相同。对我来说，这两种含义更紧密地交织在一起，因为我已经把根扎在了西安，而且开始与西安人民构建起一个精妙的联系网。

Two of the most important connections in my quest to understand China were Helen Snow, an American writer and activist, and Soong Qingling, one of China's most respected women. Helen Snow, and her husband Edgar Snow, lived in China in the 1930's and documented the beginning of the Communist Revolution, including personal interviews with Mao Zedong and others in Shaanxi Province at the end of the Long March. The people of Xi'an helped the Snows on their dangerous journeys in war-torn China.

在我探索和了解中国的过程中，有两个非常重要的人物。一个是海伦·斯诺，美国作家和社会活动家；另一个是宋庆龄，中国最受尊敬的女性之一。海伦·斯诺和她的丈夫埃德加·斯诺在上世纪30年代生活在中国，并采访过毛泽东和他的同志们。那时长征刚刚结束不久，他们用自己的笔记录了中国革命那些最初的岁月。在那个被战争煎熬的中国，是西安人民帮助他们渡过了危险的旅程。

Helen Snow connected me with Soong Qingling, whose husband, Sun Yat-sen, led the revolution in 1911 to overthrow the Imperial rule and establish the Republic of China. My friendship with both Helen Snow and Soong Qingling opened up other doors for me to meet top leaders and ordinary people. I entered China at a time in the late 1970's when China and the United States had no official relations, with very few foreigners allowed in. I was able to gain a trust level that would have been difficult without them. This was the beginning of the "thread" of connections and meaningful opportunities to witness the changes within China and changes in Chinese-American relations.

海伦·斯诺介绍我结识了宋庆龄。宋的丈夫是领导辛亥革命、推翻帝制并建立民国的孙中山。与海伦·斯诺和宋庆龄的友谊为我打开了结识中国领导人和普通民众的大门。在70年代末中美还没有建立正式外交关系时，很少有外国人被允许进入中国，而我却能够得到信任，没有她们的帮助这将是非常困难的。这是那条"线"的开始，它的意义重大，使我可以见证在中国和中美关系方面发生的巨大变化。

Sharon Crain 雪莲

Preface 3

前言 3

A Visual Diary
视觉日记

Witness to Change is my visual diary documenting what I learned during thirty years of interacting with hundreds of Chinese people who shared their fears and hopes as their lives were altered. They breathed life into the events I witnessed that transformed China after Mao to now. I think of photographs as recorded memories showing details, which reflect the larger picture. They are fragments that capture particular moments in time.

《亲历巨变》是我的一部视觉日记,它记录了在与成百上千中国人的接触中我所了解的改革开放30年的中国。在这些年的变化中他们有着自己的担忧和希望。我看到了很多改变中国的事件,而正是这些中国人给这些事件注入了生气。我觉得这些照片就是记录下来的历史记忆,它们反映了整个国家变化大图景上的一些细节。它们只是片断,但却抓住了一些特殊的历史瞬间。

Just at the time China was launching new directives within the country, China also began opening doors to the outside world. After years of isolation China would become increasingly involved in the world arena, a member of the World Trade Organization, a major international manufacturing center, a participant in global conferences and host to the 2008 Olympics.

在中国实施了新的国内政策的时候,它也开始向世界打开了国门。在多年的孤立之后,作为世界贸易组织的一员,作为世界制造业中心,作为全球性会议的参加者和2008年奥运会的东道主,中国日益深刻地卷入了国际事务。

Many new policies led to progress and prosperity unimaginable in the past, but also created myriads of complicated challenges. Individuals and government leaders still continue to struggle with the benefits and burdens emerging within a country in the midst of an historic transition.

许多新政策促成了过去难以想象的进步与繁荣,但是也带来了无数的复杂挑战。在这个国家的历史转型期,普通百姓和国家领导人都在不断地努力克服困难、改善民生。

I was privileged to witness this process in a personal way and have taken the liberty of including stories and photos of myself along with others as I share in this visual diary what I learned.

我荣幸地目睹了这个过程，这才有了我的视觉日记，从而得以与读者分享我拍摄的这些照片和它们背后的故事。

Unless otherwise indicated all of the photographs are mine. All of the ideas expressed represent my own impressions from my perspective. I am responsible for the contents.

除非特别注明，本书所有的照片都是我自己所摄，书中的所有观点都是我从自己的角度出发得出的印象。我为本书的内容负全部责任。

My aim is threefold: first, to present an overview of some of the dramatic changes that have taken place during the past thirty years, beginning in 1977 with the "reform and opening up" period. Second, to illustrate the complexity of balancing the benefits and burdens resulting from those changes. And third, to create awareness of the magnitude of current educational reforms as a forecast of future change in China.

本书写作的目的有三个。第一，对改革开放以来30年中所发生的一些巨大变化作一个全面的介绍；第二，展示在变化中平衡传统和突破的复杂性；第三，使读者了解目前进行的教育改革的宏大规模并预示中国的未来变革。

Sharon Crain　雪莲

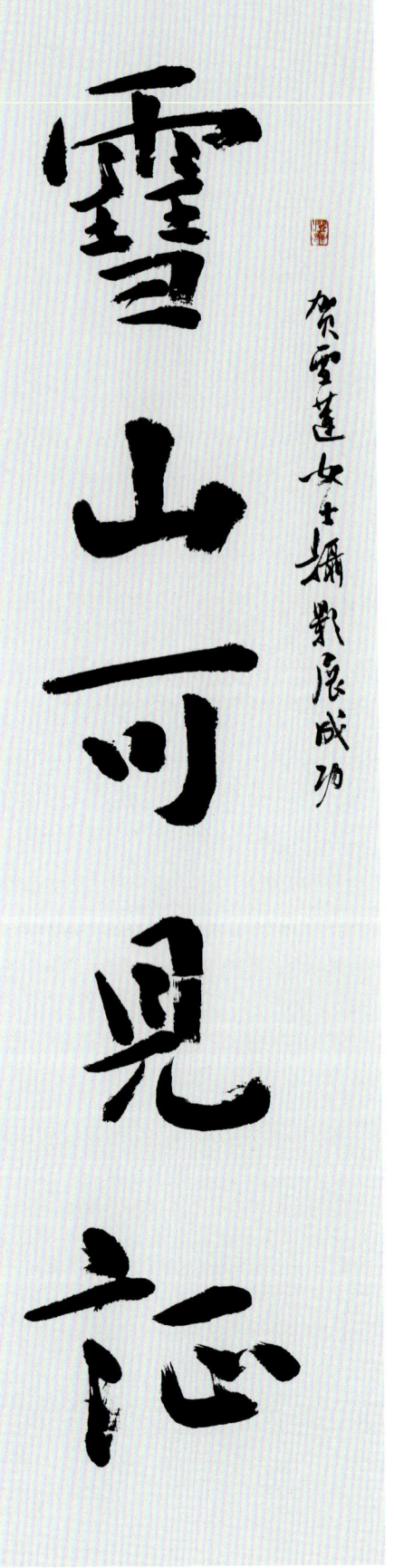

陕西书画协会副主席、书法家刘鹏题词
Calligraphy by Liu Peng

Section One
第一章

Inside China: Constant Change
持续变化的中国

亲历巨变——一位美国女性眼中的当代中国
Witness to Change: After Mao to Now

1977，广州，革命标语和打乒乓球的小伙子
Revolutionary posters and young boys playing table tennis across the bricks, Guangzhou, 1977

Introduction
导 言

  Foreigners were a rare sight when I first arrived in Shanghai in 1977. During the long isolated years of the Cultural Revolution (1966—1976) walls and barriers kept foreigners out and Chinese in. As I walked down the streets people would stop and stare. Crowds of people would gather around looking at my colorful clothes or shoes. Every man and woman wore a similar blue or green jacket, trousers and black cloth shoes. Mothers would drag their children to have a closer look, having never seen a real foreigner. The United States and China had no diplomatic relations and on both sides information was lacking. Of course there were no computers or cell phones, no private phones at all, no private televisions, no private cars and no taxis in all of China. Bikes and people pulling carts filled the streets.

  1977年我第一次到上海的时候，外国人极少。长达十年孤立的"文革"时期以后，重重阻碍使外国人很难走近中国人的生活。当我走在大街上的时候，人们纷纷停下来注视着我，围起来看我色彩鲜艳的衣服和鞋子。男人和女人们都穿着相似的蓝或绿的上衣和裤子，鞋子大都是黑布鞋。母亲们拉着她们的孩子，近距离地看着我这个她们从未见过的"真正的老外"。那时美国和中国之间没有外交关系，彼此关于对方的信息极度缺乏。整个中国没有电脑和手机，没有私人电话和电视，没有私人汽车和出租车。街道上到处是自行车和人力车。

Almost all basic food was rationed. People lined up with coupon books for cooking oil, rice, salt, sugar, and sometimes small allotments of meat per month. Vegetables were scarce and brought into the cities on horse carts. Everyone was thin. Most apartments had no central heating or running water. There was no personal mobility or opportunity for change in either residency or jobs. People lived in the same city where they were born and everyone had a required "hu kou" or residency permit. Their coupon books for food were valid only in that city. All jobs were assigned and most people held the same job for life. For government jobs pensions and salaries were often based on when a person had joined the Communist Party regardless of their expertise or work efficiency. Billboards offered only political slogans, never advertisements for material goods. Trade was virtually non-existent between China and the United States. With government control and no competition people had limited choices. No concerns existed over a gap between rich and poor because almost everyone was poor.

几乎所有的基本食品都是定量配给的。人们带着各种票证去排队购买食用油、大米、盐、糖和每月配给的极少的肉。蔬菜很缺乏，而且都是用马车运到城里。人人都很瘦。大多数公寓里没有暖气和自来水。人们也不能改变居住地和工作。他们常常生活在他们出生的城市里，每个人都需要有"户口"或者居住许可。粮本只在本市内通用。每人的工作都是被分配的，而且绝大多数人一生只做一种工作。对国家单位的工作人员来说，津贴和工资取决于他们何时"参加革命"而不管他们的工作经验和熟练程度。街上没有广告，只有政治标语。中美之间几乎没有贸易往来。由于政府的控制和缺乏竞争，人们的选择非常有限。没有人关心贫富差距，因为人们差不多都一样穷。

As I walked along the streets in the midst of hundreds of people, moving along as a giant river flowing downstream, I did not imagine that all of them throughout all of China were about to be turned in a new direction.

当我独自走在街上，走在人群中，就像掉进了一条向下沉沦的巨流。我无法想象中国人民怎样从这里迈向一个新纪元。

New policies shake old traditions
动摇传统的新政策

In the late 1970's, three bold new policies were initiated which would have life-altering effects in three major aspects of almost everyone's life in China: economic, social, and educational.

上世纪70年代末，经济、社会和教育方面相继推出了大胆的新政策，它们使几乎每个中国人的生活都发生了根本性的变化。

First, the Individual Responsibility Policy changed the economic structure. Second, the One Child Policy altered the traditional family structure. Third, the re-establishment of the National University Entrance Examination System signaled the beginning of educational reform. Throughout the next thirty years I witnessed the continuing evolution of these policies and in consequence their effect on changing the political structure as well.

第一，联产承包责任制改变了经济结构；第二，独生子女政策改变了传统的家庭模式；第三，高考的恢复标志着教育改革的起步。在接下来的30年中，我所见证的这些日益完善和持续发生效用的政策也在改变着中国的政治结构。

Change in the economic structure
经济结构的变化

The Individual Responsibility System was implemented in 1978 and marked the beginning of China's path toward a market economy. It was the first of the economic reforms by Deng Xiaoping when he became the paramount leader after the death of Mao Zedong. It would shake loose the previous economic structure of the commune system when peasants worked on a common plot of land and received allotments of grain or payment based on a point system for the benefit of the production team. According to Mao's dictum "grow gain everywhere" peasants did not have the right to choose what they wanted to plant or what might be best suited for that region. Often crops failed because of inconsistency with local conditions. With the absence of individual benefits one major problem was the lack of incentive to work hard, which resulted in low productivity. The commune system had been firmly implanted by Mao Zedong in a giant experiment of pushing communism and egalitarianism to their extreme limits.

1978年出台的联产承包责任制标志着中国开始走向市场经济，这是邓小平推行的第一项经济改革举措，那时毛泽东已去世，邓小平成为中国最高领导人。这项举措动摇了先前的人民公社制度，在那种制度下，农民都在公有的土地上劳动，并依照一种工分制度来领取粮食、现金和生产队的其他福利。根据毛泽东"大种粮食"的指示，农民无权决定他们自己种什么，无权决定什么作物最适合他们的地区，种下的作物经常由于不适于本地情况而歉收。由于没有对个人的物质奖励，人们失去了努力劳动的动力，造成产量低下。而人民公社制度是毛泽东一手扶持起来的，它把一种共产主义和平均主义的实验推向极端。

By contrast, under the new Individual Responsibility System land was contracted or leased to individual households for a period of a few years at a time. Peasants were allowed to use, but not own, the land. After satisfying state crop quotas peasants were permitted to sell their surplus crops on the open market. As individual profits increased, productivity greatly increased. Years before there had been experiments with this kind of system in limited areas of extreme poverty by the local peasants in Anhui Province and then again in Sichuan Province under the direction of Zhao Ziyang before he became Premier.

在新的联产承包责任制里，农民可以签订使用土地合同或者租用土地。他们有土地的使用权，但没有所有权。农民在满足了国家的公购粮任务后，可以在市场上出售他们的剩余农产品。这样，个人收入增加，农产品的产量也大大提高了。安徽省一些贫困地区的农民在土地承包制全面推广之前已经有了一些实践经验，接着四川省在当时的省委书记赵紫阳的支持下也进行了试点。

With growing success under Deng Xiaoping, this policy was cautiously expanded in the rural areas throughout China and later introduced into the urban areas. Deng Xiaoping called it "socialism with Chinese characteristics". This was the beginning of the shift from total central government control toward a market economy. It signaled a shift from political power to economic power.

随着联产承包责任制的成功，这个政策被谨慎地推向其他农村地区，后来又在城市推开，邓小平把它称为"中国特色的社会主义"。这也是从中央政府的全面控制向市场化转变的开始，它意味着政治权力开始向经济权力转变。

By the beginning of the 21st century China would join the World Trade Organization, would become one of the leading manufacturing centers of the world and would maintain an impressive domestic growth rate of approximately 10% for over ten consecutive years.

在21世纪初，中国加入了世界贸易组织，成为世界的制造业中心之一，并令人印象深刻地在过去的十多年间保持着大约百分之十的年国内经济增长。

Change in the social structure
社会结构的变革

The One Child Policy was initiated in 1979 at the same time as the Individual Responsibility System. If China was to continue to provide food and basic needs for its enormous expanding population, curbing its growth was vital. Premier Zhou Enlai often said in the 1970's, "China does the world a favor by feeding its own people," but it was becoming increasingly difficult to do so. The result of the One Child Policy was to alter an age-old family structure with far-reaching ramifications years later when it became apparent that this one single child received both more attention and more pressure. Traditionally parents had many children because they were needed to work in the fields and take care of their elders in their old age. Just at the time when peasants were granted the opportunity to make a profit by working harder under the Individual Responsibility System, the One Child Policy restricted the number of family members which were still needed to help in the fields and family businesses. Questions arose of how to balance the needs of a country and individual needs of a family.

1979年，和联产承包责任制同时推行的是独生子女政策。如果中国要为它日益膨胀的人口提供粮食和生活必需品，控制人口增长就成为决定性的一环。周恩来总理在70年代时经常说："养活自己的人口就是中国对世界的贡献。"但是，做到这一点越来越困难。独生子女政策使传统的中国家庭结构发生了改变，对独生子女的关注和压力也增加了。由于养儿防老的传统，中国人有很多子女。当农民得益于联产承包责任制的政策，可以通过辛勤劳作去改善自己的生活水平时，他们需要更多的劳动力，可是一胎化的政策限制了家庭人数。怎样平衡国家与家庭之间的需要成为一个问题。

Change in the educational system
教育系统的改革

The re-establishment of the National University Entrance Examination (gao kao) in 1977 returned to the centuries-old examination system based on knowledge. It had been suspended during the harsh period of the Cultural Revolution when intellectuals were criticized, looked down upon and often "sent down" to live in the countryside. Universities and colleges had been virtually closed from 1966 to 1971. As they slowly opened in the early 1970's under Mao's direction the only way for individuals to enter then was to be recommended for their ideological fervor within the three dominant categories of Worker, Soldier, Peasant. With the absence of an examination system, entrance to the university at that time depended heavily on "guanxi" or backdoor connections.

1977年高考制度的恢复使得中国教育重归以知识为基础的古老考试制度。在"文革"中，当知识分子被批判和歧视，甚至常常被下放到农村去的时候，这一制度被搁置了。从1966年到1971年，高等学校实际上被关闭了。在70年代初期，根据毛泽东的指示，这些学校又慢慢开放，但得以入学深造的只是工农兵中那些因为意识形态的热诚而被推荐的人。由于考试制度的缺乏，能否进入大学在相当程度上是依靠"关系"。

The re-instatement of the examination system in 1977 was enthusiastically welcomed as it signaled a new beginning for intellectuals by placing them in the forefront of China's economic reform. For the first time in years students were selected and admitted to universities because of their intelligence and skill demonstrated on the one national examination. In the years to follow more emphasis was placed on expanding China's educational system to the masses of people, especially in the interior regions. By 1986 China passed a nine-year compulsory elementary and secondary school law with emphasis on reaching poor rural areas. In the 1990's the number of undergraduate, graduate and postgraduate students vastly increased, accompanied by a surge of new universities throughout the country.

高考制度的恢复得到了强烈的反响，它把知识分子置于中国经济改革的前列，所以对他们来说是一个全新的开始。多年来学生的选拔第一次基于他们在高考中展示的智力和能力。接着，工作的重点放在了全民性的，尤其是内地的教育普及上。1986年，国家通过了九年义务教育法，强调农村贫困地区教育的改善。在90年代，随着一波兴建大学的热潮，本科生、研究生和博士生的数量都有了大规模的提高。

Then in 2004 a national level experiment in education was launched with the support of all eleven ministries, introducing a different focus for teacher training and new methods for student learning. The aim of the reform in education was to stimulate students to think and act differently by encouraging innovation and creativity. This represented a radical departure from previous rote memorization and recitation from books and teachers, which required uniform acceptance of information and lack of questioning. New textbooks and teacher training programs introduce ways to solicit student opinions and participation.

2004年，在11个部委的支持下，国家在教育方面实行了一项主要实验，即引进教师培训和学生学习的不同理念和新方法。这次教育改革的目的就是通过鼓励发明创造以培养学生独立思考和行动的能力。以前的中国教育强调死记硬背，要求学生一致接受书本和教师给他们的信息，不能质疑，而新的教科书和师资培训计划引入了不同的方式，欢迎学生们的意见和参与。

China's pattern for this reform was carefully monitored experimentation, beginning in trial school districts before expanding. The pattern followed the economic reform's model, which started in limited rural areas in Sichuan Province, expanded to other rural areas and then cautiously developed in urban areas. Similarly, foreign investment was first encouraged in experimental Special Economic Zones beginning in Shenzhen and other coastal cities before expanding to other parts of the country.

这次改革的模式是在推广前先行试点，是中国谨慎的监控实验的一贯模式。这种模式走的是与经济改革同样的路子。中国的经济改革就是先在四川省有限的农村地区试点，然后推向其他农村地区并谨慎地在城市中推开。鼓励外资的政策也是先在以深圳为首的经济特区试行，后来推广到其他沿海城市，最后才推向全国的。

The ultimate goal of the current educational reform is to prepare the next generation to sustain China's economic growth and to become the innovators and leaders of the 21st century. It could prove to be among the most important reforms in China's history.

目前教育改革的终极目标是培养能够让经济继续保持增长的下一代人，并且让他们成为创新者和21世纪的领导人。它可能是中国历史上最重要的改革。

Change in the political structure
政治体制的改革

Looking back to the 1970's there were, however, no bold new policies stating that the political power of the Communist Party should change. However, change is occurring because of the bold economic and educational reforms, which have provided new opportunities for individuals to take control of the decisions in their own lives.

回到上世纪70年代，没有哪项大胆的政策能够预示共产党的政治权力将有变化。不过，由于开拓性的经济和教育改革，人们得到了更多的机会去决定自己的命运。情况正在起变化。

Today students, businessmen, shopkeepers and even government officials no longer focus on memorizing ideological thoughts and theories required to survive in the past. Both private individuals and government leaders focus on practical and realistic solutions to daily problems. Because so many individuals have more mobility than ever before to move to a different city or select a different job, the government now has less control of people's lives. The residency permit (hu kou) required in the past to cash in on rationed food coupons has broken down as individuals have cash to buy food or goods in new locations where they are able to secure new jobs. Even though the central government and local governments still exercise ultimate control, there is more personal economic power and thus less political power.

今天，学生、商人、店主甚至政府官员都不必像以前那样默诵着意识形态教条才能生活。老百姓和政府领导人都在关注那些能够解决民生问题的现实可行的办法。政府放松了对人民生活的控制，老百姓现在有多得多的机会迁移到不同的城市，寻找不同的工作。过去居民必须有户口，然后才可以领取用于购买食品所必需的粮票或其他购物券，但现在这个制度被打破了。人们可以在新的地方获得新的工作，不必发愁没有户口无法谋生了。即使中央和地方政府还有着最终决定权，个人也有了更多经济权力，而政治权力的作用则减小了。

While options have increased for many individuals so have the risks for failure. The so-called "iron rice bowl" of the past is gone when almo st everything was decided and provided by the government. Many of the state-run industries have been closed or privatized and are now in the hands of individual managers. University students are no longer guaranteed and assigned jobs when they graduate. They have choices but also have the pressure to find their own jobs and even run the risk of being fired, which was unheard of a few years ago. Changes in the economic structure are beginning to shift responsibility and also control from the central government toward individuals who are making more independent decisions.

对个人来说，机会是大大增加了，但失败的危险也随之而来。过去一切都由政府大包大揽的"铁饭碗"没有了。许多国营企业关闭了或被民营企业收购了。大学生毕业时不再被保证分配工作。他们在找工作时有了选择，但也有了压力，而且还有了被解雇的危险，而这在以前是闻所未闻的。这些经济结构方面的变化使得政府不必再负那样多的责任，而个人也有了更多独立决定的权力。

It is the Communist Party members in the government ministries who are consciously bringing about these radical reforms, which consequently alter their own authority. They are nurturing the new generation to become more self-sufficient and play a more active role. The 17th Party Congress held in 2007 placed emphasis on several important new areas: Putting the people first; Developing more democracy at the grassroots level; and Fighting corruption.

正是政府机构里的共产党员有意识地推动了这些激进的变革，而他们自己的权威也最终受到了影响。他们要新的一代扮演更积极的角色并将他们培养得更加自立。2007年召开的中共十七大把重点放在了几个重要的新领域：以人为本、发展基层民主和反腐败。

Stability and harmony has been the core of the Confucian ethics for centuries throughout China's history. Now they are essential but difficult goals in the 21st century as China provides prosperity to millions of her people but seeks answers to new problems of corruption, a widening gap in wealth, pollution, finding sources of energy to supply the growing demands and addressing social unrest. Stability and harmony are important elements of balancing the changes while moving forward.

"稳定和谐"几千年来一直是儒教伦理的核心。现在，它们依然是21世纪中国核心的，但也是困难的目标。当中国为千百万人民创造繁荣的同时，它也在探索如何解决腐败问题、贫富差距问题、污染问题以及日益增长的能源需求问题，从而应对社会的不安定因素。稳定和谐是平衡变化与发展的重要因素。

1982，西安，王曾吾和雪莲
Wang Zengwu sharing stories with Sharon Crain, Xi'an, 1982

Wang Zengwu lived on Friendship Avenue in Xi'an. We were first introduced by my friend An Wei who also made arrangements for me to teach at Shaanxi Normal University. After classes I would often ride my bike through streets totally jammed with bicycles to visit him. Wang Zengwu shared with me how he and his wife survived without sons or daughters in a society dependent on children to care for parents in their old age. He sang to me from Peking Opera and recited his favorite Tang Dynasty poems. A photo of his ancestors sat on his one wooden dresser while a wooden coffin, covered with green plastic, waited for him in one corner of the room. He was proud of living in Xi'an which served as the ancient capital of China for thirteen dynasties one of which was established by Qin Shi Huang, the Emperor who unified China and prepared over six thousand terra cotta warriors for his tomb. Once Wang Zengwu gave me a sprig of bamboo as the traditional symbol of friendship. He always walked me to the gate at the end of his courtyard and with each step took me deeper into my journey to understand China.

王曾吾住在西安友谊路，是我的朋友安危介绍我认识他的。安危还帮我联系到陕西师大教学。课后我经常骑车穿过满是自行车的街道去找王曾吾。他的祖上的照片挂在木制的梳妆台上方，房间的角落里有一副为自己准备的棺材，上面盖着绿色的塑料布。王曾吾和妻子没有子女，这样在一个养儿防老的社会里他们的老年生活很艰难，但他们并不沮丧。他给我唱京剧、背唐诗，并且为生活在西安而骄傲。因为西安是13朝古都，在秦始皇时代时就是中国国都，而正是这个皇帝最后统一了中国并为自己的陵墓准备了6000多个兵马俑。有一次王曾吾送给我一条竹枝，那在传统上是一种友谊的象征。临别时他总是将我送到大门口。与他的交往让我更深入地了解了中国。

Change in the Social Structure
社会结构的变化

The bold reforms initiated by Deng Xiaoping in 1978 after the death of Mao Zedong set China on a new course affecting almost everyone's daily life as monumental changes occurred in the social structure: housing, jobs, personal choices, leadership, transportation, communication, the status of women and the traditional family.

毛泽东去世以后，邓小平在1978年发起了大胆的改革。这是一项新的事业，它影响到每个人的日常生活，从而使社会结构发生了巨大的变化：住房、工作、个人选择、领导、交通、通信、妇女地位和传统家庭。

When I first saw Shanghai in 1977 almost all of China's city streets looked like this. People's possessions were limited and similar: a few clothes, a black bike, a small area for living and a balcony to store pots or raise a hen for eggs. People on bikes and people pulling carts filled the streets and sidewalks. Crime was almost nonexistent but so was opportunity. Almost no one expressed any hope for change and it was similar when I returned in the 1980's. "I don't think I will see changes in my lifetime," one of my teacher friends told me. "Perhaps there will be change in China in 100 or 50 years. I place all my hopes someday for my children's or grandchildren's lifetime."

1977，上海，旧住房
Old housing units, Shanghai, 1977

1977，上海，公寓和小铺
Apartments and small shops, Shanghai, 1977

1977年，当我第一次看到上海的时候，几乎每一座中国城市的街道都像这个样子。人们财产有限而且都差不多：几件衣服，一辆黑色的自行车，很小的居住空间和堆着盆盆罐罐或养着下蛋母鸡的阳台。街道和人行道上到处都是自行车和人力车。几乎没有犯罪，但也几乎没有选择和机会。很少有人觉得有希望改变，到我80年代重返那里时，情况还是差不多。"我觉得在我这一生中将不会看到变化，"我的一位教师朋友告诉我，"也许100年或者50年以后会有变化。我把希望放在我孩子或者孙子身上。"

One night after visiting a Chinese friend in Beijing, my host walked me down the dark concrete stairway from his sixth-story apartment. I held tight to the railing, carefully sliding my foot to the edge to feel for the next step. My friend laughed and said, "It is just like China right now, groping in the dark." We had talked about how they had been sent to the countryside during the Cultural Revolution years in the late 1960's and had lost valuable time with no education. Those were dark years and new policies were just being formulated which would shed bright sunlight on their faces, but it was unimaginable where those policies would lead.

一天晚上，在看望了北京的一位中国朋友后，我们沿着他六层楼公寓的水泥台阶摸黑往下走。我摸着扶手，小心地用脚去摸索下一级台阶的边缘。朋友笑了，说："这就像现在的中国——在黑暗里摸索。"我们谈论着在60年代"文革"时他们怎样被送到农村，从而失去了受教育的大好时光。那是些黑暗的日子，在他们脸上撒下明媚阳光的新政策还在形成，但是很难想象这些新政策将把人们带向何方。

New apartments rise over the old "like bamboo shoots after the rain". Now cities such as Shanghai display world-class skylines and host prestigious international forums, spotlighting their growing economic importance. Modern apartments have elevators, showers and refrigerators, unheard of luxuries in the recent past. Even old buildings seen from my window where I live at Shaanxi Normal University in Xi'an have rooftop solar panels for hot water, eliminating the long walks to water

2000，上海的天际线
Shanghai skyline, 2000

2004，西安，旧公寓楼旁边新起的教工宿舍楼
New faculty apartments rise over old ones, Xi'an, 2004

stations to fill the thermos twice a day. But new buildings are often too expensive for those who once lived in the old ones. Vibrant cities expand as fields vanish. Today not all of China has been modernized, but in 1977 when I first arrived no city in China had vistas with these contemporary apartments and no one dreamed it might be possible.

旧的住宅楼旁边，新住宅楼"雨后春笋"般拔地而起。现在的城市——如上海——展示了它世界级的天际线，还开始举办权威性的国际论坛，使它们在经济增长中的地位日益凸显。现代化的公寓楼有电梯、淋浴设备、冰箱和直到最近还没有听过的奢侈品。从我在陕西师大住所的窗户里可以看到一些旧建筑，那里的楼顶上居然有太阳能热水器，而过去，人们为了打开水，每天得拎着热水瓶去热水灶，一天两次，还要走很远的路。对于住在旧公寓的人来说，新教工住宿楼的价格还是贵了些。随着农田的消失，充满活力的城市在扩张。今天，并不是中国的所有地方都现代化了，但回想我1977年第一次到这里的时候，没有中国城市像这个样子，也没有人能够想象它是可能的。

Personal choices replace ideological directives
思想解放

During the 1960's and 1970's the streets, factories and homes were filled with political slogans, both in cities and in the countryside; they were omnipresent in all public and private spaces. The predominant book available was the so-called "Little Red Book" of Mao Zedong thoughts, which everyone memorized and recited. China focused inward and exclusively on ideology. No advertisements were seen on billboards to compete for customers to buy their products since no private companies existed anywhere in China. During one of my lectures in 1984 several students had difficulty translating the word and meaning of "competition". It didn't exist in their vocabulary or in their everyday experience.

在60、70年代，不论是城市还是农村，街道、工厂和居民家里都充斥着政治标语，在公共和私人空间随处可见。《毛主席语录》是压倒一切的书，那是每个人都被要求学习甚至背诵的。那时的中国专注于意识形态，看不到争夺顾客的广告牌，因为根本没有私营企业。1984年我在陕西师大授课时，几个学生在翻译"competition（竞争）"一词时颇感困难，因为在他们的词汇或日常经验里这个概念根本就不存在。

1977，上海，革命宣传画
Revolutionary posters, Shanghai, 1977

2007，北京，名表的现代广告牌
Modern billboards with luxury watches, Beijing, 2007

2007，西安，诱人的茶广告
Tempting tea advertisements, Xi'an, 2007

Now it is estimated that over half of all Chinese companies are privatized as the private sector and competition increases. The streets, the Internet, television and magazines are filled with advertisements for products from all over the world. A peasant friend shared with me, "When I grew up the three luxuries for families in our village were to own the three circles: the circle of a watch, a bicycle, and a small sewing machine. To get married we had to prove to the bride's family that we could provide the '48 legs': 4 legs of a bed, 4 legs of a table, 16 legs of chairs, 4 legs of the stand for a wash basin and so on." He continued, "Now a woman looks for a man who has a car and microwave in a modern apartment." Yet a wide gap exists between those who still only have the "three circles" and those with luxury products widely advertised.

今天，随着民营经济的发展和竞争的加剧，估计在中国民营企业已超过50%的比例。在大街上、互联网上、电视上和杂志上，充斥着来自世界各地的商品广告。一位农民朋友告诉我："我小的时候，对我们村的家庭来说，三件奢侈品就是'三转'：手表、自行车、缝纫机。结婚的时候，我们必须向新娘的娘家证明我们准备好了'48条腿'：床4条腿，桌子4条腿，椅子16条腿，脸盆架4条腿，等等。"他还说："现在女人找对象，要看他有没有汽车和带微波炉的现代化住房。"不过，在那些还是只有"三大件"的人们与那些拥有广告宣传的奢侈品的人们之间，仍然存在着很大差距。

During the time when Mao Zedong was Chairman every man and woman wore similar blue or green so-called "Mao jackets" symbolic of the pervading egalitarian philosophy (a style originating with Sun Yat-sen after the downfall of Imperial China in 1911). All shoes were made of black cloth with only one style for males and one style for females. My husband, Bill Crain, attended the Trade Fair in Guangzhou in 1976. At the time very little difference could be noticed between the jackets, except perhaps for the quality of fabric or sometimes a slot above the pocket for one or two pens, which was worn as a subtle rank badge for higher leaders. He commented, "I could be in a meeting with ten people and never know who was the manager, the staff or the workers. There was no such thing as business cards. I needed to pay attention to who had the blue jacket with a place for two pens. That was probably the manager."

在毛泽东时代,所有的男女都穿着相似的蓝或绿的"毛式服装"(这种服装样式缘起于1911年孙中山推翻帝制的时候),它们成为渗透全社会的平均主义的象征。所有的鞋子都是黑布做的,而且男女分别只有一种样式。我丈夫威廉·柯雷参加过1976年的广交会。那时人们的服装样式几乎是一样的,唯一的区别是不同的布料和口袋上面插钢笔的孔,那是高级干部才有的特殊标志。我丈夫感叹道:"我在一次会面中也许会碰到10个人,但一点也分不清管理者和员工。没有名片这档子事。我不得不注意谁的蓝衣服的口袋上面有插两支笔的地方,那个人也许就是管理者。"

The following year in 1977 he noticed a young person wearing the blue jacket and blue trousers in Shanghai with two small red ribbons at the end of her braids. He noted, "This was the only sign of individualism I saw in two weeks." Even hairstyles were all the same: all unmarried women wore long braids, while married women wore an identical short-cropped haircut with no lipstick or jewelry. Everyone was expected to blend in and collectively move the country forward.

第二年,他在上海注意到一个穿着蓝色衣裤的姑娘在辫子上系上了红丝带。他说:"这是我在两个礼拜里见到的唯一个人主义的标志。"甚至发型都是相同的:未婚女子都留着长辫子,已婚妇女则大都剪成短发,没有口红和首饰。每个人都被期待着融入集体,将国家推向前进。

Now individualism is flourishing in everything from dress, choice of jobs, residency, and marriage as men and women make more independent decisions.

现在个性化的高涨不仅体现在穿着上,也体现在工作、居住地和婚姻的选择上。男人和女人都越来越独立地作出决定。

1977，北京的街道，千人一面的衣服样式
One-style of clothing for all men and women, Beijing street, 1977

1977，上海，商店橱窗里的鞋子只有黑布鞋
Store window with the only style of black cloth shoes, Shanghai, 1977

2007，北京，天安门广场，个人风格
Individual style, Tian'anmen Square, Beijing, 2007

Tian'anmen Square: then and now
天安门广场今昔

As I walked in Tian'anmen Square in 1977 for the first time I was jolted by the bigger-than-life size portraits of Lenin and Stalin next to the Great Hall of the People. I felt the lingering influence of the Russians from the days when Mao Zedong had turned to the Soviet Union for guidance along the road to Communism. On the other side of the Square near the Museum of History were giant portraits of Marx and Engels, authors of *Manifesto of the Communist Party*. Throughout the country millions of huge photos of Mao Zedong were prominently displayed in every factory, school, office, restaurant and household. On the streets very few cars were seen and very little evidence of any Western influence.

1977年，我第一次在天安门广场散步的时候，就被人民大会堂旁列宁和斯大林的巨幅画像震惊了。我感受到俄罗斯挥之不去的影响，这种影响从毛泽东转向苏联式共产主义道路的时候就有了。在广场的另一面，历史博物馆那一侧，是《共产党宣言》的作者马克思和恩格斯的巨幅画像。而毛泽东的大幅照片那时被醒目地悬挂在全国每一个工厂、学校、办公室、餐馆和居民家里。汽车极少，西方的影响几乎无迹可寻。

Today one enormous portrait of Mao Zedong hangs at the entrance to the Forbidden City, the old

1977，北京，天安门广场。雪莲在列宁和斯大林画像前
Tian'anmen Square, Lenin and Stalin photos and Sharon Crain, Beijing, 1977

1977，北京，天安门广场马克思和恩格斯的画像
Tian'anmen Square, portraits of Marx and Engels, Beijing, 1977

2004，北京，毛泽东的画像面对着天安门广场和疾驶的汽车
Mao Zedong facing Tian'anmen Square and speeding cars, Beijing, 2004

Imperial Palace, overlooking the fast-paced cars heading toward "socialism with Chinese characteristics".

今天，悬挂在天安门城楼上的毛泽东画像俯瞰着下面急速驶过的汽车，它们都在急匆匆地开往"中国特色的社会主义"。

A Chinese Ambassador having dinner at our house in the early 1980's explained to me, "A person or a country must be careful which direction to follow. If you only go to the right or only go to the left you will go in circles." This represented a new openness for a government official at that time and a new direction for China.

80年代早期，一位中国大使曾在我家里与我们共进晚餐。他对我说："不论是一个人还是一个国家，都必须认真考虑走什么样的道路。如果只是左，或者只是右，你都会走弯路。"他的话代表了那个时候一个政府官员的开阔胸襟，也为中国指出了新的方向。

Leaders shift focus toward practical issues
转向实际问题的领导人

After Mao Zedong died in 1976 students in classrooms sang the praises of Chairman Hua Guofeng who became their leader for a brief period. Posters in the streets signaled the downfall of the "Gang of Four" including Mao's wife—Jiang Qing who had tightly controlled music, art and literature during the Cultural Revolution and who sought political control after Mao's death. By 1978 Deng Xiaoping emerged as the "paramount leader". He pushed forward the Four Modernizations, which marked the beginning of China's economic reforms in agriculture, industry, technology and defense.

1976年毛泽东去世后，教室里的学生们唱起了华国锋主席的赞歌。华国锋在一段不长的时间内成为中国的领导人。大街上的宣传画告诉人们包括江青在内的"四人帮"倒台了。江青在"文革"中曾严密控制音乐、艺术和文学等宣传部门，并在毛泽东去世后试图掌握政治权力。到了1978年，邓小平成为"最高领导人"。他推动的四个现代化——农业、工业、科学技术和国防领域的现代化——标志着中国经济改革的开始。

Jiang Zemin came to power in 1989 as Secretary General of the Communist Party and then President of China from 1993 to 2003.

1989年江泽民成为中国共产党总书记开始执政，并从1993年到2003年期间担

1977，北京，小学生在毛泽东和华国锋画像前表演节目
Mao Zedong and Hua Guofeng, elementary school children, Beijing, 1977

2007，西安，讲授邓小平和江泽民的思想
Teaching about Deng Xiaoping and Jiang Zemin, Xi'an, 2007

2007，西安，胡锦涛和社会主义荣辱观
2007，改革中的实际问题，《纽约时报》和《华尔街日报》
Hu Jintao and eight vices and eight virtues campaign, Xi'an, 2007
Practical issues, The New York Times and The Wall Street Journal, 2007

任中国国家主席。

Deng Xiaoping gave up his official titles but continued to be regarded as the prime force pushing China to become a modern industrialized nation. In 1992 in a famous speech in the south Deng Xiaoping unleashed a further surge of entrepreneurialism when he sought to oppose those who were against economic reform and openness. Practical solutions replaced ideology when Deng Xiaoping stated, "some must get rich before others" and emphasized the necessity of developing the wealth in coastal areas first before expanding to the interior. He is often credited with the popular statement "to get rich is glorious".

即使在邓小平辞去官方职务以后，他仍然被认为是推动中国成为现代工业化国家的主要力量。1992年，在他著名的南方谈话中，邓小平掀起了新一轮的改革浪潮。他主动出击，批评那些反对改革开放的人。当他表示"让一部分人先富起来"，并强调让沿海地区先于内地积累财富的必要性的时候，实际的考虑就取代了意识形态。他经常被称道的一句话是"致富光荣"。

Hu Jintao assumed leadership as Secretary General of the Communist Party in November 2002.

2002年11月，胡锦涛当选为中共中央总书记。

In recent years these leaders continue to face constant international and domestic challenges of quality control, trade issues or problems of corruption. In 2007 posters throughout China displayed The 8 Dishonorable Vices and The 8 Honorable Virtues as part of a campaign to overcome corruption, which is stifling progress and undermining people's confidence in the government. The list encouraged eight ways to cultivate personal values and eight ways to avoid dishonest practices. Chinese leaders have often utilized numbers when describing their goals: Deng Xiaoping stressed the "Four Modernizations" for new development in China; Jiang Zemin talked about the "Three Represents" emphasizing what the Chinese Communist Party represented; and Hu Jintao focused on the double eights.

近些年，这些领导人继续面对国际国内的挑战，诸如质量控制、贸易问题以及腐败问题。2007年，遍及全国的"八荣八耻"的标语成为反腐战役的组成部分，因为腐败问题已经阻碍了国家的发展，也危及人民对政府的信心。这个口号提倡用八种方式去培养个人道德并避免不好的行为。中国领导人描述他们的目标时经常使用数字：邓小平用"四个现代化"强调中国新的发展；江泽民用"三个代表"强调中国共产党的代表性；而胡锦涛则强调两个"八"。

Years ago a young university student explained to me a difficult problem in simplified terms, "At the top level, the leaders of China are very good. At the bottom level, the people are hard working. Unfortunately, those officials in the middle level can block good policies at the top from ever reaching the people at the bottom." His words reflect continuing concern by people today.

几年前，一位学生用简单的语言对我解释了一个困难的问题，他说："中国的高层领导人是非常好的，基层民众也工作得很努力，不幸的是，一些中层干部使得上面的好政策无法落实。"他的话反映了人民对这个问题的继续关切。

Changes in transporting people and goods
交通的变化

Scenes like these were common in the 1970's, 1980's and 1990's as I too rode my bike to visit friends or go shopping. Bicycles and people filled the roads selling or buying goods or taking grandma to the hospital wrapped in a blanket and pulled in the back of a cart. Often the entire family settled onto their one bike, with vegetables tied to the front and eggs in a mesh bag held in their hands as they negotiated their way through busy bumpy streets. Other bikes supported heavy or fragile loads: stacks of chairs or a wide sofa with a person perched on top. Sometime, a fat squealing pig was tied across the back of a bike or live chickens dangled upside down from the handlebars to arrive fresh at the market.

这些是20世纪70到90年代我骑着自行车访友或购物时看到的寻常场景，那时街道上满是自行车和行人。正如在照片中所看到的：有的买卖货物；有的拉着车子，将裹在毯子里的奶奶送去医院；还有的全家人骑一辆自行车，前边挂着蔬菜，手里还提着一网兜鸡蛋，小心翼翼地穿过拥挤的街道。自行车常常成为载物的工具：人们用它拉着很多椅子或是一个长沙发，甚至还有人坐在上边。有时候，车子后边会绑上一只尖叫的肥猪，或在车把上吊着活鸡，赶往市场。

At this 1977 bicycle parking lot in Beijing the only difference between the all-black bikes was the identification number on the back. For a few cents people could lock and leave them in the care of a "watcher" while they went to work. On rainy days on the long journey home a plastic cape covered the bike, the rider and their belongings as they cycled at a slow steady pace through the middle of the streets.

1977年，在这个北京的自行车保管站，一色黑色自行车的唯一区别是它们不同的登记号。人们花上几分钱，把车子交给"看车人"，然后去工作。雨天里，在漫长的回家路上，骑车人穿上塑料雨披，遮住自己和他们的物品，慢慢地前行。

In recent years cars and ring roads take people quickly to their destinations but create new demands for fuel and cover farmland for highways; they increase pollution in the cities while adding commuting time for individuals who move to outlying areas to enjoy modern apartments and breathe better air. In the

1984，甘肃，送奶奶到医院
Taking Grandma to the hospital, Gansu Province, 1984

1989，西安，驮在自行车上的家庭
Balancing the family on their one bicycle, Xi'an, 1989

1981，上海，送货
Transporting goods for delivery, Shanghai, 1981

1977，北京，自行车保管站
A place to park bikes, Beijing, 1977

2004，上海，三环路上的汽车
Cars on the third ring road, Shanghai, 2004

past, the dream of the peasants was always to leave the countryside and live in the cities. Now ironically this is reversing as those in the city yearn to live in the distant suburbs beyond polluted crowded cities.

  近些年，汽车和环形公路使人们的交通更为迅捷，但对燃料和耕地（用于修建高速公路）的需求也在增加，同时加剧了城市的污染。人们用于路上的时间也增多了，因为他们搬到郊区去享受现代化的公寓和新鲜的空气。过去，农民的梦想就是离乡进城。现在，带有讽刺意味的是，人们又纷纷渴望住在郊区，远离拥挤而且被污染的城市。

Control of information yields to instant communication
便捷的信息传送取代了对信息的控制

In the 1970's and early 1980's strictly limited information and government regulations were posted on the walls, which I saw along the streets in Beijing. The other dominant source of information came from loud speakers, which intruded into everyone's range of hearing from high poles near the schools, factories, apartments, office buildings and farm houses. At that time almost no television broadcasts or publications brought news about the outside world.

上世纪70年代到80年代初，当我走在北京的大街上时，墙上贴着的只是有限的信息和政府的规定。消息的主要来源是大喇叭，不管是在学校、工厂、公寓、办公楼，还是在农村，到处都能听见它们的声音。电视和出版物上几乎没有关于外部世界的消息。

In the 1980's while teaching at Shaanxi Normal University I often visited my old friend Deng Wanfang in Xi'an. In the middle of discussions about changes in China and life in the United States our words were constantly interrupted by the blaring of directives from the loud speaker outside her apartment window about health campaigns prohibiting spitting on sidewalks or important new rules governing the economic reform.

1977，北京，贴在城市墙上的政府公告
Government directives pasted on city walls, Beijing, 1977

80年代在陕西师大教书时,我经常找老朋友邓万芳。在谈论中国的变化和美国的生活时,我们的谈话经常会被窗外大喇叭的嘹亮声音所打断。那里边讲的都是一些公告,诸如禁止随地吐痰或关于经济改革新的重要政策。

At the university where I taught I never needed an alarm clock because every morning at exactly the same time the loud speaker outside my room blasted: "Yi-er-san-si" (1-2-3-4)... as the voice led people all over China in the same exercises and then announced all the vital information on regulations or new policies that might have been initiated overnight. In a time of rapid radical change it was an efficient way to insure that everyone was informed and in step with new policies. No one could say they didn't know about the new directives but what they truly understood was very limited.

在我教学的学校从来不需要闹钟,因为每天早上的同一时刻,我屋外的大喇叭就会响起来。"一、二、三、四……"随着广播员的声音,全国的人们都开始做广播体操,接着还会发布有关各种规定和政策的新消息。那是一个急剧变化的时代。大喇叭也是一种颇有效率的方式,可以保证每个人都了解最新的消息,并且跟上新政策的步伐。没有人不知道这些新的政策,但他们真正知道的又那样少。

Today individuals such as Dr. Li Yanping, with cell phone in her hand, enjoy many resources for gathering and utilizing information. As an educator benefiting from new opportunities she has conducted research in England, Australia and the United States that has helped in her teaching about comparative education. It is estimated that over half a billion cell phones are in use throughout China with a growing Internet use. China skipped hard line personal telephones and moved directly into the cell phone technology. Computers are still comparatively expensive so the cell phones are also used for instant text messaging of information from everywhere. New technology has greatly facilitated the development of trade and investment within China and in other countries.

就像拿着手机的李延平博士一样,今天的人们利用许多资源收集和使用信息。作为一个受惠于新机遇的教育者,她在英国、澳大利亚和美国做过研究,这些研究对她的比较教育教学有很大的帮助。据估计已经有超过5亿的中国人拥有手机,使用互联网的人数也在迅速增加。中国越过了个人电话的时代,直接进入手机时代。由于电脑还比较昂贵,手机也被用作接发短信。新技术使得中国不论在国内还是国外的贸易和投资都更为便利。

In the remote rural village of An Shang, I walked down a narrow muddy path at the peak of the corn harvest when almost every parent, grandparent and child was

2004，西安，陕西师范大学，使用手机的李延平博士
Dr. Li Yanping with cell phone, Shaanxi Normal University, Xi'an, 2004

2006，安上，田间耕作的农民用手机通话
Peasant in the cornfields with cell phone, An Shang, 2006

working in the fields. It surprised me to see this peasant taking a break with the ever-present cigarette and his cell phone. Even today many peasants throughout China have never left their villages, generation after generation, but now they are able to widen their connections and gather information with cell phones and computers.

我去过一个偏僻的小村子安上。那时正是秋收时节，家家的青壮年、老人和孩子都在田里劳作。走在逼仄泥泞的乡间路上时，我很惊奇地发现这个农民在休息时一边抽烟一边用手机通话。即使在今天，中国还有许多农民祖祖辈辈没有离开过他们的村庄，但现在他们可以通过手机和电脑扩展他们与外界的联系，得到更多的信息。

People in both urban and rural areas are voicing their opinions and complaints more openly. The easy spread of ideas and reportage from other places via Internet and cell phones has provided conveniences for personal and business needs.

不管城市还是农村，人们现在都更公开地表达他们的观点和抱怨。通过手机和互联网，思想和信息的传播更为方便，这样就为个人和商业活动提供了便利。

Changes for women: "Women hold up half the sky"
妇女的变化："妇女能顶半边天"

"Women hold up half the sky" was a phrase used by Mao Zedong implying that women were equal to men. In reality what women shared equally with men was hard physical labor. This woman working in a park steadied an entire burdensome tree trunk on her shoulder as I watched her move a huge pile of them across the courtyard to a work site. She represents women throughout China who continue to balance a full time job while caring for their family.

"妇女能顶半边天"是毛泽东的话，意指男女平等。在现实中，妇女承担着和男人一样繁重的体力劳动。这个在公园劳动的妇女将一根沉重的木料稳稳地扛在肩上，我看着她就这样穿过院子走到工作地点。她代表了中国的妇女：她们既要全职工作又要照料家庭。

Men are beginning to assume more responsibility for childcare and household chores but the heavier burden is still felt by the women. Traditionally, a woman married into her husband's family and lived there forever to care for her husband's parents: she was expected to be obedient to her mother-in-law and to her husband.

1977，北京，在公园里劳动的妇女
Woman carrying a heavy pole while working in a park, Beijing, 1977

男人们开始担负起更多的照看孩子和家务劳动的责任，但是妇女肩上的担子还是更重。传统上，已婚的妇女就应该永远生活在婆家并且侍奉公婆。人们期望她在婆婆和丈夫面前是恭顺的。

Since the majority of women has now joined the work force and are earning money on their own, many are assuming more control of their lives and are entering new careers, holding high-level positions never available to them before. Increased mobility and job opportunities often take women away from their hometowns and beyond traditional household roles of the past. However, many women and men must leave children behind in the care of aging grandparents who in turn have no one left to care for them.

由于现在大多数妇女有了工作和收入，许多人有了更多的决策权，从而过上了一种新的生活。她们在家庭中拥有了过去从未有过的地位。另外，越来越多的农村妇女出外打工，这也常常使得她们离开了家乡，远离了她们过去扮演的传统角色。但是，许多年轻父母将子女留给了年迈的爷爷奶奶照看，而这些老人自己却无人照顾。

Remnants of the past
过去的痕迹

These women walking and talking appear as remnants of the past, when feet were tightly bound to make them smaller which was the preference of men at that time. It was a custom practiced for over a thousand years until officially outlawed by Sun Yat-sen in 1912.

在这些行走和谈话的妇女身上可以看到过去时代的影响，那时她们不得不缠足，因为男人喜欢小脚。作为一种习俗，缠足在中国的延续超过了千年，直到孙中山领导的辛亥革命时才被正式废止。

In ancient times if a woman was at home alone when someone knocked on the door she would respond, "No one is here," because she had no responsibility and men made all decisions. When asked how many children there were in the family she replied only with the number of boys, as girls were not counted. Often girls were not given a name until they married.

在中国古代，如果一个女人独自在家，听到有人敲门，她会回答："家里没人。"因为男人决定一切，而她负不起任何责任。当被问到家里有几个孩子时，她也只说男孩的数目。女孩结婚之前经常连名字也没有。

1977，上海，过去的痕迹：缠过脚的妇女
Remnants of the past: women with bound feet, Shanghai, 1977

2007、西安，提着公文包、穿着高跟鞋的苗妮娅
Miao Niya with briefcase and high-heeled shoes, Xi'an, 2007

In recent years women increasingly hold positions of leadership as owners and managers and enjoy fashionable high-heeled shoes. Miao Niya is the Director of the Shaanxi Xin Qian Jing Printing Company, one of the most successful printing companies in Xi'an, a city of over 8 million people. She told me, "I treat my employees with respect whether they are men or women. We all work together as a team, as a family, to make progress for the company." Like many women today she carries a briefcase filled with many options and opportunities for the future.

今天，越来越多的中国妇女走上领导岗位，成为管理者和业主，穿上了时尚的高跟鞋。苗妮娅是陕西新前景印务有限公司董事长。在有800多万人口的西安市，"新前景"是最成功的印务公司之一。她告诉我："我尊重我的雇员，不管他们是男性还是女性。为了公司的发展，我们一起工作，像一个团队，一个家庭。"像许多今天的妇女一样，她提着公文包，装满未来的发展计划。

The Women's Culture Museum and a secret women's language
妇女文化博物馆和神奇的"女书"

Qu Yajun is the Director of the Women's Culture Museum, one of the largest museums in the world dedicated totally to women and the only one of its kind in China. It is located at Shaanxi Normal University, Xi'an.

屈雅君是妇女文化博物馆的馆长。这个博物馆位于陕西师范大学校园内,是世界上最大的妇女博物馆之一,也是中国唯一一家专以妇女为主题的博物馆。

The wedding costumes of the different minorities illustrate local customs through the centuries. For example, when a bride of the Moinba ethnic culture arrived at the husband's house she wore special wedding clothes prepared by the husband, which meant from then on she became a member of that family and was no longer counted in her own. Traditionally, since daughters "married out" and left their own families, emphasis was placed on having sons because they were needed for hard work in the fields and because the oldest son and his wife were expected to stay in the household to care for his parents in old age.

妇女文化博物馆内收藏的不同民族的婚礼服装展示了千百年来形成的地方习俗。比方说,门巴族新娘到婆家的时候穿的是丈夫特意为她制作的结婚服装,这意味着从此她就成了婆家的一员,而不再是娘家人了。传统上,由于女儿要嫁出去,离开娘家,家庭的重点就放在生儿子身上,因为儿子才能支撑家庭,而且长子和他的妻子要留在家里,照看年迈的父母。

The Women's Culture Museum has many rare examples of a unique women's language. The peculiar characters, originally embroidered on fans and handkerchiefs reveal a secret language known only by women in one particular area. These came from Jiangyong County, Hunan Province. Scholars have various views of when it first came into being, tracing it possibly to the end of the Ming Dynasty or beginning of the Qing (middle 17th century). The "secret women's characters" share certain forms originally developed in the Shang Dynasty over three thousand years ago when inscriptions were written on bones and tortoise shells.

妇女文化博物馆收藏了一种独一无二的神秘女书。这些特殊的文字最初绣在扇子和手帕上,是一种只有一个特殊地区的女人才了解的文字。它

2007，西安，妇女文化博物馆馆长屈雅君
Qu Yajun, Director of the Women's Culture Museum, Xi'an, 2007

2007，陕西师大，妇女文化博物馆，神秘"女书"的文字
Characters of a secret women's language, Women's Culture Museum, ShiDa, 2007

们来自湖南省江永县。学者们对这种文字何时出现尚有争议，但可能是在明末清初。"神秘的女性文字"与商代的甲骨文有些相似之处。甲骨文最早出现在3000年前的商代，文字是刻在兽骨和龟甲上的。

Also on display at the Women's Culture Museum is a blanket with traditional Chinese characters prepared by a woman who was dissatisfied with her arranged marriage. She wove her unhappy feelings, including extramarital affairs into the cloth. Fortunately, her illiterate husband could not read it.

博物馆的展品中还有一床带有传统汉字的毯子，它是一个不满自己包办婚姻的妇女织的。她把自己的不满之情——乃至婚外情——都织了进去。幸运的是，她的丈夫不识字，读不懂。

A new beginning for women
妇女的新开端

Many women today, such as Liu Ying, exude confidence in themselves and happily arrange their own marriage. Photographed here with her husband Liu Ying combines East and West, old and new, in her Western wedding gown near the Small Wild Goose Pagoda (707 AD). After her university graduation she followed her dreams to Shanghai and works with a company promoting creative and artistic new concepts that were unheard of a few years ago.

今天的许多女性,如刘颖,都很自信而且心情愉快地安排了自己的婚姻。在小雁塔旁与丈夫的合影里,刘颖穿了一件西式婚纱,将东方与西方、传统与现代结合了起来。大学毕业后,她追寻自己的梦想去了上海,在一家公司工作。在那里,她的创造性和前所未有的艺术感被激活了。

西安,刘颖和丈夫在小雁塔
Liu Ying with her husband at the Small Wild Goose Pagoda, Xi'an

Change within the family structure: the One Child Policy
家庭结构的变化:独生子女政策

The One Child Policy introduced by Deng Xiaoping in 1979 radically changed the traditional family structure and shifted the focus from large families with many children who worked in the fields and cared for their elders to a single child per family. This policy was initiated to solve population problems for the country but simultaneously created new social challenges for the family.

由邓小平1979年提出的独生子女政策急速地改变了传统的中国家庭结构,那种有许多孩子在田间劳作并且赡养老人的大家庭转为独生子女家庭。这个政策的初衷是解决国家的人口问题,但也伴随产生了一些新的社会难题。

The effects of the One Child Policy are evident throughout China as two parents and two sets of grandparents focus their affection and their hopes for the future on one child. Both attention and pressure on this one child have greatly increased with this 6:1 ratio. According to the Chinese saying "It takes thirty years for a boy to become a man," one of the graduate students in my class explained. "We are now in our thirties, this policy started when we were born. None of us has brothers or sisters. Our childhoods were different from our parents who had many brothers and sisters. Now we feel the responsibility as the only person to take care of our parents but also increased stress to get good

1981，北京，竹制婴儿车里的女童
Young child in bamboo-frame stroller, Beijing, 1981

2007，西安，名字叫"苹果"的小姑娘和父母及爷爷奶奶在一起
Young girl named "Apple" with her parents and grandparents, Xi'an, 2007

grades and then good jobs to fulfill their dreams." Another student added, "China still has such a huge population and we have to fight for our dreams."

独生子女政策的影响在全国都是显而易见的,因为父母、爷爷奶奶、外公外婆都把他们的爱及对未来的希望寄托在一个孩子身上。伴随这种六比一的比例出现,关爱和压力都成倍地增长了。中国的老话说:"三十而立"。我班上的一个研究生曾解释说:"我们现在已经30岁了,而独生子女政策在我们出生时就有了。我们都没有弟兄姐妹,这使我们的童年与父母的不一样。现在我们感到作为独生子女对父母的责任,同时也增加了压力,要取得好成绩,找一份好工作,去圆他们的梦。"另一个学生补充说:"中国仍然有如此庞大的人口,我们不得不为我们的梦想而奋斗。"

Frequently, parents and teachers talk about how the one child has been spoiled as parents and grandparents dole out special toys, clothes or extra snacks. For the first time in China's history many children are overweight, reflecting economic progress and abundance of food but also demonstrating one example of overindulgence of children by their families. In recent years there has been some flexibility within the one-child policy regulations to allow for a second child.

父母和老师经常谈论独生子女怎样被溺爱,因为长辈们总是给他们买玩具、衣服和零食。中国历史上第一次出现了许多孩子超重的现象,既反映出经济的发展和食品的丰富,也折射出家庭对孩子的溺爱。这些年独生子女的政策有所松动,有了生第二胎的余地。

Discussions also focus on the increased suicide rate with overachieving young students in high school and college who are struggling to cope with tremendous stress and pressure to succeed. New programs are being initiated to train counselors and place them in schools throughout the country to provide basic counseling. But many students are resistive to seeking help, unable to overcome traditional stigmas against searching for help for personal problems outside the family.

优秀而天赋突出的高中生和大学生中日益升高的自杀率也引起了关注,这些学生不得不挣扎着应对那种期望他们"成功"的巨大压力。新的培训心理咨询顾问计划已经实施,他们将为全国各地的学校提供基本的心理咨询服务。但是许多学生仍然不愿就个人问题求助,因为把事情捅到家庭以外传统上认为是不光彩的。

Change in the Economic Structure
经济结构的变化

Since the founding of the People's Republic of China in 1949 the entire economic structure was governed through central control by the Communist Party. All major decisions in agriculture and industry came from leaders in Beijing and were scrupulously implemented.

1949年中华人民共和国成立后，中国实行的是中央计划经济。所有工农业方面的重大决定都是由中央领导人作出的，然后被严格地加以执行。

The radical changes that turned China toward a market-oriented economy were first experimentally introduced in rural areas in the late 1970's and then expanded to urban areas. This experimentation with blending communism, socialism and a market economy is still evolving and affecting the lives of more than 1.3 billion people within China and others throughout the world in the process.

70年代末，首先在农村试行的激进改革将中国推向以市场为导向的经济，接着又将这种改革推向城市地区。这种混合了共产主义、社会主义和市场经济的实验仍在进行，并影响着13亿多中国人的生活，以及整个世界。

Beginning of the market economy: rural areas
市场经济的开端：农村地区

1999，安上，秋收季节的一个农民家庭
A peasant family during corn harvest season, An Shang, 1999

The Individual Responsibility System: planting new seeds
联产承包责任制：播撒新的种子

The Individual Responsibility System was first introduced in the rural areas in 1978, completely changing the economic structure of China. Peasants were encouraged to work harder and most importantly allowed to sell their produce for profit after satisfying government quotas. Peasants were given more responsibility to decide what crops to grow based on demand, profitability and local conditions.

联产承包责任制最先是在1978年实行的，它完全改变了中国的经济结构。农民由此得到了努力劳动的动力，更重要的是他们被允许在交纳了公购粮以后可以出卖他们的农产品。他们也有了更多权利去根据市场的要求、可能的获利和本地的情况自主决定种什么。

This bold new policy of allowing for individual profit was the beginning of the shift from total central government control toward a market economy. Starting in limited experimental farm areas it met with astonishing success, gradually spreading to other rural areas throughout the country before eventually being introduced into urban areas.

这种允许个人获利的大胆新政策是中国的经济从中央计划经济向市场经济变革的开端，它首先是在某些地区开始试点的，取得了惊人的效果。由此这个制度逐渐地推向全国农村，最后推向城市地区。

Products and profits: from the countryside to the city
生产和利润：从农村到城市

New policies however took time to implement in the cities. Even into the late 1980's examples of the old system were seen at harvest time as cabbage was dumped from trucks onto the street by state-run enterprises. Damage and rotting often occurred at the bottom of the heap. Women filled their woven baskets on the back of their bikes with mounds of cabbage that was usually pickled to last for the winter. Vegetables and fruits were limited and only available from local areas during that growing season.

不过，新政策在城市的落实得花时间。即使到了80年代末，旧体制的印记依然随处可见。在大白菜收获的季节，可以看到国营公司的卡车把它们运来并被卸在大街上，而菜堆下面的菜会慢慢腐烂。妇女们用自行车驮着装满了大白菜的编织袋，这些大白菜通常要被腌起来吃一冬。蔬菜和水果不丰富，而且都是生长期间才有的本地产品。

With time the expansion of the market economy in rural areas brought more produce into cities, along with new pride. With improvements in transportation and refrigeration a

1989，北京，大街上的大白菜
Piles of cabbage on a city street, Beijing, 1989

wide variety of produce became available year-round. By gaining a profit, individuals prudently and carefully cultivated better produce; both sellers and buyers benefited. While shopping in local city markets I witnessed fierce competition as people searched and haggled for the best products at the best prices.

农村市场经济的发展为城市带来了更多的农副产品，这也是改革值得骄傲之处。交通和制冷业的发展使得一年到头都会有丰富的水果蔬菜。为了更多的收入，农民们精心种植，买卖双方都从中获益。在市场上采购时，我也看到了激烈的竞争。人们讨价还价，争论不休。

2000，西安，菜市场里，一个姑娘正在细心地整理新鲜蔬菜
A girl carefully arranging fresh vegetables in a city market, Xi'an, 2000

The widening gap within the countryside
农村日益扩大的差距

    Feng Jiedong showed me the cave house where he lived as a boy until 1980 in his small rural village. It was similar to cave houses I have seen in Yen'an where Mao Zedong and others lived in the 1930's and 1940's in northern Shaanxi. Cave houses were often dug into the sides of mountains in areas with limited farmland. While some people still live in these cave-style houses, Mr. Feng now lives with his family in a two-story tiled house where

2002，安上，冯杰东在他儿时住过的窑洞前
Feng Jiedong in front of his childhood cave house, An Shang, 2002

2007，安上，学生们在冯杰东家的新瓦房前
Students gathered at Feng Jiedong's new tiled house, An Shang, 2007

students often come to discuss schoolwork or local issues. Feng was elected by the villagers to become the Chairman of the Education Committee in a process of grassroots democracy.

在他生活的那个小村子里，冯杰东带我看了他过去住的窑洞，在那里他一直住到1980年。那个窑洞很像我在延安见过的那些窑洞，毛泽东和他的同志们在长征结束到达陕北后就住在这样的窑洞里。由于耕地有限，人们从黄土坡的一面挖进去就成了窑洞。现在有些人还住在这样的窑洞里，但冯先生一家已经住在一栋两层小楼里了，他的学生经常去那里和他讨论功课和一些地方上的问题。在基层民主选举中，冯被选为安上村教育委员会主席。

Government policies have shifted from total central control to allowing peasants more freedom in deciding what crops to grow and sell on the open market to make a profit. Thus many peasants have benefited financially from this opportunity and often choose to raise certain fruits such as kiwi to sell for a higher price.

政府的政策已经改变了，不再是过去那样的全面调控，而是给农民更多的自由去决定种什么对他们更有利。这个政策使许多农民受益，他们经常选择去种水果，例如卖价比较高的猕猴桃。

However, sometimes shortages occur throughout the country when peasants decide not to plant crops such as cotton or even rice because it is more difficult to grow. While some peasants earn profits to build new houses others continue down muddy roads to small dank houses after hard labor in the fields. Still other peasants have totally lost their land to new development and industrialization as the growth rate of the GDP impatiently increases the pressure for more land to build factories and roads.

2002，安上，通往农民住房的泥泞小路
Muddy roads leading to peasant houses, An Shang, 2002

2007，户县，现代农民住房
Modern peasant houses, Huxian County, 2007

不过，有时候农民不愿意种那些种植起来比较困难的作物，如棉花，甚至水稻，从而造成市场短缺。有些农民挣了大钱，已经住上了现代化的新房子，其他人虽然田间劳作很辛苦，但之后也只能沿着泥巴路回到他们阴暗潮湿的小屋里去。由于GDP的快速增长，国家发展和工业化建设需要更多的土地，还有很多农民完全失去了耕地。

Many suffer injustices from the lack of an effective legal system. Policies to protect peasants' rights can be written at top levels but not implemented at local levels; complaints at the lower level may never reach the top. Some peasants who lose their land search for different jobs in the countryside while millions have become migrants seeking work in the cities. Some peasants are given money for their land and have been able to seek profitable jobs elsewhere, creating wide differences within the countryside as well as a gap between rural and urban areas.

缺乏有效的司法制度也使许多人深受其苦。中央把保护农民权益写进了政策条文，但在基层并没有落实，那里的申诉很可能永远无法到达上层。一些失去土地的农民在本地寻找种田以外的工作，更多的农民抛下家庭到城市里找工作。有些农民从他们失去的土地上得到了经济补偿，能够去其他地方寻找工作，结果就像城乡差别在扩大一样，农村内部的差别也在扩大。

户县，农民赶着骡子运送收获的庄稼
Peasants at the height of corn harvest with mule, Huxian County

In 2006 the government announced a major policy to end heavy taxes levied on peasants which had existed for decades, such as taxes on trees to grow apples, or on roads leading to the school. Taxes or fees had been collected for almost anything, often at the discretion of local leaders unjustifiably. Habitually taxes outweighed profits.

2006年政府宣布了一项重大的新政策，就是不再征收已经持续了几十年的农业税。过去征税的对象包括果树、去学校的道路，几乎什么都要上税，而交什么税经常是地方上随意决定的，这是不公平的。税收经常超过了农民的收益。

At the same time economic reforms allowed peasants to earn more money through hard work, the government shifted responsibility for paying the high cost of education and healthcare onto the shoulders of individuals, creating additional burdens.

经济改革允许农民通过自己的辛勤劳动挣得收入，但同时政府又改变了对个人的教育和医疗支出大包大揽的做法，这就给人们增加了新的负担。

University tuition, previously funded by the government, is now out of reach for most peasant families. To help alleviate this problem a new policy was announced in 2007 to provide tuition and a stipend for some students who can attend selected teacher-training universities if they agree to serve as teachers for at least ten years. The aim of this policy is twofold: to allow more students from the countryside to receive higher education and to improve the level of teaching in rural areas in the future.

大学学费以前都是国家负担的，而现在国家不负担了，这就超出了大多数农民家庭能承受的限度。2007年出台的新政策试图解决这个问题，就是国家为一些师范学生提供学费和生活费，条件是他们承诺毕业后从事中小学教育十年以上。这项政策的目的有两个：让更多的农村学生接受高等教育；提高农村地区的教学水平。

These policies reflect widespread concern for the inequalities that exist for those from the countryside. Leaders are aware of and concerned about widespread rural unrest. More mobility and expanded forms of communication have increased access to information and heightened awareness of relative deprivation for those living in remote areas.

这些政策反映了对农村不公平现象的广泛关注。领导们意识到农村存在的广泛的不安定。日益增长的流动性和沟通方式的扩展使得边远地区的居民了解到更多的信息，提高了他们对自己相对贫困状态的认知。

Expansion of the Market economy into urban areas
市场经济在城市的扩展

Market economy transforms state-run factories
市场经济下的国营工厂

Economic policies allowing for individual profit had been developing in the countryside in the 1980's for years before being introduced in urban areas.

80年代，保护个人所得的经济政策在农村实行了多年以后，开始推广到城市。

Looking back to 1977 when I first visited this factory in Guangzhou, all the workers were paid according to a set scale, unrelated to productivity or individual effort. Their salaries were frequently dependent on ideology and "guanxi" (backdoor connections) or on when they joined the Communist Revolution rather than based on their own skill or experience. Revolutionary posters surrounded their workspace. Correct understanding of ideology was the main criteria for selection of "model workers". No such thing existed as a monetary bonus in recognition for excellence.

1977年我第一次访问广州这家工厂的时候，工人的收入是根据一个等级制度决定的，与他们生产的产品数量及个人的努力没有关系。工资主要取决于他们的思想、关系（走后门）以及何时参加革命，而不是他们的技术和经验。工作地点四周都是革命标语。思想好是成为劳动模范的主要标准。没有奖金这种东西。

A certificate and clanging of a gong were the bonuses in the 1970's. Throughout China the major form of recognition for model teachers or model workers or for a factory making its required quota was the arrival of a big army truck with red flags and government officials. They would beat the drums and clang the gongs. I listened as school children paraded with portraits of Mao Zedong and Hua Guofeng when the truck arrived for a ceremony at their school for the publication of the *Selected Works of Mao Zedong* (Volume Five) in Shanghai in 1977.

在70年代的中国，如果有人成为模范教师、劳动模范或者工厂完成了生产任务，证书和锣鼓会成为奖励他们的主要形式，同时也会来一辆载着政府官员、插着红旗的部队卡车，人们敲锣打鼓地庆祝。1977年，我在上海看到一辆这样的汽车来到一所学校参加那里举行的庆祝《毛泽东选集》第五卷出版仪式，学生们举着毛泽东和华国锋的画像列队迎接。

Later outside a factory, I watched another truck approach and again heard the loud beating of drums and clanging of gongs as local officials read the names of "model workers". A list was posted on the factory wall next to rules and regulations. This was the only bonus for outstanding work at that time except for an occasional bottle of cooking oil to offset widespread shortages: no

01　1977，广州，国营工厂工人和革命标语
Workers in state-run factory with revolutionary posters, Guangzhou, 1977

1977，上海，学校举行庆祝《毛泽东选集》第五卷出版仪式
A ceremony at school for the publication of the *Selected Works of Mao Zedong* (Volume Five), Shanghai, 1977

other incentive existed to work harder. The supply of goods produced by factories was decided by the central government in Beijing and was often inconsistent with demand.

后来，在一家工厂外面，我看到另一辆这样的大卡车开过来，并再次听到敲锣打鼓的喧闹声。地方官员在这样欢快的气氛中宣布劳动模范的名字，他们的名单被贴在工厂的墙上，旁边是厂里的各种规章制度。这是那时对优秀工人的仅有的奖励。但偶尔有些模范还能得到一桶食用油，补贴一下配给油的不足。没有其他的物质刺激。物质供给由中央政府决定，它们经常不敷需求。

In recent years to encourage productivity, monetary bonuses were introduced to compensate individuals who achieved a successful work level in their factory or industry. In addition bigger offices or better housing became part of rewards and incentives that were offered to higher level positions.

改革开放以后，为了提高生产效率，也建立了奖金制度，以鼓励那些成功地完成生产任务的工人。除此之外，更大的办公室和更好的住宅也成为对高层管理者奖励的一部分。

New job opportunities have greatly increased freedom of mobility which never existed before when individuals were restricted by their official residency permit (hu kou) requiring them to remain in one place in order to secure housing and receive food from the rations booklets. People now purchase food on their own and often secure jobs in different locations. However, not everyone is benefiting from this flexibility.

新的工作机会使得人们有了很大的迁徙自由，而这在以前是从未有过的，那时人们都被严格限制在他们的户口所在地，以取得住房和配给的食品。人们现在买食品不再需要粮票，还可以在不同地方找到工作。不过，不是所有人都能从这种变化中受益。

2007，西安，新办公室成为额外的奖励
New offices become added bonus, Xi'an, 2007

2004，西安，作为福利的新公寓楼
New apartments provide benefits, Xi'an, 2004

The widening gap: within the cities
城市中的两极分化

2007，西安，旧公寓楼
Old concrete apartment units, Xi'an, 2007

2007，北京，现代豪华别墅
Modern imperial mansion, Beijing, 2007

While enormous disparity in wealth exists between urban and rural residents it is also glaringly evident within cities as illustrated by my visit to two friends living in modern cities. One retired couple with limited money lives in this dimly lit cold concrete apartment complex with few amenities. Nothing has been repaired in years. Broken bikes and boxes crowd the narrow stairwells. We sat around their small metal table on chairs taped together and talked about the high cost of medical bills. In contrast a few weeks before I had relaxed on a leather sofa with another family who lives in a European style luxury complex with their car in the garage and fresh flowers in the dining room.

贫富差别不但存在于城乡之间，也存在于城市内，而且已经非常明显。最近我访问了境况非常不同的两个朋友。一个是老人，夫妻都已退休，养老金有限，生活在一栋黑洞洞、冷冰冰、条件简陋、年久失修的公寓楼里。狭窄的楼道里堆着散了架的自行车和一堆箱子。我们坐在一个小桌子旁，谈起了昂贵的药费。相比之下，几星期前我访问了另外一个朋友。他家住在豪华的欧式住宅里，有车，还有车库，餐厅里摆放着鲜花。我们坐在他们的皮沙发里惬意地交谈。

Students, teachers, government leaders and shopkeepers on the street talk about how to solve the problem of increased wealth for some and unemployment or low income for others. It is a topic of serious concern to people in cities and countryside.

学生、老师、政府领导人、大街上的私营店主，大家一直在谈论如何解决一些人富裕起来而另一些人又失业和低收入的问题。不论对城市人还是农村人，这都是一个严肃的话题。

Because of the huge population and overcrowded schools it is still extremely difficult or very expensive to find housing in many cities. Most children must officially still attend the schools in the area where they were born and have their "hu kou" or residency permit which creates difficulties for parents who are offered new positions that require a move or for migrants whose children must remain back home in a different city. Awareness of these difficulties is beginning to bring about changes in the "hu kou" system.

由于大量的人口和过于拥挤的学校，要在城市里找到住房极其困难，要不然就是太贵了。大多数的孩子必须在他们出生或有"户口"的地方上学，这给那些在异地找到了新工作而且必须迁移的人造成了很大困难。他们的孩子不得不留在当地成为"留守儿童"。意识到这些困难是对"户口"制度进行改革的开端。

Satisfying basic needs : one country, decades apart
满足基本需求：一个国家——几十年的差别

How to balance the enormous chasm between urban and rural, coastal and interior, wealth and poverty within a country of more than 1.3 billion people stretching three thousand miles from east to west?

怎样才能使一个东西跨度5000多公里、人口超过13亿的国家在城乡之间、沿海和内地之间、贫富之间的巨大差别得到一种平衡？

Hauling water from a distant well is heavy for these children but essential for their families in Kashgar since frequent droughts create loss of crops and severe water shortages. Government policies push economic progress to interior regions where hundreds of millions have been taken out of poverty while others continue to struggle.

从很远的水井往家抬水，对这些孩子们来说，这活太累了，但对他们在喀什的家来说，这又是很重要的，因为那里水资源严重缺乏，经常发生旱灾，使得庄稼歉收。政府的政策将经济发展推向内地，那里成百上千万的人已经脱贫，但其他的人依旧在努力。

After sleeping in a yurt in Xinjiang Uyghur Autonomous Region with nomads in the far

1995，喀什，往家里抬水的孩子们
Children hauling water home, Kashgar, 1995

1995，新疆，牧民正在转移他们的畜群和家当
Nomads moving their herds and belongings, Xinjiang, 1995

northwestern region of China I watched as others moved their herds in search of a better location. They were moving their collapsible homes (called yurts) and all of their belongings on the backs of camels. Their basic needs included finding drinking water and enough food for their animals.

在中国西北遥远的新疆，我曾睡在牧人们的蒙古包里。起来后，我看着他们赶着畜群去寻找更好的营地。他们把自己的蒙古包和一切家当放在骆驼背上，然后迁徙。他们的基本要求是为他们的畜群找到饮用水和足够的食物。

Bright neon lights spotlight luxury goods in this Tang Dynasty-style shopping complex in the ancient capital of Xi'an. Fashionable suits and quality watches lure shoppers past the historic Drum Tower, which once rang out the time of day. China's expanding upper and middle classes provide the domestic stimulus for economic growth while others yearn to achieve the same success.

2007，西安，古城内唐代风格的现代店铺（李思远 摄）
Tang Dynasty-style modern shops in the ancient capital, Xi'an, 2007(Photo by Li Siyuan)

2007，西安，豪华商店
Modern shops with quality goods, Xi'an, 2007

  这是古城西安一家唐代风格的店面，闪亮的霓虹灯映照着里边的精美商品，显得珠光宝气。这家商店位于历史悠久的鼓楼附近，那里的鼓声曾送走了无数的日子，而今天它却用时尚的套装和高品位的手表吸引着那些来到鼓楼的游客。中国不断扩大的中产阶级刺激着国内的经济增长，而其他人也渴望取得与他们同样的成功。

  In vivid contrast, I learned the difference in what was considered a "basic need" from a friend who searched for a fine quality jacket for her husband and a new computer for the family in these modern shops in the city. She was miles apart in distance and lifestyle from the herdsmen.

  作为一个明显的区别，我从一个朋友身上发现了一些与前面所说的牧民朋友迥然不同的"基本需求"。她在这些现代化的商店里给她的丈夫找高档上衣，还打算为家里买一台新电脑。和那些牧民比起来，他们的差别可真是难以计算——不但是地理上的，更是在生活方式上的。

It is not only the distance of several thousand miles that separates the people of Kashgar in the far northwest from those in progressive Eastern coastal cities such as Shanghai, where modern facilities and goods are in abundance. In developmental terms the people's living standard can be decades apart from one area of China's vast country to another. Even a surface glance of these two extremes provides an insight into the enormity of the tasks facing China in the future.

现代而繁华的东部地区对贫困的西部而言已经成为一个不同的世界，所以将遥远西北的喀什和繁华的东部沿海城市——如上海——区别开的不仅是几千公里的距离。中国地域辽阔，地区间的生活水平差别会有几十年。即使只是对这两个极端的地区匆匆一瞥，我们也会对中国未来面临的艰巨任务有所体会。

2007，扶风县，菜市场上的讨价还价
Negotiating for vegetables, Fufeng County, 2007

"That's too much!" A villager in An Shang protests the price and pleads to add a bit more to the scale. An abundance of food and goods is colliding with rapidly rising costs. For decades the price for a kilo of rice or flour was controlled and subsidized by the government. Now with a market based economy, inflation and the rising cost of energy, people in both the countryside and in cities are shocked at the prices. Salaries have increased but for most not enough.

"太贵了！"一个安上村的村民表示不满，还要求再加一点。充足的食品和商品与急速上升的成本相矛盾。过去，在长达几十年的时间里，所有的物价都被政府控制，一公斤米和一公斤面的价钱许多年没有变过，同时政府也给予补助。现在，随着市场经济、通货膨胀和能源价格上涨的到来，农村和城市的居民都经常被上涨的物价吓一跳。工资上调了，但对大多数人来说还不够。

Coping with Change
应对变革

Unprecedented growth spurs unintended consequences
经济高速增长的代价

China's unprecedented growth has unquestionably benefited hundreds of millions but has created situations unintended and unwanted. While cranes crowd the skyline building offices and shops, ring roads circle the cities. Improved infrastructure provides a constant flow of goods and people while increased incomes allow residents to buy refrigerators and new cars. This rapid growth also causes severe energy crises, traffic congestion and pollution. Constant construction has increased the need for workers as migrants flow into crowded cities.

中国经济史无前例的增长毫无疑问使亿万人受惠，但也带来了一些意料不到的情况。一方面，到处是吊车、摩天大楼和商场、围绕着城市的环行路，改善了的基础设施带来了无尽的物流和人流，增加了收入的居民可以买冰箱和汽车；另一方面，这种急速的增长也引起了严重的能源危机、交通堵塞和污染问题。持续的建设导致对大量建筑工人的需求，农民工涌入了已经拥挤不堪的城市。

Careful balancing and new laws are urgently needed to insure safety for the workers who stretch on scaffolding poles with little or no protective programs or social services. Likewise, expanded innovation will be required to prevent devastating destruction to water, air and land. China's impressive

2004，陕西，高新区的吊车
Cranes in high-tech zone, Shaanxi Province, 2004

2007，陕西师大，脚手架上的工人
Workers balance their footing on scaffolding, ShiDa, 2007

rapid progress, unchecked, could destroy the country.

为了工人的安全，对新的法律的期待变得越来越迫切。那些在脚手架上工作的人几乎——或者根本——没有保险及社会福利。同样的，需要广泛的创新以防止对水、空气和土地的污染。中国令人印象深刻的经济过热如不加约束是很危险的。

Migrant workers building the new economy
建设新经济的民工们

These two migrant workers slept beside the work site after long hours of building the new economy. They lack decent wages, health benefits or safety protection and send most of their money back to far away family members. The estimated 140 million migrants who float to new construction sites create individual burdens and social unrest. Seeing these men sleeping beside the work site outside with no home I reflected on the similar plight of migrants in the United States in the past when they fought for basic rights of water and shelter and schooling for their children. Migrants often do the jobs rejected by many but then are looked down upon by others.

这两个农民工在工作了很长时间后，在工地旁睡着了。他们没有像样的工资，没有医疗保险，没有安全保护，还把他们的大部分收入寄回家。这样的农民工全国估计有一亿四千万人。他们来到城市的建设工地，同时也带来了个人的问题和社会的不安定。看到这些露宿街头的人们，我想起了过去那些美国流浪者同样的窘境，他们为了水、安身之所和孩子上学这些基本权利而奋斗。农民工们经常干那些别人不愿意干的工作，而且得忍受别人的冷眼。

2007，睡在工地旁的农民工
Migrant workers sleep beside the work site, 2007

Some workers stand on the corner with a pole and paintbrush seeking daily employment, others carry their belongings on their back looking for work. One of my graduate students spoke about the challenges facing China today: "Social inequality is a potential threat to the stability of our society," she said in front of the whole class. "Because of the economic reforms some people have gotten rich and that is good. But the differences are becoming greater. Some are at the bottom of society and work very hard but cannot lead a good life. If they lose their balance the situation can become dangerous." Chinese leaders and individuals are struggling to balance the unprecedented growth with the unintended consequences.

一些农民工拿着工具站在角落里,等待雇主上门,找一些临时的活;其他人背着行李找活干。我有一个学生是研究生,她在谈到中国今天面临的挑战时曾说:"社会不公正对我们社会的稳定是一个潜在的威胁。"她在班上发言说:"由于经济改革,有些人富了,这是好事,但是贫富的差距也在加大。有些人在社会的底层,他们努力工作,但还未能过上好的生活。如果情况失去了平衡会很危险。"中国领导人和老百姓都在这种前所未有的增长和意想不到的后果之间寻求一种平衡。

Environmental costs
环境的代价

Vivid progress, as evidenced by this long line of sleek apartments stretching to the sky, vanished two days later when air pollution blotted out these distant tall modern buildings. This is the view from my window where I live at Shaanxi Normal University in Xi'an. In previous years I could see to the nearby countryside with the outline of mountains in the distance and even had a view of the Tang Dynasty Big Goose Pagoda. Now the modern skyline and mountains disappear from one day to the next as thick pollution blurs the view of modernization.

就像那一长排伸向天际的整齐的住宅楼,这种表现生动的进步两天后就消失了——空气污染使得这些远方的现代化高层建筑变得模糊不清。这就是我从陕西师范大学的房间窗户看出去的景致。就在前些年,我还能看到附近的农村和远山的轮廓,甚至看到唐代建筑大雁塔。现在由于浓重的污染,那些现代的天际线和远山都一天天地消失了。

2007，西安，从我的房间窗户看出去的漂亮的新住宅楼
Beautiful new apartments seen from Crain's window, Xi'an, 2007

2007，西安，两天后在同一位置拍摄的照片
Looking out from the same window two days later, Xi'an, 2007

Reclaiming the land
开垦土地

In Gansu Province I watched in amazement as hundreds of worker carved out ledges in the rocky sandy soil in order to plant and water one tree at a time. A massive project to plant millions of trees was designed to help save the arid environment, where sand and dust fills the air and clogs the lungs. It appeared as if they were building the Great Wall, one brick at a time, to protect the country from being destroyed. Years of deforestation have resulted in violent dust storms stretching to regions hundreds of miles away from the far northwest to the modern capital of Beijing in the east.

2007，甘肃，数百人植树
Hundreds of workers planting trees, Gansu Province, 2007

在甘肃省，我看到几百个工人在沙石的土壤里挖出树坑，栽树浇水，这使我很惊讶。这是一个规模宏大的植树造林、拯救环境工程，那里干旱少雨，空气里都是沙土，能呛了肺。看起来他们就像是一砖一瓦地在修建长城，以保护这个国家不被毁掉。多年的植被破坏造成了从边远的西北地区到东部现代化城市首都北京，跨度几千公里的广大范围受到沙尘暴的肆虐。

2009，陕西，山上的梯田（李思远 摄）
Terraced farming up the mountainside, Shaanxi Province, 2009 (Photo by Li Siyuan)

In some regions regulations attempt to reclaim the land by prohibiting people from cultivating crops and allowing only natural vegetation to flourish. Preventing peasants from terrace-farming certain mountainside areas can be beneficial for the environment but disastrous for a family dependent on climbing up the mountainside to plant seeds and harvest their crops, as they have done for generations. Often no other arable land is available to them.

一些地区限制使用耕地，"退耕还林"，还禁止农民造梯田。这种措施保护了环境，但对那些依靠这种梯田种粮为生的农民来说却是灾难性的，因为他们祖祖辈辈都是这样生活，而那里也没有其他的可耕地可以利用。

Xiao Chai, a bright university student in my class, talked openly about solutions to environmental problems and a need for more individual participation. "I think some laws must be passed and strictly enforced to save the rivers and protect the air from factories dumping chemicals but more attention should be paid to the education of individuals so everyone will help with environmental protection." Another student added, "If we can't breath, all the progress of the last few years doesn't help anyone."

小柴是我班上一个聪明的学生，他也坦率地谈到环境保护的措施问题，认为应该有更多人加入到环保活动中去。他说："我觉得应该通过相关的法律，严格限制工厂倾倒化学废料，保护水和空气；其次，应该投入更多的精力对人民实行教育，使大家都来保护环境。"另一个学生说："如果我们不能呼吸，过去这些年的所有进步就没有意义。"

This was the message I often heard from intellectuals, peasants and top leaders concerning many of the critical issues facing China today: laws are needed but education is equally important to break many of the old habits and old thinking of the past.

这种有关中国正在面对的紧要问题的话我经常听到，说话的人有知识分子，也有农民和领导者。法律是需要的，但对人民的教育同样重要，这样才能破除过去的旧思想和旧习惯。

Healthcare and mental healthcare concerns
医疗事业和精神病治疗

Basic education is also desperately needed to improve healthcare. Current policies struggle to meet overwhelming challenges of an aging population, easy spread of diseases, mass-migration of workers and a lack of available services.

医疗状况需要通过基本教育加以提高。中国目前的政策正在努力应对人口老龄化、疾病的轻易传播、大规模的流动农民工以及医疗服务缺乏带来的挑战。

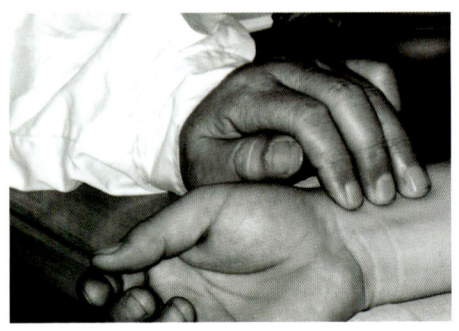

陕西，张医生正给病人把脉
Dr. Zhang reading the pulse of a patient, Shaanxi Province

In the 1970's there was a program for minimal training of peasants in the countryside to provide basic healthcare for other peasants. They were the so-called "Barefoot Doctors" because they worked in the fields, often barefooted as they planted rice. Most rural areas still lack trained doctors and necessary equipment making it necessary for people to travel to district or provincial hospitals far from their homes for treatment. Recently the government is putting new emphasis and new funding to address healthcare concerns.

在70年代，在农村医疗方面中国有一个做法，即对农民进行简单的医疗培训，以给农民

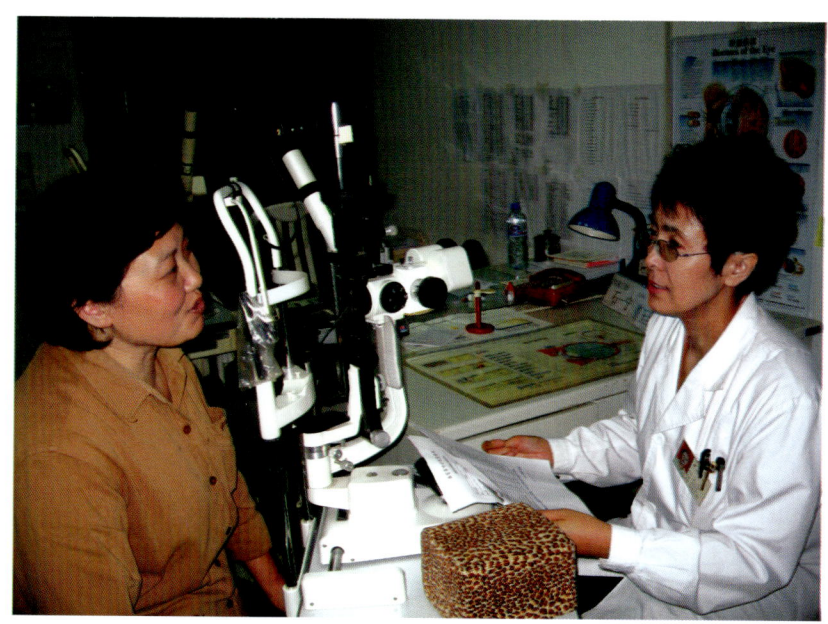

2007，西安，石一宁医生给病人问诊
Dr. Shi Yining listens to the concerns of one of her patients, Xi'an, 2007

以基本的医疗服务。他们就是所谓的"赤脚医生"，因为他们不脱产，还在田间劳动，插秧时经常赤着脚。绝大多数农村地区还是缺乏经过培训的医生和必要的设备，人们得到离家很远的地区医院或省上的医院去求医问药。近些年来，政府已经对农村医疗事业投入了更多的关注，提供了更多的资金。

In urban areas healthcare facilities have steadily expanded. Clinics and hospitals have been built with excellent equipments and improved training of personnel but often with high costs to the patients. Healthcare in the past was extremely limited but provided by the government. Now, many people cannot afford needed medical treatment. Government leaders are seriously debating how to handle medical problems more effectively. One new area of concern beginning to be discussed more openly is the issue of mental healthcare to help individuals cope with the intensity of stress in their daily lives.

城市的医疗设施已经相当强化了。已经建成的诊所和医院拥有很好的设备和经过专业培训的医生，但是医疗费用上涨了。过去的医疗服务非常有限但由政府提供。而现在，许多人付不起治病的费用。政府领导人正在认真地考虑怎样有效地解决这个问题。一个新的关注点是精神疾病的治疗问题。这个问题已经开始被更加公开地讨论，以帮助人们应对日常生活中越来越大的压力。

Mental healthcare issues
精神疾病的治疗问题

Change to the unprecedented degree experienced over the last thirty years has deeply affected the Chinese people. Modernization is clearly beneficial in some aspects yet it also challenges established behavior and customs, creating scenarios never encountered by previous generations.

过去30年史无前例的变化已经深刻地影响了中国人民。现代化在某些方面带来的好处是显而易见的，但它也对久已形成的行为和习惯提出了挑战，造成了以前从未遇到过的局面。

Further, the effects of change may be multiple and experienced in quick succession arising from the One Child Policy, new educational demands, mobility, greater personal choice and more individual responsibilities. All of these and more have contributed to transforming China in a breathtakingly rapid period of time. People's lives have been radically jolted.

这种变化的影响很快在接踵而来的社会现象中被体验和放大了：独生子女政策、新的教育需求、人口迁徙、更多的个人选择和责任等等，所有这些都使得中国的社会转型进入了一个让人喘不过气的迅猛时期。人们的生活被猛烈地撼动了。

Throughout China's history individuals were expected to handle emotional problems within their families or on their own. Until recently no counseling or guidance programs were available to train or help individuals cope with stress or depression.

在整个中国历史中，个人总是被期望依托家庭或由他们自己来处理感情问题，没有有关的咨询计划去培训或者帮助人们应对心理紧张和沮丧的问题。这种情况直到最近才有了变化。

According the World Health Organization China has one of the highest suicide rates in the world, yet there have been almost no facilities or trained professionals to address mental healthcare issues. Increasingly it is circulated that top students in excellent universities and managers in leading companies account for many who take their own lives.

根据世界卫生组织的统计，中国是世界上自杀率高的国家之一，但是精神治疗方面的机构和经过培训的专业人员还是寥寥无几。更加令人不安的消息是，自杀者中很多人都是名牌大学里的尖子学生和知名公司里的经理人。

Help with student stress
帮助学生减压

陕西师大，面对高中的心理咨询师暑期培训计划
Summer training program for high school counselor, ShiDa

The Chinese word "压力" (ya li) meaning "big pressure on the shoulder" is a frequent topic of vital concern in schools and at home. Teachers worry about their students who feel the immense pressure to succeed as the only child in their family. Managers who have been thrust into positions with increased responsibility but lack experience are finding it difficult to cope with the multitude of issues that arise. China is in the midst of transition, which is changing century-old and deeply ingrained patterns of the past.

"压力"是一个在学校和家庭中不断被提起的重大话题。老师担心他们的学生由于是家庭的唯一希望而感到太大的压力。那些在重要岗位上的管理者们，由于缺乏经验却又承担着越来越多的责任，发现很难处理那些源源而至的大堆问题。中国仍然处在过渡和实验的阶段，正在改变那些长时间形成的、根深蒂固的思维和行为模式。

Currently some significant initiatives are sprouting in pilot programs throughout the country, both government-sponsored and privately-initiated. Experimental training programs are teaching basic mental health skills to individuals who then serve as counselors in the schools, to be available for students to discuss sensitive issues that were previously only whispered in private at home or not at all. One of these trained high school counselors from Sichuan told me, "Sometimes students will only call me anonymously on my cell phone after school so no one else will see them or know they need help."

在这方面已经有一些大胆创意。一些遍及全国的开拓性计划开始施行，其中有政府资助的，也有民间创办的。这些实验性的培训计划向那些将成为学校心理咨询师的人们教授基本的技巧。他们将会见学生并与他们讨论那些以前只跟家里人启齿，或永远埋藏在他们心里的敏感问题。一个四川的高中心理咨询师告诉我:"有些学生只在放学后匿名给我打手机,这样就没人知道他们需要帮助。"

I met with the psychologist who led training sessions in 2007 at Shaanxi Normal University for eighty high school teachers from surrounding areas. She said the program was required by the government but was funded by the individual schools. After initial training during the summer, follow up sessions were scheduled within each school to share with other teachers what had been taught and to analyze the success of the program. When I met with the principal of one of the private high schools that had a newly trained counselor on staff, she shared, "Students have difficulty overcoming feelings of shame or embarrassment. It will take time for them to gain confidence to talk with someone openly about problems, but I believe it is a step forward to begin to have people with more training within an elementary or secondary school to try to help."

2007年,我见过一位在陕西师范大学领导着一个此类培训计划的心理学家,学员是来自周围地区的大约80位高中老师。她说这个计划是由政府要求成立的,但却由一些学校资助。在暑假的首期培训后,每所学校还有进一步的培训班,让参加过首期培训的人给同事们传授他们已经学到的知识,并分析培训计划的成功之处。我曾见到一位民办高中的校长,她的雇员中也有一位心理咨询师。她说:"学生在需要心理咨询时感到害羞和不好意思,所以要经过一段时间学生才能有信心和别人敞开地谈他们的问题,但是我相信让中小学老师接受更多这方面的培训是向前迈出的一步。"

One model to help deal with stress
帮助减压的一个范例

2009,北京,徐浩渊医生在培训心理咨询师
Dr. Xu Haoyuan training counselors, Beijing, 2009

Recognizing that many people needed help in responding to stress, anxiety, fear, and loss, Dr. Xu Haoyuan, a psychotherapist trained in China and the United States, decided to promote positive mental health through the use of anonymous online counseling services (www.ht2ht.com) and distance education programs for teachers and parents. Both approaches have successfully reached out to millions of individuals throughout China. Dr. Xu Haoyuan established the WorldLink Foundation in a cooperative effort with an American board of directors and advisors to provide people with coping strategies to help them respond to a multitude of pressures experienced in everyday life.

徐浩渊是一位在中国和美国接受过心理治疗方面培训的心理医疗师。她认识到许多人在应对压力、焦虑、恐惧和失落时需要帮助，所以决定通过网上匿名咨询服务（www.ht2ht.com）和对教师及家长进行远程教育的方式推广正面的心理治疗。这两种方式都很成功，使数以百万计的人们接受到了有关的知识。徐浩渊医生还与一个美国（心理）指导者理事会共同努力建立了美国威灵基金会，帮助人们应对日常生活中的各种压力。

After the tragic earthquake in Sichuan, Dr. Xu and a team of counselors returned for a second time in 2009 to contribute intensive training programs for teachers and parents who continue to suffer and have difficulty coping with traumatic stress. They trained teachers to help parents and students who struggle to rebuild their lives. Together with WorldLink, this program was made possible with assistance from the China Institute Earthquake Relief Fund in New York, which has contributed to rebuilding sustainable schools in the earthquake areas. Through cooperative efforts individuals in China and America are working together and learning about mental healthcare needs and services within both countries.

在汶川大地震灾后，徐医生和一个心理咨询小组于2009年再次回到四川，为那些依然不能从悲剧阴影中走出来的教师和家长建立了一个心理咨询的强化培训班。他们对教师加以培训，去帮助那些试图重建生活的家长和学生。这个培训班由纽约华美协进社的地震救助基金和威灵基金会共同资助，而前者是专为建设灾区的永久性学校而成立的。中美双方的有关人员正在共同努力，了解两国对心理医疗和服务的需要。

The egg seller and psychology
卖鸡蛋的人和心理学

"Have you eaten?" was the common Chinese greeting used for centuries in the past when the predominant concern for everyone was having enough food to survive for the day. It is still frequently used as a greeting and is a way to express polite concern toward others. Each day I met Yu Ruixue she would first ask, "Chi le ma?" (Have you eaten?) We had gotten to know each other when I frequently bought fruit in the market where she sold eggs to the local people. An old professor had told me when he was growing up he only had eggs twice a year: one on the New Year and one on his birthday as a very special occasion. Now they are bought and sold in abundance.

"吃了吗？"过去是中国人通常的问候语，那时人们最关心的是是否有足够的食物以求温饱。现在这种问候语还不时被使用，表示客气和对他人的关心。每天我见到余瑞雪，她都会问我："吃了吗？"她是卖鸡蛋的，我去市场上买水果的时候认识了她。一位老教授告诉我，在他小的时候鸡蛋是稀罕物，一年只能吃两次：一次是过年，一次是过生日。现在每天都有大量的鸡蛋成交。

One night the egg seller Yu Ruixue invited me to come with her to a meeting where friends gathered to discuss concerns about stress in their daily lives. They talked about methods of helping their children at home or students in the classroom. It was an open discussion of individuals sharing their fears and hopes and represents a new kind of forum for handling issues that were traditionally hidden within the household or totally suppressed. On many occasions such as this people shared with me the complexity of coping with multiple changes in their lives.

一天晚上，余瑞雪邀请我和她一起参加朋友们的聚会，讨论有关日常生活中的心理压力问题。他们谈到了在家里帮助孩子或在学校帮助学生的方法。这是一次开诚布公的讨论，每个人都谈了自己的担心和希望。它是一个新的论坛，目的是解决那些传统上不示于人的心理问题。在许多类似的场合，人们都跟我谈到他们应对无穷变化的复杂性的经验。

2007，西安，在市场上卖鸡蛋的余瑞雪
Yu Ruixue selling eggs in the market, Xi'an, 2007

2007，西安，一群朋友讨论"紧张"和"压力"（李思远　摄）
A group of friends discuss stress and pressure, Xi'an, 2007(Photo by Li Siyuan)

Section Two
第二章

Heroes : Then and Now
今昔英雄

Introduction
导言

In assessing all of the changes that have resulted in the China of today, many people whom I met stand out as exceptional. Each of them I value and respect for what they lived through and contributed to their country. Many are well known and eminent in China and elsewhere. Here I honor them for their achievements and express my gratitude for their contributions to my understanding of China for over thirty years. Through them and others I began to weave a thread of connections with people in diverse positions and different locations who guided me across many bridges of understanding in my own journey inside China. They taught me about China in a very personal way, often allowing me to touch history through their stories.

在评价导致今天中国的这些变化时，必须谈到许多我见到过的人，他们是这样的令人印象深刻、与众不同。对于他们的生活和对国家作出的贡献，我高度评价，十分尊重。许多人才华出众、中外知名，这里我对他们的成就表示敬意，对他们在过去30多年中使我更好地理解中国表示由衷的感谢。通过他们和其他人，我开始织就了一簇与不同职位、不同地区的人们联系的"线"，是这些人让我在中国的旅途中搭建了许多理解的桥梁。他们以自己个人的方式为我诠释了什么是中国。通过他们的故事，我经常"触"到历史。

People Who Influenced Change
影响巨变的人们

Mao Zedong was seen as a hero in the eyes of millions of Chinese who unquestionably followed him for decades after he established the People's Republic of China in 1949. There were other high-level leaders and common citizens who dramatically or unpretentiously also influenced change and became heroes in the minds of many.

毛泽东是亿万中国人心目中的英雄。1949年中华人民共和国成立后，中国人民埋头跟着他几十年。还有很多人，也许是高层领导，也许是普通老百姓，都潜移默化而又深刻地影响了中国的变革，成为人们心目中的英雄。

西安，画家刘文西与他画的毛泽东
Artist Liu Wenxi with his painting of Mao Zedong, Xi'an

Liu Wenxi: Mao and heroes of the past
刘文西：毛和昔日的英雄

Mao Zedong, Zhou Enlai, Zhu De and Liu Shaoqi, four heroes of the past, are immortalized on a huge canvas that hangs in the Great Hall of the People in Beijing. I watched as Liu Wenxi, a nationally treasured artist, painted four of China's most prominent revolutionary leaders and observed his own striking resemblance to Mao Zedong.

毛泽东、周恩来、朱德和刘少奇，四位过去的英雄，被绘成巨幅画像，悬挂在北京人民

刘文西所绘的毛与人民在一起的画
Mao with the people, painted by Liu Wenxi

大会堂里。刘文西是一位全国知名的画家。当他在巨大的帆布上画这四位杰出的中国革命领导人时，我就在一旁观看，并且发现他与毛泽东（长相）惊人的相似。

For years Liu Wenxi recorded with his brush classic images of Mao Zedong surrounded by compelling portraits of peasants when giant posters and sayings of Mao were prominently displayed throughout all of China. Now as quotes on the stock market replace quoting political slogans Mao Zedong is most commonly seen in the hands of the people on all monetary denominations of Chinese currency (RMB, renminbi, means the people's money). Liu Wenxi also drew the portrait of Mao Zedong, which appears on those printed currencies.

在很长时间里，刘文西一直用自己的画笔描绘毛泽东的经典形象。在他笔下，毛泽东总是被表情生动的农民簇拥着。那时候，毛泽东的宣传画和语录风行全国。现在，股票市场取代了政治标语，最经常看到毛泽东的地方就是人们手中的人民币。而这些毛泽东像也是刘文西画的。

刘文西与他所画的毛泽东、周恩来、朱德和刘少奇
Painting of Mao Zedong, Zhou Enlai, Zhu De and Liu Shaoqi by Liu Wenxi

Helen Snow (1907—1997): bridge builder of Sino-American understanding
海伦·斯诺（1907—1997）：中美理解之桥的建造者

"The Great Wall between China and the rest of the world seemed very far away. This was basic grassroots Chinese-American friendship. Never would I do anything to break this special relationship, woven of such a few fragile threads in a world where merciless swords cut at international understanding."

Helen Snow Inside Red China

"中国和世界其他地区之间似乎并没有一座万里长城，因为相互间的民间交往是中美友谊的基础。在当今的世界上，各民族间的相互理解时常会遭到无情的破坏，而我绝不会做任何事去损害这种脆弱的特殊关系。"

——海伦·斯诺《续西行漫记》

1937，身着军装的海伦·斯诺与一个年轻战士在延安的合影（这张照片被用在她自己的著作《续西行漫记》的封面上）
Helen Snow dressed in her army disguise with a young soldier in Yen'an in 1937(on the cover of her book *Inside Red China*)

2007，海伦·斯诺30年代的照片（在西安举行的她诞辰100周年的研讨会上展出过）
Photo of Helen Snow in the 1930's(displayed at the 100th Anniversary Symposium of her birth), Xi'an, 2007

These words reflect Helen Snow's thoughts as she said goodbye to the young Chinese boy who had helped her through war-torn zones in northern Shaanxi Province. Helen Snow was young, beautiful and brave as she journeyed deep into China's interior to interview Mao Zedong, Zhou Enlai, Zhu De and others in Yen'an in 1937. They were the young heroes who had survived the Long March and who would dramatically alter the course of China's future.

这些话反映了海伦·斯诺那时的想法，她正和一个中国小伙子告别，而正是这个小伙子帮助她通过了陕北的交战地区。那是1937年，她年轻、美丽、勇敢，深入到中国内地去采访毛泽东、周恩来、朱德和其他人——那些经过了长征的年轻英雄们，他们日后将影响中国的未来发展进程。

Helen Snow and her husband Edgar Snow each made their separate and dangerous journeys and provided rare and valuable accounts in their books *Inside Red China* and *Red Star Over China* respectively, which remain as classic documentations of the Communist Revolution. For many within China and the outside world their words were the first eyewitness accounts. The information Helen Snow gained from those strong men and women in Yen'an and from her ten years of active involvement in China became the substance of over twenty books and innumerable unpublished manuscripts, including *My Yen'an Notebook, Women in China,* and *My China Years*. She recorded in painstakingly accurate detail the painful struggles of the Chinese people on their march to establish a new China in the midst of civil war with the Kuomintang and the War of Resistance with Japan. Helen and Edgar Snow dedicated their lives to building bridges of understanding and friendship between the Chinese and American people and continue to be greatly admired.

海伦·斯诺和她的丈夫埃德加·斯诺各自单独完成了他们充满危险的旅程，并且分别在他们的著作《续西行漫记》和《西行漫记》中作了非常有价值的描述，这两本书仍然被认为是有关中国革命的经典文献。对很多中国人和外国人来说，这两本书是他们第一次读到的中国革命见证人的描述。海伦·斯诺从延安那些坚强的男人和女人那里以及她生活在中国的10年中得到了大量的信息。它们成为她超过20本书和难以计数的未刊手稿的基本内容，包括《我的延安笔记》《中国妇女》和《我在中国的岁月》。她以精确的细节记录了中国内战和抗日战争期间中国人民为建立新中国而进行的艰苦卓绝的斗争。海伦和埃德加·斯诺毕其一生的精力去搭建中美人民友谊和理解的桥梁，并且将继续为两国人民所敬仰。

In 2007 several symposia to commemorate the 100th Anniversary of Helen Snow's Birth were held in Beijing, Xi'an, Yen'an and Baoji following in the footsteps of her journeys in China, organized by the Society for Friendship Studies in Beijing and by An Wei throughout Shaanxi Province. A large photograph portrays a youthful and courageous Helen Snow during her early China years.

2007年，循着海伦·斯诺在中国的行迹，几场纪念她诞辰100周年的研讨会分别在北京、西安、延安和宝鸡举行。这些研讨会分别是由北京的中国国际友人研究会和安危组织的。在这些研讨会上展示了一幅海伦·斯诺的画像，是早年中国岁月里那个年轻而勇敢的海伦。

Helen Snow and Deng Xiaoping
海伦·斯诺和邓小平

In a way it was because of Deng Xiaoping that I was first introduced to Helen Snow. While immersed in Chinese studies at Duke University in the 1960's I had read Helen and Edgar Snow's books and had been to China in the 1970's. Then one Sunday in 1979 at our house in Madison, Connecticut I read a long article in *The New York Times* which said Helen Snow had been invited to Washington D.C. to attend a reception with Deng Xiaoping in celebration of the official establishment of diplomatic relations between China and the United States.

从某种意义上说，我是因为邓小平才认识海伦·斯诺的。早在上世纪60年代在杜克大学专攻中国研究时，我就读过海伦和埃德加·斯诺的书。70年代我访问了中国。1979年的一个星期天，我在康涅狄格州麦迪逊的家里读到了《纽约时报》上的一篇长文，上面提到海伦·斯诺受邀赴首都华盛顿，参加欢迎邓的国宴，并共同庆祝中美两国正式建立外交关系。

1983，美国。海伦·斯诺在雪莲康涅狄格州麦迪逊市的家（卡罗·帕特森 摄）
Helen Snow at Sharon Crain's house in Madison, Connecticut, U.S., 1983 (Photo by Carole Patterson)

It described how Helen Snow and Deng Xiaoping had never met although they were both in Shaanxi Province in 1937 when Helen made her dangerous journey to Yen'an. As she was leaving after her five-month stay Mao Zedong wrote a letter with instructions for Deng Xiaoping who had just been appointed Deputy Director of the Political Department of the 8th Route Army. Mao folded the paper and handed it to Helen Snow asking her to give it to Deng Xiaoping on her way back to Xi'an before returning to Beijing. Helen traveled on horseback and foot to the Sanyuan area near Xi'an where Deng Xiaoping and the 8th Route Army had been stationed. However, due to continuous fighting and shifting of locations to avoid enemy attacks, Deng Xiaoping's unit had left just the night before Helen arrived. She missed Deng Xiaoping by twelve hours.

这篇文章写到，海伦·斯诺和邓小平以前从未谋面，虽然1937年时他们都在陕西。那一年，海伦历尽艰险来到延安，并在那里待了5个月。在她离开时，毛泽东写了一封介绍信给时任八路军政治部副主任的邓小平，并把信折好后交给海伦·斯诺，请她在路经西安返回北京的途中把信交给邓小平。海伦时而骑马，时而步行，一路兼程到达三原时，由于在与敌周旋过程中的不断战斗和转移，邓小平的部队刚刚在前一天晚上离开了。仅仅相差12个小时，她错过了这次会面。

Forty-three years later in 1979 in Washington D.C. Helen Snow, in a red silk Chinese jacket, dramatically presented the letter from Mao Zedong to Deng Xiaoping with her words, "You are a hard man to catch up with!"

43年后的1979年，华盛顿，身着一件红色中国丝制上衣的海伦·斯诺，戏剧性地将那封信交给了邓小平，并说："你是一个让人难以追赶的人！"

In conclusion *The New York Times* article said, "Helen Snow resides in the quiet town of Madison, Connecticut." I had no idea we lived in the same town until I read that article. So it was Deng Xiaoping's visit that introduced me to Helen Snow in my own community. The next day I looked up her number in the phone book and called: "My name is Sharon Crain, I have studied about China and read the books by you and your husband. It would be a great honor if I had the opportunity to meet you."

《纽约时报》的那篇文章在结束的时候说："海伦·斯诺住在康涅狄格州一个安静的小镇——麦迪逊。"在我读那篇文章之前，我一直不知道我们住在同一个镇上，而且就在我的社区，所以可以说是邓小平的访问把我介绍给了海伦。第二天我就在电话册上查到了海伦的号码，并且给她打了一个电话："我叫雪莲，一直研究中国，也读过您和您丈夫的书。如果有机会见到您我将不胜荣幸。"

Helen's life in America
海伦在美国的生活

No one had ever mentioned that Helen Snow lived there. She had turned inward and had become a hermit in her own house. She and Edgar Snow moved to Madison in the 1940's after they returned from China. Later they suffered hostile anti-communist thinking during the McCarthy era in the United States in the 1950's. In China they had struggled through dangerous blockades to get to the front to capture firsthand stories and record the essence of the Chinese revolution. Neither of them was ever a member of the Communist Party in China or America. However when they returned to their own country they found people in the United States were more suspicious than receptive about their experiences in China.

没人提到过海伦住在那里。她变得内向了，成了足不出户的隐士。她和埃德加·斯诺在上世纪40年代从中国回来后就搬到麦迪逊。在反共的麦卡锡时代，他们受了很多苦。在中国他们历经艰险去前方了解并记录了有关中国革命的第一手资料，但他们两人既不是中国共产党员，也不是美国共产党员。不过当他们回到自己的国家后，发现人们并不接受，甚至怀疑他们在中国的经历。

Back in the small historic town of Madison, Connecticut Helen and Edgar Snow were no longer the daring team they had been in China, risking their lives to witness and document the crucial events unfolding. They could not get anything published about China, even though they had more firsthand information than almost anyone in the United States at that time.

回到麦迪逊这个历史小镇以后，海伦和埃德加不再是他们曾经在中国那样的敢死队了，可以冒着危险去亲历和记录那些正在发生的关键事件。即使拥有超过几乎任何美国人的第一手资料，他们仍然没有就中国问题发表著述的权利。

In 1949, the same year that the People's Republic of China was founded, Helen and Edgar Snow were divorced. Edgar then married Lois Wheeler and moved to Switzerland where they had two children. Their daughter was named Xi'an, "western peace", the same as China's ancient capital. Edgar Snow died of cancer the very week that Mao Zedong met with President Nixon in Beijing in 1972, opening again relations between China and the United States. Premier Zhou Enlai had sent a team of Chinese doctors to assist Edgar Snow and they stayed with him until the end. According to his wishes, Edgar Snow's ashes were equally distributed between Beijing University where he had taught when it was called Yanjing University and along the Hudson River on the east coast of the United States, where the Atlantic Ocean flows outward toward China and other parts of the world.

1949年，即中华人民共和国成立的那一年，海伦和埃德加·斯诺离婚了。埃德加接着和路易斯·威勒结婚，并移居瑞士，在那里他们有了两个孩子。他们的女儿取名"西安"。1972年他因癌症去世。就在他去世的那个星期，毛泽东在北京会见了尼克松，揭开了中美关系史上的新篇章。周恩来总理曾在埃德加·斯诺生前派了一个医疗队去帮助他治疗疾病，并一直到他的生命终点。按照斯诺的遗愿，他的骨灰一部分埋在他教过书的北京大学——那时叫燕京大学，还有一部分撒进通往大西洋的哈德逊河，而大西洋会把美国和中国以及世界其他地区连接起来。

In Madison, Helen lived alone in an old New England house built in 1752 with wood-planked floors, low ceilings and a nine-foot wide stone fireplace. She loved the house, she loved her old Remington typewriter, which she had carried to China and back, she loved the raccoons, which came in from the surrounding woods, but most of all she loved writing. She didn't care about form or style or the meticulous editing that Edgar Snow did, she just wanted to record information accurately and quite frequently with subtle humor.

在麦迪逊，海伦独自生活在那所建于1752年的老式新英格兰房子里，那里有宽且厚的木地板、低矮的天花板及9英尺宽的石头壁炉。她爱这栋房子，爱她的旧莱明顿打字机，那是她带去中国又从中国带回来的。她也爱浣熊，它们来自周围地区。但她最爱的还是写作。她并不在意写作的形式和风格，也不像埃德加·斯诺那样仔细地修改，她想做的只是将她所知道的准确又不失幽默地记下来。

What I noticed immediately when I first met Helen Snow at her house in Madison in 1979 were the piles of typed pages, floor to ceiling, in small cut off cardboard boxes. Thousands of pages that recorded information about China were stacked in room after room in her house. When I asked if I could help, since she did not drive and was alone, she replied, "Well, you can help me publish my thirty unpublished manuscripts about China."

1979年，我第一次在海伦·斯诺的家里见到她时，就注意到从地板到天花板，到处堆的是装在小纸板箱里的打印稿。成千上万张有关中国的打印好的稿件堆满了她家的一间又一间屋子。因为她不开车，又是独居，我问可以帮她点什么，她说："嗯，就帮我把这些有关中国的30部书稿出版了吧。"

The door was opened: She had allowed me to enter her secluded world. Her meeting in Washington D.C. with Deng Xiaoping had been one of the very few times she had ventured out in public since returning from China over thirty years earlier. She lived alone because she wanted to write and because she feared that others still thought negatively about China.

海伦将门打开了：她让我进入了她的秘密世界。从中国返美以后的30多年来，她极少在公众场合露面，与邓小平在华盛顿的会面是这少数露面中的一次。之所以深居简出是因为她想写作，也是因为她担心其他人仍然敌视中国。

Helen Snow and "Gung Ho"
海伦·斯诺与"工合"

Our friendship deepened as we spend hundreds of hours over a period of nearly twenty years working together to try to publish more of her books and manuscripts in China and America. Helen Snow opened for me a world of China that would not have been available without her and challenged me to "carry on the torch" to build new bridges of understanding. She took me back to the 1930's and the birth of modern China. She became my invaluable "primary-source material" from which I would learn about the early goals of Mao Zedong in 1937; about the warmth and strength of Zhou Enlai's wife, Deng Yingchao, and the everyday struggles of the young boys who had left their families to become soldiers and follow Mao; and about the hardships of some of the old people who lived in the small caves and worked in surrounding fields to help eke out food for the Communist troops.

在将近20年的时间里，我们的友谊深化了，因为我们花了大量的时间一起工作，为的是让她更多有关中国的著作和手稿在中美两国得以出版。海伦·斯诺为我打开了一个中国的世界，如果没有她这对我来说是无法实现的；而这件事本身也向我提出了挑战，即接过她的火炬，继续建设理解的桥梁。她将我带回到上世纪30年代和现代中国刚刚诞生的时期，成为我无可替代的"主要材料来源"。从她那里，我知道了1937年时毛泽东的目标，知道了周恩来夫人邓颖超的热情和力量，知道了跟随毛成为战士的年轻人的日常斗争，知道了一些老人的艰辛——他们住在窑洞里，在田间辛苦劳作，却将打下的粮食支援给共产党的军队。

Helen Snow was also a social activist and one of the leading initiators of the Industrial Cooperative Movement to provide urgent relief to China in the late 1930's. These cooperatives were called "gung ho", which in Chinese means "work together". Today in the United States the same words are commonly used to describe someone who is enthusiastic or "gung ho" about something, which originated with Helen Snow in China. Her book *China Builds for Democracy* described these Industrial Cooperatives and was used by Premier Nehru as a guide for developing similar cooperatives in India.

2007，海伦·斯诺的书《中国为民主奠基》在西安出版
Helen Snow's book *China Builds for Democracy*, published in Xi'an, 2007

The book was finally published in Shaanxi Province in 2007 and translated into Chinese by Jian Hua, Zhong Lun and An Wei.

海伦·斯诺也是一个社会活动家，是工业合作化运动的主要发起者之一，这一运动为上世纪30年代后期的中国提供了急需的救济。"工合"在中文里意思是"一起工作"。今天在美国，同样的词通常被用来形容那些热情的人或者用合作态度对待事情的人，而这样的运动就是由海伦·斯诺等在中国发起的。她的著作《中国为民主奠基》描绘了这些"工合"运动者，并被尼赫鲁总理用做在印度发展此类合作的指导性文件。这本书最后于2007年在陕西出版，译者是剑华、仲伦和安危。

After Helen Snow's death in 1997, a memorial service was held in the Great Hall of the People in Beijing as well as in Madison, Connecticut. Ambassador Huang Hua and his wife He Liliang made the long journey from Beijing to Madison to attend. China's Ambassador to the United States, Li Daoyu, also made the journey from Washington D.C. along with more than two hundred people from five countries and twelve states in America. Old friends from China, such as An Wei and Gong Pusheng, many presidents of U.S.-China organizations, and several writers came to pay their respects to Helen Snow who had built bridges of understanding between the two countries for decades.

1997年海伦·斯诺去世后，北京的人民大会堂和康涅狄格州麦迪逊市都为此举办了悼念仪式。黄华大使和夫人何理良专程从北京赶来；中国驻美大使李道豫也从华盛顿赶来；参加悼念仪式的还有来自5个国家和美国12个州的200多位来宾。海伦的许多中国老朋友，如安危和龚普生，许多中美友好团体的负责人，以及一些作家都赶来了，对这位几十年来始终致力于搭建中美理解之桥的杰出人士表达敬仰之情。

An Wei: trusted translator of Helen Snow's books
安危：海伦·斯诺著作的特约翻译

An Wei first learned about the Snows when he was sent to Yen'an as a student in the late 1960's during the harsh Cultural Revolution years. There he lost time for formal study but gained knowledge about the early leaders of China. He became interested in learning more about the Snows' active involvement in China. When Helen Snow returned to China in the 1970's An Wei was her interpreter and they developed a meaningful friendship. Later she trusted him to become the key translator for her books so the younger generation could learn from the past.

安危第一次知道斯诺夫妇是在延安，那是60年代末混乱的"文革"期间，他是一个被派往那里的学生。在那里，他失去了在学校学习的机会，但却了解了中国的早期领导人，并且对斯诺夫妇与中国的关系产生了兴趣。当海伦·斯诺70年代重返中国时，安危成为她的翻译，并且与她建立了深厚的友谊。后来她委托安危为她著作的主要翻译，以使年青一代可以从历史中受益。

As the thread of our connections continued Helen introduced me to An Wei who in turn made the first arrangements for my teaching at Shaanxi Normal University in Xi'an, which has continued for decades. An Wei and I have collaborated on educational projects between China and America for nearly thirty years. As a visiting scholar for a year at Trinity College in Connecticut An Wei utilized his time to work with Helen Snow and continue his research into her life. He has translated into Chinese and published many of her books in China and now serves as President of the Edgar and Helen Snow Center in Xi'an.

1985，康涅狄格州麦迪逊市，安危在海伦家
An Wei at Helen Snow's house in Madison, Connecticut, 1985

作为我们友谊的继续，海伦把我介绍给安危，安危又在1982年帮我联系到在西安的陕西师范大学教书。在将近30年的时间里，安危和我在许多中美间的教育项目上展开了合作。安危在康涅狄格州的三一学院曾做过一年的访问学者，他利用这段时间和海伦一起工作，继续他对海伦一生的研究。他翻译出版了许多她的著作，现在还担任设在西安的"埃德加·斯诺夫妇研究中心"的主任。

An Wei and his wife, Niu Jianhua, have devoted their lives to promoting friendship and understanding between Chinese and Americans. Helen Snow encouraged them both to build strong relations between our two countries, which they have admirably accomplished.

安危和妻子牛剑华致力于中美两国人民间的友谊和理解。虽然他们在这方面已经做出了令人钦佩的成绩，海伦·斯诺还是鼓励他们做得更多些。

Ambassador Chai Zemin: "Understanding"
柴泽民大使："理解"

1980，华盛顿，柴泽民大使、隋永洁和雪莲
Ambassador Chai Zemin, Jeannette Sui and Sharon Crain, Washington D.C., 1980

Jeanette Sui (Soong Qingling's adopted daughter) was a 20-year-old university student in the United States when she and I attended the National Day celebration at the Chinese Embassy in Washington D.C. with Ambassador Chai Zemin, who became China's first Ambassador to the United States after the establishment of diplomatic relations between China and the United States in 1979.

我和隋永洁（宋庆龄的养女）在参加中国大使馆举行的国庆招待会时曾与柴泽民大使合影，那时她还是一个20岁的大学生。柴是中美1979年正式建交后中国派驻美国的第一任大使。

We met together and talked about Soong Qingling and Helen Snow and the fact that our countries were on the verge of new opportunities with the recent opening of relations after thirty years of closure. I asked Ambassador Chai what he believed was needed the most for the development of relations in the future. He replied with just one word: "Understanding."

我们谈起了宋庆龄和海伦·斯诺,以及我们两国隔绝30年后随着最近的开放而面临的新机遇。我问柴大使未来两国间关系最需要的是什么,他的回答只有一个词:"理解"。

Ambassador Wang Bingnan: Warsaw Ambassadorial-level talks and China's stock market
王炳南大使:中美大使级会谈和中国股票市场

Soong Qingling had given this coffee pot to Helen and Edgar Snow for their wedding in the 1930's. Helen asked me to return it to China to be placed in the Soong Qingling Museum with the help of Wang Bingnan, President of the China People's Association of Friendship with Foreign Countries.

30年代海伦和埃德加·斯诺结婚时,宋庆龄送给他们一个咖啡壶作为结婚礼物。海伦请我把它带给王炳南,并放置在宋庆龄博物馆里。那时王炳南是中国对外友协的会长。

1982,北京,王炳南和雪莲
Wang Bingnan and Sharon Crain, Beijing, 1982

This Friendship Association in Beijing and in Shaanxi Province made arrangements for many of the delegations of Americans I took to China in the 1980's and 1990's.

80年代和90年代,我曾带领很多美国代表团访问中国,而所有这些访问都是北京和陕西的对外友协安排的。

For many years, Ambassador Wang represented China in a series of Ambassadorial-level talks during the Warsaw Pact meetings in Geneva in the 1950's before the U.S. and China had reopened diplomatic relations. Many years later, Ambassador Wang Bingnan's son, Wang Boming, helped us initiate a Scholars' Program at China Institute in New York for the first visiting scholars who came to the United States after diplomatic relations were formalized in 1979. Wang Boming studied in the United States for years before returning to help establish China's very first Stock Exchange in Shanghai.

在中美正式建立外交关系前,中美两国50年代在日内瓦举行过一系列的大使级谈判,王炳南代表中国担任了多年的大使。多年后,王炳南大使的儿子王波明帮助发起了纽约华美协进社的学者交流计划,这个计划是为了中美关系正常化后第一批来自中国的访问学者而建立的。王波明在美学习多年,后来回到中国,参与建立了上海的股票交易所。

Foreign Minister Huang Hua: a circle of friendship and Sino-American relations
外交部长黄华：友谊之轮回和中美关系

Ambassador Huang Hua and his wife He Liliang visited with their old friend Helen Snow in her living room in America in the 1980's, where I first met them. They reflected on when they had often met in the Snow's living room in Beijing when making plans for the 1935 December 9th Student Movement against Japanese aggression. Huang Hua was then a young student at Yanjing University when he was asked by Edgar Snow to be the interpreter during his dangerous journey to interview Mao Zedong.

黄华大使和妻子何理良80年代在美国海伦·斯诺的家里访问她时，我第一次在那里见到了他们。他们回忆起30年代的事情。在筹划反对日本侵略的"一二·九"运动时，黄华经常和斯诺夫妇在他们家的客厅里会面。埃德加·斯诺在历经艰险去陕北采访毛泽东时，邀请黄华做他的翻译，当时黄华是燕京大学的年轻学生。

Years later when Mao established the People's Republic of China, Huang Hua served as Foreign Minister, as Vice Premier and as an Ambassador to the United Nations. In an interesting circle of events Huang Hua became the key negotiator and essential link leading to the Nixon-Mao visit in 1972 and the subsequent establishment of relations between China and the United States in 1979.

中华人民共和国成立后，黄华担任过外交部长、副总理和驻联合国大使。他是促成1972年尼克松访华和1979年建立中美外交关系的主要谈判者和关键联系人。

I later learned that Huang Hua was the one who had carefully crafted the wording from Mao Zedong indicating that Nixon would be welcome to come to China as the United States President or as a private citizen. Huang Hua's old friend, Edgar Snow, was originally asked to convey that message. After many secret voyages by the United States Secretary of State Henry Kissinger, President Nixon arrived in Beijing in 1972. The United States and China opened doors for the first time since Mao Zedong assumed power in 1949.

后来我才知道毛泽东邀请尼克松访华的邀请函措辞——不论是尼克松作为美国总统还是普通公民来访，我们都表示欢迎——是由黄华精心翻译的。本来这个邀请是委托给黄华的老朋友埃德加·斯诺转达的。在基辛格国务卿多次秘密访华后，尼克松总统的访华之旅终于在1972年成行，自中华人民共和国成立后中美之间第一次敞开了大门。

1983，黄华、何理良、雪莲和海伦·斯诺在海伦康州麦迪逊的家里

Huang Hua, He Liliang and Sharon Crain with Helen Snow at her house, Madison, Connecticut, 1983

Chen Hanpo: like pages of a history book
陈翰伯：历史大书中的篇章

Chen Hanpo was a journalist in the 1930's in Xi'an and helped Helen Snow on her journey to Yen'an. Later in Beijing he became the director of all publishing throughout China for many years. When he came to the United States in 1980 he visited his old friend Helen Snow, who insisted on introducing him to the benefits of American "fast foods" to allow more time for what Helen called "long thoughts". So we ate McDonald's hamburgers at my house as they talked about the dangers of riding through the dark streets in Xi'an in a rickshaw evading the Kuomintang guards who were trying to prevent Helen Snow from reaching the Communist front. As we sat on the deck on a clear sunny day their words and recollections flowed like pages of a history book about the struggles of the Chinese people in the 1930's when it was unclear what path China would follow.

陈翰伯30年代在西安时是一名记者，在海伦·斯诺前往延安的时候，他曾提供了帮助。后来在北京他曾统管全国出版界多年。当他1980年访美时，也看望了老朋友海伦·斯诺。海伦坚持一起吃"快餐"，因为可以有更多时间"长谈"。这样大家就只是在我家一起吃从麦当劳买来的汉堡，并谈起了在西安时的往事。那时海伦·斯诺要去延安，遭到了国民党特务的严密监视。但她最终乘了一辆人力车，穿过黑暗的街巷，摆脱了监视。他们就在我家的露台上畅谈，那里阳光明媚，历史的回忆像泉水一样涌出。那是30年代，中国的路还不明朗。

1980，陈翰伯、海伦·斯诺和雪莲在麦迪逊市雪莲的家
Chen Hanpo with Helen Snow and Sharon Crain at the Crain's home in Madison, 1980

Ambassador Ling Qing: one family and Hong Kong
凌青大使：一个家庭和香港

1997，凌青和妻子张联在北京家中
Ling Qing and his wife in their home, Beijing, 1997

1997，中国媒体宣布香港的历史性回归
The Chinese press announced the historic return of Hong Kong, 1997

Ambassador Ling Qing and his great-great grandfather are heroes within one family. Ling Qing served as China's Permanent Representative to the United Nations (1980—1985) just as Deng Xiaoping's economic reform was opening China to the world. He became a very effective and respected voice representing China.

凌青大使和他的高祖父都是他们时代的杰出人士。从1980年至1985年，正值邓小平的改革开放之时，凌青出任中国驻联合国代表，踏实能干，赢得了尊敬。

His great-great grandfather, Lin Zexu, had also played a pivotal role back in 1839 when he was the Special Commissioner in Canton who gave the orders to burn the foreign shipments of opium flowing into China and who ordered the ports to be closed, leading the British to retaliate with the Opium Wars. After the war one of the concessions was that Hong Kong was ceded to Britain. The British had introduced opium into China as a way to gain money for buying silk, porcelain and jade.

凌的高祖父是林则徐，是鸦片战争中的关键人物。1839年他出任钦差大臣，下令焚烧运往中国的鸦片，并封锁广州港，英国随即报复，鸦片战争由此爆发，战争的结果之一是香港被割让给英国。鸦片是英国人倾销入中国的,为的是获取白银以购买丝绸、瓷器和玉石。

When Ambassador Ling Qing was at the United Nations in New York in the 1980's he and his wife frequently came to dinner at our home in Connecticut and we became good friends. (In those days they first had to secure permission from the U.S. government to travel beyond 25 miles; the same was true for U.S. officials living in China at that time.) Ambassador Ling Qing shared with us that he was proud of his ancestral roots and the courage of his great-great grandfather, who is still considered a real hero in the eyes of the Chinese people. In 1997 Ambassador Ling Qing told us he was also proud when Hong Kong was returned to China.

80年代凌青大使在纽约联合国总部任职时,常和妻子一起到我在康涅狄格的家与我们共进晚餐,我们成了好朋友。(由于被禁止去离纽约40公里以外的地区,他们来之前必须得到美国政府的许可——在中国的美国外交官也受到同样的限制。)凌青大使说他很为自己的家族自豪,为他高祖父的勇气而自豪。在中国林则徐始终被认为是真正的英雄。1997年香港回归时他告诉我他为此而骄傲。

His wife (Zhang Lian) became Ambassador to Sri Lanka making them the first couple in China to serve as Ambassadors simultaneously. Both Ambassador Ling Qing and his wife have earned the deep respect of those in China and many other countries who have worked with them and admire their honesty and ethics.

凌青的夫人张联曾任中国驻斯里兰卡大使。他们是中国第一对大使夫妻。在与他们共事过的人中有中国人也有外国人,他们都钦佩凌青夫妇的坦诚和道德风范。

An economic advisor: a gift of Swan Lake
经济顾问:"天鹅湖"

A key economic advisor, here unnamed, has also taught me about China. After dinner and long discussions in the cafeteria at Beijing University in 1992 this Chinese friend gave me a gift of musical glass swans. For many years he has been one of the most important advisors to top leaders in the government concerning analysis and recommendations for economic policy planning. As the glass swans began to turn and play the songs from Tchaikovsky's Swan Lake he solemnly told me that his father was a teacher who died during the Cultural Revolution when intellectuals were criticized and Swan Lake was banned as being bourgeois and unnecessary. That was a time when the so-called "Gang of Four" strictly controlled all music and art in China.

一个我不方便提到名字的高层经济顾问也曾让我了解了中国经历的岁月。1992年的一天,我和这位中国朋友在北大餐厅共进晚餐并进行了长谈,过后他送了我一个带有两个玻璃天鹅的音乐盒。这位朋友曾是政府领导人最重要的经济顾问。当玻璃天鹅音乐盒响起柴可夫斯基的"天鹅湖"时,他严肃地告诉我,他的父亲是一名教师,死于"文革"期间,那时知识分子遭到批判,而"天鹅湖"也被认为是资产阶级的和不必要的。在"文革"时,"四人帮"严密控制了中国的音乐和艺术。

In preparation for his role as economic advisor my friend had studied at key universities in the United States and then attended a top-level leadership-training program. He could have stayed in the U.S. and been very successful but he chose to return to China and work within the government to develop thoughtful plans to move China forward and avoid a return to the past.

这位朋友曾在美国的一些知名大学学习,还参加了一个高层领导人培训计划,为他的经济顾问角色作准备。他本来可以留在美国,并且在那里成就一番事业,但他还是选择了回国。他在政府里工作,用他的智慧去制订使中国一直前行的计划。

Whenever we met he always spoke with incredible compassion about the need for cultivating good values and ethics and adopting policies that would help alleviate the diverse needs of people throughout China. He is in a position to advise government leaders. Each time I listen to his thoughts I feel a sense of optimism about many of the current decisions and decision-makers in China.

1992,北京,玻璃天鹅音乐盒
Musical glass swans, Beijing, 1992

只要我们相聚,他就会以令人难以置信的热情谈起他的设想:建立良好的价值观和伦理观,满足全国人民的多样化需求。他是政府领导决策的顾问。每一次听到他的想法,我就为中国的决策和决策者感到高兴。

Madame Lu Cui: a hero in her youth
陆璀女士：英雄年轻时

1996，北京，陆璀
Lu Cui, Beijing, 1996

Lu Cui was a young girl when students protested outside the city wall surrounding Beijing in 1935 against Japanese imperialism in Manchuria and Northeast China. They were calling on the governing Kuomintang and Chiang Kai-shek to end the civil war with the Communists and to defend China against further aggression by Japan. The students were angry that they were not allowed to enter the city walls, calling for greater freedom to speak out. On December 9th, as several thousand students demonstrated Lu Cui slipped under the big wooden gates and unlatched the doors from within so the students could enter. This student protest, known as the December 9th Student Movement, led to further demonstrations and to a successful nationwide resistance against Japanese aggression.

1935年，当北京城外的学生聚集，抗议日本帝国主义侵占中国东北时，陆璀还是个少女。这些学生们呼吁国民党政府和蒋介石结束内战，一致对外。学生们得知他们不能进城时很愤怒，呼喊要争取更大的言论自由。12月9日，当数千学生游行的时候，陆璀从巨大的城门下钻了进去，把城门打开让学生进了城。这次以"一二·九"著称的学生运动进一步促进了全国性的抗日风潮。

In the 1980's Lu Cui told me how she had been arrested immediately that day by Kuomintang soldiers and put in a truck with others to go to jail. She said Edgar Snow caught her eye, jumped on his bike and followed the truck to the jail where he was able to meet with her. That was the start of her friendship with Edgar and Helen Snow. Unknown to her at the time, the Snows had been meeting with

1997，北京，陆璀、陆的丈夫朱子奇和雪莲在人民大会堂海伦·斯诺的纪念会上
Lu Cui and her husband Zhu Ziqi with Sharon Crain at the commemoration for Helen Snow in the Great Hall of the People, Beijing, 1997

student leaders secretly in their home to help make plans for that protest. Huang Hua, Chen Hanpo and others were among the young student leaders who protested to bring about change.

80年代，陆璀曾告诉我那天示威后她马上被国民党士兵抓起来了，并被押上卡车，和其他人一起被投入监狱。她说埃德加·斯诺亲眼看到她被捕，并且马上跳上自行车，一路尾随卡车到监狱，并在那里见到了她。这是她和埃德加·斯诺夫妇友谊的开始。那时她还不知道斯诺夫妇一直在他们家里秘密会见学生领袖，帮助策划这次运动。学生领袖中有黄华、陈翰伯和其他一些人。

Just before Helen Snow died she dictated a letter for me to send to Madame Lu Cui, remembering the courage of the young hero who became her friend. As Helen spoke she was wearing the purple sweater Lu Cui had sent her. After Helen Snow passed away in 1997 there was a ceremony in the Great Hall of the People in Tian'anmen Square in Beijing. Among the many leaders and old friends honoring Helen Snow were Madame Lu Cui and her husband Zhu Ziqi, a well-known beloved poet.

海伦·斯诺去世前还口授了一封信给陆璀女士，并让我寄给她，信中回忆了她的老朋友年轻时的勇气。当她向我口授的时候，她还穿着陆璀送给她的紫色毛衣。1997年海伦·斯诺去世后，在北京人民大会堂有一个悼念她的仪式。参加仪式的领导人和老朋友中包括陆璀女士和她的丈夫朱子奇——一位知名诗人。

Gu Pin'e: flowers can bloom again
顾品锷：鲜花可以重新绽放

Ambassador Gu Pin'e has served his country well, working to further China's relationships with many other countries: in the Foreign Ministry for over thirty-five years; Ambassador to Saint Lucia, and as Secretary General of the China Society for People's Friendship Studies.

顾品锷大使一直很出色地为他的国家服务，并且努力发展中国同其他国家的关系。他在外交部工作超过35年，曾担任驻圣卢西亚大使，后来成为中国人民对外友好协会的总干事。

When he was Deputy Consul General in New York City he often visited Helen Snow and in 1996 accompanied Ambassador Mei Ping to present the Honorary Ambassador Award to Helen Snow. She became only the third recipient to ever receive this high award from China. Helen told me it was one of the most meaningful moments of her life and made her feel that all of her lifelong efforts concerning China were worthwhile. They also presented her with beautiful yellow roses, which they knew were her favorite. It was in stark contrast to the past when flowers were crushed and considered decadent and bourgeois during the turbulent Cultural Revolution years. Now, flowers blossom once again throughout China.

在担任中国驻纽约副总领事时，他经常造访海伦·斯诺。1996年他陪同梅平总领事出席了授予海伦·斯诺荣誉大使奖的仪式。海伦是第三个被授予这个来自中国的崇高荣誉的人。海伦告诉我那是她一生中最有意义的时刻之一，她感到她关于中国的毕生努力都是有价值的。他们带来了她最喜欢的美丽的黄玫瑰，它展示了一个与动乱的"文革"绝不相同的场景。那时的花被认为是颓废的、资产阶级的，从而被毁弃。现在美丽的花儿再一次在中国遍地开放。

2002，北京，顾品锷大使和雪莲
Ambassador Gu Pin'e and Sharon Crain, Beijing, 2002

Influential Writers Documenting Change
记录变化的知名作家

Bingxin (1900—1999): an optimistic writer whose life spanned a century
冰心（1900—1999）：一位与20世纪同在的乐观作家

1982，北京，冰心、她的女儿吴青和雪莲
Bingxin, her daughter Wu Qing and Sharon Crain, Beijing, 1982

Bingxin is considered one of China's most highly regarded and prolific writers. Her writing career began as a university student during the time of the May Fourth Movement of 1919 and continued for seven decades. She received a master's degree in literature from Wellesley College in the United States and taught in Japan but always returned to China to continue her teaching and writing. She wrote prose, poetry and short stories, which spanned the 20th century. One of her important works was her collected essays, *To Young Readers*, whose wisdom influenced many.

冰心是中国20世纪最享有盛誉和最多产的作家之一。她在五四运动时开始创作，那时她只是一个大学生，但她的创作生涯持续了70年。20年代，她赴美留学，在威尔斯利学院获得文学硕士学位，后来曾在日本教学，但基本上是在中国国内教书和写作。从20年代到90年代，她写了为数众多的散文、诗歌和小说，其中最为人称道的是她的散文集《致小读者》。她的智慧影响了很多人。

Her daughter Wu Qing continues her spirit and was one of the first to establish a network to promote the study of English in China. In recent years Wu Qing became co-founder of a training center in Beijing to help poor rural and migrant women.

冰心的女儿吴青传承了她的精神，并且是中国最早的英文学习网络的倡导者之一。近些年来，她成为帮助农村贫困妇女和外来务工妇女的一家培训中心的共同发起人。

When I met with Bingxin in her home in Beijing I brought her Helen Snow's autobiography, *My China Years*. Helen had told me how much the Chinese people admired Bingxin for her writing and her optimism. They had been friends in Beijing in the 1930's.

我是在北京冰心的家里见到冰心的,并且转交给她一本海伦·斯诺送她的自传《我在中国的岁月》。海伦告诉过我中国读者多么喜欢冰心,不但因为她的作品,也因为她的乐观。当斯诺夫妇30年代在北京的时候,他们就已经是好友了。

Ding Ling(1904—1986): prolific writer and political activist
丁玲(1904—1986):多产作家和政治活动家

Ding Ling was one of China's most prominent and popular writers of the 20th Century and one of the first to openly speak for the rights of women. She stated they should be able to select whom they wanted to marry not according to old customs of arranged marriages. By the 1920's she was well known for her book, *Miss Sophia's Diary*, and boldly continued expressing her ideas in three hundred works spanning fifty years.

丁玲也是20世纪中国最出色和最受欢迎的女作家之一,同时也最早为妇女权利大声疾呼。她反对包办婚姻的陋习,声言妇女应该有权利选择自己的结婚对象。早在20年代她就以小说《莎菲女士的日记》而闻名,在50年的时间里她写了300多部(篇)不同类型的作品,而且一生直言不讳。

1984,北京,丁玲和丈夫陈明在他们的公寓
Ding Ling and her husband Chen Ming in their apartment, Beijing, 1984

As a political activist she was placed under house arrest for years in the 1930's by the ruling Kuomintang (the Nationalists), then labeled by the Communists during the Anti-Rightist Campaign in 1957, and put in jail for five years during the Cultural Revolution. She endured twelve years of manual labor before being rehabilitated.

作为政治活动家,丁玲在30年代曾被国民党软禁数年。1957年,她被打成右派,而且在"文革"中坐了5年牢。在她的右派问题平反前,丁玲经受了长达12年的劳改。

When she was invited to participate in the University of Iowa's International Writers' Program in the United States in the 1980's Ding Ling visited her old friend Helen Snow. She was saddened to see the poor conditions in which Helen lived all alone and told her she hoped she would return to China. However, Helen Snow often expressed how much she loved her old house in Connecticut where she spent time each day to continue her writing about China.

80年代她应邀赴美参加爱荷华大学的国际作家写作计划,并利用这次机会访问了老朋友海伦·斯诺。看到海伦贫穷和孤身独居的状况,她很难过。她对海伦说希望她能够重返中国。但海伦·斯诺经常表示她非常恋家,喜欢住在康涅狄格,并每天在这里继续写她有关中国的书。

Lu Yao (1949—1992) and other writers : reveal the past
路遥（1949—1992）和其他作家：揭示过去的岁月

1982，西安。作家们在西安事变旧址（从左至右）：安危、董得理、李小巴、杜鹏程、雪莲、任仕增、陈贤仲、杨韦昕、路遥
Writers at the site of the Xi'an Incident, Xi'an, 1982 (R to L) Lu Yao, Yang Weixin, Chen Xianzhong, Ren Shizeng, Sharon Crain, Du Pengcheng, Li Xiaoba, Dong Deli and An Wei

In 1982 an impressive group of contemporary writers gathered at the exact place where Communist leaders negotiated with Chiang Kai-shek after he had been kidnapped during the famous Xi'an Incident of 1936. Du Pengcheng was well known for his novel, *Defend Yen'an*, while others had recently published and received literary awards for their books about abuses during the Cultural Revolution, which had ended about six years before.

1982年，一群令人印象深刻的中国当代作家聚集在西安事变的旧址，其中杜鹏程因为他的长篇小说《保卫延安》而知名，其他人则在前不久发表作品对六年前结束的"文革"给予了揭露，有些还因此获奖。

One of the authors, Lu Yao later received the prestigious Mao Dun Literary Award in 1988 for his novel *Ordinary World*. A friend described his impact on her, "I learned how to treat my parents with respect by reading Lu Yao's books as a child."

路遥是这些作家中的一个，他后来因为创作长篇小说《平凡的世界》而在1988年被授予茅盾文学奖。一位朋友这样形容路遥对她的影响："我从小时候就读路遥的书，从那里我知道了怎样善待父母。"

Zhang Jie and Wang Meng: describe decades of struggles
张洁和王蒙：描写斗争的年代

1990，美国康涅狄格州维斯大学，张洁（左），雪莲和王蒙（右）
Zhang Jie (L), Sharon Crain and Wang Meng (R), Wesleyan University Connecticut, U.S., 1990

Two of China's contemporary and most renowned writers have brilliantly documented the struggles and emotions of the Chinese people in the midst of change during their decades of writing.

张洁和王蒙是两位中国当代最著名的作家。在几十年的创作生涯中，他们出色地记录了改革年代里中国人的矛盾和情感。

Zhang Jie, one of China's most outstanding female writers, is the only two-time winner of the coveted Mao Dun Literary Award: first, for her *Heavy Wings* in 1982 and again for her epic novel *Without Words* in 2005, which has been acclaimed internationally and is considered a classic account of the Chinese people during the 20th century as well as a distinguished literary work. Our friendship began when Zhang Jie was a visiting Writer-in-Residence at Wesleyan University in Connecticut near my home.

张洁是中国最杰出的女作家之一，也是唯一两次获得享有盛名的茅盾文学奖的作家：第一部作品是《沉重的翅膀》（1982），第二部作品是史诗性小说《无字》（2005）。《无字》受到了国际性的赞扬，被认为是20世纪中国人民生活的经典描述，也是一部杰出的文学著作。我是在张洁在康涅狄格州维斯大学做住校作家时结识她的，从那时起我们就成了朋友。

Wang Meng was China's Minister of Culture from 1986 to 1989. As a popular and respected writer for over fifty years his books have been translated into twenty languages. He was nominated for a Nobel Prize in literature. Like many writers and intellectuals in China he suffered during the Anti-Rightist Campaign in 1957 and again in the Cultural Revolution in the 1960's and 1970's when he was sent to Xinjiang Uyghur Autonomous Region in the far Northwestern region of China. During sixteen years of living there he learned the Uyghur language and songs. It is always a joy to hear him sing and feel the warmth of his respect for the common people.

王蒙曾在1986年至1989年间任中国文化部长。在他从事文学创作的50年里，他一直是一个受读者喜欢和尊敬的作家，并被提名为诺贝尔文学奖的候选人。他的作品被翻译成20种文字。像许多中国作家和知识分子一样，他在1957年的反右运动中被打成右派，60年代被送往偏远的新疆，"文革"中遭受迫害。在新疆的16年间，他学会了维吾尔语，还会唱维吾尔歌曲。听他唱维吾尔歌曲是一种享受，也能感受到他对普通人的热情。

Wang Meng, Zhang Jie and I first met through our mutual friendship with Vera Schwarcz, Professor of ancient and contemporary Chinese history and Director of the Mansfield Freeman Center for East Asian Studies at Wesleyan University in Connecticut. She is a noted scholar of Chinese history and serves as a bridge between Chinese and Americans through her own teaching and extensive writing about China.

我是通过康涅狄格州维斯大学的中国古代和当代历史教授舒衡哲与张洁和王蒙成为朋友的。她是维斯大学曼斯菲尔德·弗里曼东亚研究中心主任，著名的中国史专家。她通过对中国问题的教学和写作，搭建起中美间的桥梁。

Xiao Qian (1910—1999): democracy in writing
萧乾（1910—1999）：写作民主

Xiao Qian was one of China's important writers and journalists who covered the war years in England in the 1940's. In addition he translated some of Shakespeare's plays and James Joyce's *Ulysses* into Chinese in his later years. He wrote short stories and essays filled with vivid details and emotions describing the suffering of the lower classes and injustices that existed in society.

萧乾是中国最重要的作家和记者之一。40年代他在英国就战争进行了广泛的报道，晚年翻译了一些莎士比亚的戏剧和詹姆斯·乔伊斯的《尤利西斯》。他写过短篇小说和散文，以生动的细节和充沛的情感反映了下层人民遭受的苦难和社会的不公正。

His life was a microcosm of the changes in China before and after Mao Zedong. He suffered during the Cultural Revolution and like most writers was prevented from writing for years before being rehabilitated. His friendship with Helen and Edgar Snow in the 1930's led to our friendship in the 1980's. In his apartment in Beijing he taught me about the subtle flavors and healing elements of

1993，北京，萧乾在他北京寓所的桌旁
Xiao Qian at his desk in his apartment, Beijing, 1993

Chinese tea and about the vicissitudes of life in China.

他的生活是毛泽东生前和去世后中国变化的缩影。他在"文革"中饱经磨难，而且在平反之前像大多数中国作家一样被长时间禁止写作。由于他和海伦以及埃德加·斯诺在30年代就结成的友谊，我们在80年代也成了好朋友。在他北京的家里，他让我了解了中国茶的精妙之处和药用功能，也了解了他一生的沉浮。

When I visited him in the hospital shortly before he died at the age of nearly ninety, he shared with me what he strongly believed: "Democracy means being able to write the truth in books or in newspapers and have it published." Xiao Qian had spent his whole life trying to write the truth.

在他将近90岁高龄的时候，我去医院看望了他，而在那以后不久他就去世了。那一次他对我说，他坚信"民主就意味着能够在书中和新闻中道出真实，并使之得到发表"。他用了自己整整一生去写那个真实。

Ordinary Citizens Affected by Change: Shopkeepers, Peasants and Minorities
被巨变影响的普通人：店主、农民和少数民族

I was fortunate to know many Chinese leaders, writers and heroes but equally important to me were the ordinary people who have made their own contributions to China. Many became close friends and influenced my perception of China. Over these thirty momentous years I closely observed the citizens of China, almost no one remained unaffected by change. A few pages from my dairy record fragments of their lives: a shopkeeper and her daughter, a poet and retired teacher, four generations of one peasant family and special Tibetan and Uyghur minorities.

我幸运地认识了许多中国的领导人、作家和杰出人士，但对我来说，那些为中国作出了自己贡献的普通人同样重要。许多这样的普通中国人成了我的好朋友，影响了我对中国的看法。在这意义重大的30年里，我近距离地观察了中国的普通公民，发现无人不受巨变的影响。我的一些日记记录了他们生活的片断：一个店主和她的女儿；一位诗人和退休教师；一个四世同堂的农民之家；还有藏族人、维吾尔族人。

Shopkeeper Ma, beyond the ancient Silk Road
古代丝绸之路之后：马老板

Near the old Drum Tower in Xi'an along one of the narrow passageways leading to the Great Mosque was Ma's shop where I have gone for twenty-five years to buy "old treasures". As China modernized it has become more difficult to find the traditional hand-made silk embroideries, carved jade, or old porcelains, which were the goods for which the merchants made the long and dangerous journey centuries ago along the ancient Silk Road to buy and trade with China.

马的店铺在西安鼓楼附近，沿着一条狭窄的街道，可以通向清真大寺。25年来，我总是在那里买"古董"。随着中国的现代化，越来越难在那里发现传统手工制作的丝绣、玉器和陶瓷，这些货物正是古代丝绸之路时期商人们不畏艰险、长途跋涉来中国的原因。

Ma was a Muslim of the Hui minority, which has had a large community in Xi'an for centuries. The Great Mosque where they worship is one of fifteen mosques in Xi'an and one of the oldest in all of China. It was built in 742 during the Tang Dynasty, considered the Golden Era of Chinese history when Xi'an was the ancient capital and goods and ideas were exchanged between East and West. Now, many of these small shops are being torn down and replaced with modern complexes filled with

2000，西安，马老板和雪莲
Shopkeeper Ma and Sharon Crain, Xi'an, 2000

2007，西安，雪莲和马老板的女儿在摄影展上
Sharon and Ma's daughter at photo exhibition, Xi'an, 2007

international merchandise or machine-made souvenirs for foreigners.

马是回族,一个在西安生活了几个世纪的、有相当大社群的少数民族。她们去做礼拜的清真大寺是西安的15座清真寺之一,也是中国最古老的清真寺之一。清真大寺建于唐代,公元742年,那是中国古代辉煌的时期。那时西安是都城,也是东西方货物和思想交汇的地方。现在许多这样的小店铺被拆掉了,代之以现代化的商厦,里面摆满国外商品和专为外国游客制作的纪念品。

Ma's shop was one of the few remaining where such treasures might still be found and over the years we became friends, especially in 1989 when my eldest son Wes Crain and I were both teaching in Xi'an. Ma always greeted us with a big smile and was thrilled to know that a mother and son were teaching in her city. Everyone in the surrounding shops, including us, called her "Mama".

马的店铺是仅存的几家依然能够发现珍奇的地方。交往得多了,我们竟成了朋友,尤其是在1989年,我和大儿子巍斯·柯雷来西安执教以后。马迎接我们时总是带着灿烂的笑容,而且知道有一对(美国)母子在她的城市教书,她很激动。周围店铺的人都叫她"妈妈",我们也这么叫。

At that time two money systems existed in China: the Foreign Exchange Currency (FEC) and the renminbi (RMB) the people's money for the Chinese. Wes and I frequently bought things from her shop and often traded money as well. FEC could be used by Chinese to purchase foreign made goods such as a radio or television, not easily available to them at the time.

那时的中国有两个货币系统:对外国人的外汇券和对中国人的人民币。巍斯和我经常在她的店里买东西并和她换钱。中国人可以用我们的外汇券购买外国商品,如收音机和电视机,都是那时不容易得到的东西。

Years later when my son got married I gave him a blue and white porcelain box as a wedding gift from Ma's shop. In 2007 when I held a photo exhibition in Xi'an Ma's photo appeared prominently. I was saddened that she had passed away but thrilled when Ma's daughter attended to represent her mother. Friendships begun through exchanging goods and ideas, as in the days of the Silk Road, continue through the next generation.

多年后,当我儿子结婚时,我送给他一件从马的商店买来的青花瓷瓶作为礼物。2007年,我在西安举办了一次图片展,其中有她的照片,挂在很显眼的位置,但是马已经去世了,这让我很伤心。不过,让我高兴的是,她的女儿出席了这次展览。从丝绸之路的时候起,友谊就从货物和思想的交换开始,现在它随着新一代人在延续。

The jiaozi makers and China on the move
做饺子的人和前进中的中国

Across the busy street from "my" university where I frequently returned to teach was a small open-air restaurant where we often enjoyed plates of dumplings (jiaozi) with hot sauce and a bowl of broth for a few cents. Zhang Changmin and his wife Zhao Xueqin rose early every morning seven days a week to buy vegetables and meat to create hundreds of jiaozi all day, cooked in a huge wok over the hot fire. They were there until late each night eking out a living in the same place for years until a big shopping center opened and their tiny restaurant was torn down as progress pushed them out. They then moved to a nearby small street, until that shop too was torn down as a modern apartment building went up.

在我经常回去教书的大学的对面,有一家露天饺子馆。我经常去那里,只要花一点钱就可以吃上一碟饺子,以及醋汁和热汤。张常民和妻子赵雪琴每天都起得很早去采购,接着忙活整整一天,做成百上千的饺子,并在一个大锅里将它们煮熟。他们起早贪黑,就这样在那里维持生计,一直很多年,直到被一个大的购物中心取代。他们的摊档被拆毁了,社会向前的步伐使他们不得不离开那里。他们搬到了临近的一条小街上,直到新的铺面再一次被拆迁。一座公寓楼在那里拔地而起。

A teacher friend bought one of those apartments so her family would have a better place to live with central heating, a shower and more space. The exact location brought positive benefits to one friend and difficulty to another.

我的一个教师朋友在那座公寓里买了一套单元房,一个比原来的住所好得多,带有暖气、淋浴设备的宽敞单元房。同一个地方给我两个朋友带来的却是不同的东西:一个更好了,另一个却更困难。

The jiaozi-makers moved across town and started yet again, until her husband suddenly passed away. Zhao Xueqin now works harder than ever before in the new location by herself; she was able to scrape together enough money for her only daughter to attend a college in Hunan, the province where Mao Zedong was born. Zhao is left alone but she told me, "My daughter has a job and moved to Beijing. She was able to get an education, which I could not get because of Mao's Cultural Revolution. My daughter has moved far away, but her life is better than mine." With construction and constant changes everywhere, China is on the move.

做饺子的人搬离了,到城市的另一端重新开张。后来张常民突然逝去。现在赵雪琴在她的新店面里自己干,但比以前更努力了。她为独生女儿凑足了去湖南上大学的学费,那里是毛泽东出生的地方。赵是孤独的,但她告诉我:"我女儿已经有了工作,到北京去了。由于'文化大革命',我没有受过良好的教育,但我的女儿受了。她现在走得很远,不过生活好多了。"随着无处不在的建设和持续变化,中国正在前进。

2000，西安，张常民、他的妻子和老饺子馆
Zhang Changmin and his wife and the old jiaozi restaurant, Xi'an, 2000

2007，西安，长安路上的新店铺
New shops on Chang'an Road, Xi'an, 2007

1986，西安，家中的邓万芳
Deng Wanfang in her apartment, Xi'an, 1986

Deng Wanfang, retired teacher and poet
诗人和退休教师邓万芳

Deng Wanfang was long retired from teaching at the Metallurgical College in Xi'an when we first met in 1982 at an old friend's home where she often went to provide help and advice. Eager to make friends with an American she quietly whisper in my ear, "Come to my apartment."

1982年，我们第一次在一个老朋友的家里见面时，邓万芳早已从西安冶金学院的教师岗位上退休了。她经常去这个老朋友那里帮忙，也出出主意。她很热心和一个美国人交朋友，所以悄悄地对我耳语道："到我家来。"

During the next twenty years each time I returned to China she was one of the first people I would want to visit and would eagerly ride my bike across town and climb the steps in her concrete building to enter her small apartment. She was always there except for the occasional practice with what she called "the old people's chorus", in which she loved to participate. She often quoted Abraham Lincoln or Deng Xiaoping and share stories of how she and her husband suffered during the Anti-Rightist Campaign when intellectuals were asked to speak up but were then criticized and looked down upon. Almost always she presented me with some of her poetry, beautifully brush-painted on old newspapers and

1989，西安，巍斯·柯雷和雪莲在邓万芳的两侧，以及她的儿孙们和郭迎、郭捷
Wes Crain and Sharon Crain on each side of Deng Wanfang with her children, grandchildren and special friends Guo Ying and Guo Jie, Xi'an, 1989

generously shared meals even when almost all basic food was rationed. Later, she moved in with a grandchild to a larger apartment, which had heat, a refrigerator and more plentiful supply of food.

在接下来的20年里，每次我回到中国，第一批要去拜访的人之一就是她。我总是急匆匆地骑着自行车穿过城区，然后爬上她家水泥大楼的台阶，走进她那个小小的公寓。除了偶尔与那个她热心参加，并被她称为"老年合唱团"的团体一起排练外，她总是在家里。她经常引用亚伯罕姆·林肯和邓小平的话，并给我讲述她和丈夫在"反右"中受迫害的故事。在"反右"过程中，知识分子被要求讲真话，但接着就被批判和歧视。她总是给我读她用毛笔写在旧报纸上的诗，慷慨地邀请我与他们共享配给的基本食品。后来，她和一个孙子一起搬进了有暖气和冰箱的大公寓，食品供应也丰富得多了。

I also met her friend Guo Ying, handicapped from childhood, who benefited from the compassionate care of his sister and her husband. They helped to carry him and his wheelchair down the narrow stairwell from their second floor apartment but looked up to him with admiration for his positive attitude. Through the years Guo Ying, who had taught himself English, would translate letters and poetry mailed between Deng Wanfang and myself. She would write in Chinese and I in English, but even without translation we seemed to communicate with a language of our own. After attending the wedding of her granddaughter one year (when she was becoming quite frail) she expressed her wish to me, "My dear friend, I hope our children's children will continue our friendship forever." People such as Deng Wanfang are the links in developing international relations and are the unsung heroes of China.

我也见到了她的朋友——幼时就患有残疾的郭迎,他得到了他姐姐和姐夫的精心照料。郭迎行动困难,出门时需要姐夫和姐姐把他和轮椅从二层楼上沿着狭窄的楼梯抬下来,但他们对他的积极生活态度感到很钦佩。通过多年自学英语,郭迎可以为邓万芳和我翻译我们之间的信和诗。邓用中文,而我用英文——其实不用翻译我们似乎也可以用自己的语言交流。有一年我应邀参加了她孙女的婚礼(那时她身体已经很虚弱),她向我表达了她的愿望:"好朋友,我希望我们的子孙能永远延续我们的友谊。"像邓万芳这样的人就是发展国际关系的纽带,也是中国的无名英雄。

Peasants in the countryside : change within their families
乡村农民:家庭的变化

"Talk with the kings but walk with the people"
"和帝王交谈,与百姓同行"

Other special friends who taught me so much about China lived in the countryside. Visiting with families outside Xi'an recalled for me the deep respect my parents instilled in me for peasants (farmers). My father grew up on a farm in the middle of America and taught me the expression, "Talk with the kings but walk with the people." In the 1980's I often rode my bike to visit nearby families. Peasants then numbered over 85% of the people throughout China and had limited education and almost no mobility to move to a different location. Land south of the university was all farmland then but now much of it is covered with high-rise apartments and other buildings. Families were large and the grandparents played a leading role taking care of grandchildren while the parents toiled in the fields. For many young children grandma was their hero. An ancient poet described the peasants' endless plight:

我有一些特别的农村朋友,他们使我对中国了解很多。对西安郊外农家的访问让我想起了我的父母,是他们让我知道了要非常尊敬农民。我的父亲在美国中部的一个农场长大,他教给我一句话:"和帝王交谈,与百姓同行。"80年代我经常骑着自行车走访附近的农家。那时农民超过全国总人口的85%,他们受教育有限,也几乎没有能力去别的地方。我教书的大学以南都是农田,但现在全是高层住宅楼和其他建筑。农民家庭一般很大,祖父母是家长。孩子的父母下田时,祖父母就帮着他们照看孩子。对很多孩子来说,祖母就是理想的化身。一位古代诗人曾经这样描写了他们没有尽头的苦难生活:

1982，陕西师大附近，农民家庭和雪莲
Peasant family and Sharon Crain, near ShiDa, 1982

1994，户县，丰收季节农家小院里的农民和他的孩子
A peasant and his children hanging corn during the harvest season, Huxian, 1994

From break of day	从日出，
Till sunset glow	到日落，
I toil.	我劳作：
I dig my well,	挖井，
I plow my field,	犁地，
And earn my food	挣一口吃喝。
And drink.	
What care I	如果我平静地离开，
Who rules the land,	谁会在意？
If I am left in peace?	谁来经营这土地？

    In the fall of 1989, I returned to China to teach and learn, continuing my visits to the countryside. One weekend I went with a Chinese teacher and his American wife to stay with his family in a rural area. My friend was the first in his village to ever marry a foreigner. While we were there one neighbor came to the house pretending to borrow a washboard for scrubbing clothes but actually just wanted to catch a glimpse of the foreigner. That night when we each had a bowl of corn soup the son told me, "That is all we eat every night during the corn harvest."

    1989年秋，我重回中国，教书学习，继续走访农村。一个周末，我和一位教师朋友去他在农村的家。他娶了一位美国姑娘，也是这个村子第一个和外国人结婚的人。当我们在那儿的时候，一个邻居过来借洗衣板，实际上只是想看一眼真正的外国人。那天晚饭我们每人喝了一碗玉米糊糊。我的朋友告诉我："秋收的时候，我们每天的晚饭就是这个。"

    In their house, newspapers were glued to the walls and windows to keep out the wind. We slept in our long underwear and heavy clothes to keep out the cold but it was harder to keep out mice from the piles of corn and husks in the inner courtyard. A single light bulb was suspended from the ceiling where we gathered to eat but stayed lit only briefly. For generations peasants have known to how to survive in the cold and the dark. Now, new policies push progress and widespread advertising promotes modern products as peasants reach out to improve their living standards. Widespread expansion of electricity, heat and modern appliances are drastically straining resources to meet their needs.

为了挡风，他们房子的墙上和窗户上都糊了报纸。我们穿着秋衣秋裤睡觉，为的是保暖。老鼠在院内的玉米堆里乱窜，没办法把它们赶走。在我们吃饭的屋子里有一盏电灯，但不常开。世世代代的农民都知道怎样在寒冷和黑暗中生活。现在，新政策促进了发展，无处不在的广告普及了现代产品，农民们在努力提高他们的生活水准。电、热和现代家用电器的广泛使用满足了他们的需要，但也极大地耗费着资源。

So often during my visits with peasant families throughout China during the last thirty years, I have thought of the words of Helen Snow describing the peasants of China in the 1930's. In some areas of China today the peasants' lives are the same as they were centuries ago. In other areas seismic changes have transformed their living standards where they enjoy modern conveniences and educational opportunities never imagined even a few years ago. As recorded in the preface of Helen Snow's book *Inside Red China*:

在过去30年我访问各地的农民家庭时，我经常想到海伦·斯诺形容30年代中国农民的话。在今天中国的某些地区，农民还过着千百年来同样的生活；但在另外的地方，他们的生活发生了巨大的变化，开始享受现代生活的便利及更多的受教育的机会，而这些即使在几年前也是难以想象的。在海伦·斯诺的《续西行漫记》的前言里，作者这样写道：

"The laboring classes of China have no peer. They ask less of life and give more than the people of any race. They are so intelligent of hand and brain, so capable of endurance and ceaseless struggle, so competent in any given field of work, that to know them is to admire them without question and to wish to see them rise to the stature to which they are entitled."

"中国的劳工阶级是独一无二的。他们对生活要求很少，但给予的却比其他任何种族的人民都多。他们聪明勤劳，忍辱负重，顽强斗争，在任何工作领域都有竞争力，所以了解他们就会无条件地尊敬他们，就会希望看到他们过上他们应得的生活。"

Four generations of one peasant family
一个四世同堂的农民家庭

Fan Zhihua's family is a clear example of new opportunities experienced by some of the younger generation, unfathomable to the peasants of the past. His father worked in the fields from dawn till dusk with no hope for the future. The traditional cloth was wrapped around his waist, which could be used to secure his one pair of patched trousers, carry an extra load of vegetables. He had no formal education and never talked about change. After he died a marker for his grave rested at the end of the tiny plot of land where he had farmed all his life.

年轻的一代有了新的机会，樊志华的家庭是这方面的典型，而这对老一代农民来说是难以理解的。樊志华的父亲从早到晚在田里劳作，对未来没有奢求。他穿着老式的衣服，腰里系着一根布带，裤子打着补丁，挎着的篮子里装满了菜。他没受过正式的教育，从来没有谈到过变化。去世后他的坟就被置于他劳作一生的那块地的地头。

Fan Zhihua (similar to his father) grew up as a peasant but was able to have an elementary education. During the time of the Great Leap Forward (1956—1957) Mao Zedong tried to push China forward with revolutionary zeal by enlisting individual efforts, such as arming peasants with brushes to paint propaganda posters. Peasants in Huxian County, Shaanxi Province were given brushes, paints and minimal training and were asked to promote the revolutionary goals of the country through painting. Fan Zhihua, Liu Zhide and Li Fenglan were among the first to be called "peasant painters".

跟他父亲相似，樊志华也是地道的农民，但上过小学。在大跃进期间，毛泽东试图激起每一个人的革命热情来将中国推向前进，比如让农民来画宣传画。陕西户县的农民就这样得到了最基本的美术训练，然后被要求用绘画宣传的方式服务于国家的革命目标。樊志华、刘

1989，甘亭镇，樊志华的父亲在他的小块地里收获红辣椒
Fan Zhihua's father harvesting red peppers on his small plot of land, Ganting town, 1989

志德、李凤兰是第一批被称为"农民画家"的人。

After the disastrous collapse of the Great Leap Forward, Fan Zhihua continued to paint, combining farming with teaching art in the local primary school. Today over two thousand peasant painters work in Huxian, greatly admired as folk heroes locally and by people from around the world who collect their artwork. In the late 1980's the Ministry of Culture officially designated Huxian as the "home of modern Chinese folk painting".

灾难性的"大跃进"过后,樊志华继续他的美术创作,并在田间劳作之余在本地一所小学做美术老师。现在户县大约有两千多名农民画家,他们作为民间成功人士很受当地人的羡慕,他们的作品也在世界范围内被收藏。80年代末期,文化部正式将户县命名为"中国现代民间绘画之乡"。

Going beyond his father's limited elementary education Fan Gaoqi (Fan Zhihua's son) was able to receive a high school education and then took courses at the Foreign Language Institute in Xi'an to learn English. Learning from his father he has become an exceptional painter. He has received national awards in China and also held a one-man show in Helsinki, Finland where his paintings of *Santa Claus's visit to China* were published in a book. Another exhibition was held in Connecticut in the United States with paintings of Fan Gaoqi, Liu Zhide and other peasant painters. Unfortunately they were not granted a visa by the United States to attend this event. Fan Gaoqi is always home for planting and harvest seasons but now has a job working in a small gallery in Xi'an, which promotes peasant painting.

2004,户县甘亭镇,樊志华、妻子及雪莲在剥玉米
Fan Zhihua and his wife with Sharon Crain shucking corn at their home, Ganting town, Huxian County, 2004

相对于樊志华所受的有限的小学教育，他的儿子樊高奇幸运得多。他是个高中毕业生，还到西安外语学院学习过英文。他继承父业，现在已经成为一名优秀画家。他曾被授予全国美术奖，还在赫尔辛基举办过个人画展，他的《圣诞老人中国之旅》的画册也在芬兰出版。美国的康涅狄格州也举办过一次有樊高奇、刘志德和其他农民画家作品的画展。遗憾的是，他们没有获得签证，因而不能亲自赴美参加这次画展。农忙时樊高奇仍在家务农，但也在西安一家经营农民画的小画廊有了一份工作。

Representing the fourth generation of the Fan family, Li Rui (Fan Zhihua's granddaughter) was accepted to the Xi'an University of Post & Telecommunications in 2007. She is excited about her

2007，长安，樊志华的外孙女李瑞在她的大学宿舍
Fan Zhihua's granddaughter Li Rui in her university dorm, Chang'an, 2007

2007，甘亭镇，户县，樊志华（左起第三），雪莲和樊全家共进晚餐
Fan Zhihua (third L) with Sharon Crain and his family at dinner in their home, Ganting town, Huxian County, 2007

future as the first person in the history of their family ever to achieve this level of education.

樊家第四代人的代表是樊志华的外孙女李瑞，她于2007年考入了西安邮电学院学习。她很激动，因为她是樊家接受高等教育的第一人。

Fan Zhihua and I began our friendship in 1989 during the planning of a major exhibition of peasant paintings to come to the United States for the first event of our newly established Sister City Relationship between Xi'an and Kansas City, Missouri. Fan Zhihua along with two hundred peasant paintings came to the United States to serve as Ambassador of Good Will to promote friendship and understanding between our two countries.

我在1989年与樊志华成了朋友，那时我们正在筹划在美国举行一个大型中国农民画展，那是西安和密苏里州堪萨斯市建立姊妹城市后的第一个活动。樊志华携200多幅农民画来到美国，作为"亲善大使"来增进两国之间的友谊和理解。

My strong bond with his family is one of the reasons I keep returning to China. When we eat together we often toast with the meaningful traditional Chinese saying: "Wo men shi yi jia ren," we are the people of one family.

我与樊家的紧密联系是我不断回到中国的原因之一。一起进餐时，我们经常干杯，并说一句中国的老话："我们是一家人。"

Fortunately, many Americans are learning from Fan Zhihua's family and from other peasants in Huxian. Several on-going educational exchanges take place with American students from the Greenwich School in Connecticut who have a Sister School in Xi'an and with teachers and students from programs at China Institute in New York who frequently go to Huxian. For many it has been a rewarding experience to learn from those in the countryside at a personal level beyond the classroom, where the peasants are their teachers.

令人高兴的是，许多美国人也正在了解樊志华的家庭和户县的其他农民。一些与美国学生交流的教育计划已经在实行，成员包括康涅狄格州的格林威治中学——它是西安一所中学的姊妹学校；也有来自纽约华美协进社的师生们，他们经常到户县去。这些计划给学生们提供了在教室以外与中国农民亲自互动的宝贵经验，在那里农民成为他们的老师。

During a Folk Festival of twenty thousand peasants in Huxian in 2002, I was extremely proud to be given the official designation of Honorary Peasant, which echoes my deep admiration and respect for the peasants of China.

2002年在户县举行的有两万农民参加的民俗节上，我非常自豪地被授予"荣誉农民"的称号，它也反映了我对中国农民深深的尊敬。

Seeds of democracy in the countryside
农村中的民主种子

In 2005 in the village of An Shang the first real election in the history of the village was held when the villagers themselves selected candidates whose plans and specific programs to carry them out had been presented to them. Formerly the township leaders had chosen candidates, as in the prior 2003 election.

2005年，安上村进行了村史上第一次真正的选举。村民们自己选择候选人，而候选人在选举前必须陈述他们的计划，以及实现这个计划的具体步骤。以前的候选人都是由镇领导选定的，就像2003年的选举。

Walking along muddy narrow paths toward the polling place to vote for Chairman, Vice Chairman and three members of the Villagers' Committee was a first time experience for these villagers. Grassroots participation was a welcome change, where votes were cast privately and the final tally publicly announced.

村民们沿着泥泞狭窄的小道到达选举地点，选举村民委员会的主席、副主席和三名委员。对他们来说，这种选举是破天荒的：选举人不记名投票，但最后会公开唱票。这种基层的民主参与是一个积极的变化。

Later at a folk festival in An Shang in 2007 hundreds of villagers waited eagerly to watch an open-air Peking Opera performance. However, as we watched together no opera appeared but an on-stage vigorous verbal struggle took place where those who had lost the last election angrily began protesting and shouting through stage microphones. The opera was cancelled, but the election results by the majority of the people held.

2007年，我参加了安上村的一个民俗节，几百名村民聚集在那里等着看一场室外的戏曲演出，可台上上演的却是一场口水战。那些在选举中失败的人们开始通过麦克风愤怒地大喊和抗议。演出被取消了，但是被大多数人认可的选举结果依然有效。

A few months later at the 17th Party Congress in Beijing, Premier Wen Jiabao said that development of grassroots democracy in the countryside is one of the top priorities in the country. The seeds are planted.

几个月后，在北京召开的中共十七大上，温家宝总理说，发展农村基层民主是国家要进行的头等大事之一。这奠定了民主的基础。

2005，安上村，村民在排队选举
Peasants lining up to cast their vote, An Shang village, 2005

Ethnic minorities, balancing beliefs and burdens
少数民族：信仰与负担

Learning from peasants in the countryside about their everyday life and from various ethnic minorities about their particular beliefs has expanded my understanding and appreciation for the people throughout China.

对农民日常生活和不同少数民族特殊信仰的了解使我对中国人民的理解更加全面了。

A complex set of change is reaching China's minorities, represented by fifty-six ethnic groups. The Han comprise 92% of China's population with the remainder spread between fifty-five minorities. Most of those have strong religious customs and beliefs with their own set of heroes passed down through generations. For example the Uyghurs in Xinjiang are mainly Muslims while the Tibetans practice Buddhism and others hold onto folk traditions and beliefs unique to their particular ethnic group. In some autonomous regions minority children attend specially designated school to learn their own ethnic language and practice traditional songs and dances.

一系列复杂的变化也正在影响到少数民族地区。汉族占中国人口总数的92%，其余的人口散布在55个少数民族中。绝大部分少数民族都有强烈的宗教习俗和信仰，有自己代代相传的英雄故事。比方说，新疆的维吾尔族人多数信仰伊斯兰教，而藏族人则笃信佛教，其他民族也有自己独特的民间传统和信仰。在一些民族自治地区，少数民族的孩子在特定的学校就学，学习自己民族的语言，演习传统的歌舞。

However, in China and most countries throughout the world, it is not easy to look different, speak a different language and practice customs dissimilar from the majority. A friend in Shanghai told me the minorities are lucky because they can have more children, while Han are limited to the One Child Policy. A friend from Inner Mongolia told me about the winds that whip across the grasslands in the winter, where there are few people and wide open space. Many of the minorities live in the desert areas of Xinjiang or the mountain areas of Tibet, where populations are sparse because of the lack of arable land.

不过，与众不同的长相、语言及不同的生活习惯，这对世界上大多数国家的人来说生活都是困难的。一位上海的朋友告诉我少数民族很幸运，因为他们可以要更多的孩子，而汉族家庭为政策所限，只能要一个孩子。一位内蒙古来的朋友告诉我，他们那里冬天的风席卷草原，人口很少，地方极开阔。许多少数民族生活在新疆戈壁地区和西藏山区，那里由于可耕地缺乏，人口也很少。

Parents struggle to pass on their language and customs but are faced with practical issues and difficult choices and often send their children to schools which teach mandarin Chinese in hopes their children will be better prepared to find a job in the future.

父母都努力将自己的语言和生活习惯传延下去，但是他们也面临一些实际问题和困难的选择，所以常常把孩子送往用普通话教学的学校，希望自己的孩子将来能找到好工作。

For example, Daxing is a town nestled amongst moss covered mountain peaks in one of China's very poorest regions in Guizhou Province. It was closed to foreigners in the 1990's when I lived with a family of the Miao ethnic minority, which is prevalent in that area. The wife of this family showed me a trunk with a few old blue and white woven clothes, typical of the Miao dress, and a large cloth headdress that was traditional for Miao women. She said she never wore them now because she did not want to stand out as being different. She said no laws existed about the clothes but it was better to just blend in. Her oldest son walked through the dark woods at night to go to school because not enough classrooms or teachers existed for all the children to attend school during the day. Her husband was a teacher who had not been paid for a long time.

比方说，大兴是贵州省的一个小镇，掩藏在青翠的大山之中，是中国最贫穷的地区之一。90年代我曾在那里的一个苗族家庭生活过。那时，大兴对外国人来说还是封闭的。那里是苗族聚居区，那家的女主人给我看过她的衣箱，里面衣服不多，都是旧的，颜色也就是蓝的和白的，典型的苗族样式。还有很大的包头布，传统上是为妇女准备的。她说她从没有穿过这些衣服，因为她不想与众不同。她解释说，穿衣并没有什么规矩，但最好能够与大家融合在一起。她的大儿子晚上要穿过黑暗的树林步行去学校，因为白天在学校没有足够的教室和老师。她的丈夫是教师，但已经很久没发工资了。

Also in Xinjiang is Kashgar, populated largely by Uyghur Muslims. More than two thousand years old, Kashgar was the first city merchants entered from the ancient Silk Road. It still maintains its history of trade, holding one of the largest outdoor Sunday bazaars in the world where there can be fifty thousand people from surrounding areas come to buy basic grains and live goats (often loaded onto donkey carts with family members to travel back home).

在新疆喀什，主要人口是信仰伊斯兰教的维吾尔族人。它是沿着丝绸之路进入中国的第一站，两千多年前西方的商人就是从这里进入中国的。在喀什仍然可以看到它的贸易史，今天它依然拥有世界上最大的室外巴扎。星期天会有大约五万人从相邻地区来到这里购买粮食和羊。人们经常将买到的货物装上驴车，然后和家人们一起回家。

1993，喀什，本地拥挤的巴扎——小车和负重的人
Local bazaar crowded by carts and people with heavy loads, Kashgar, 1993

1997，喀什，一次学校演出时的维吾尔族孩子和家长
Uyghur children and parents at a school performance, Kashgar, 1997

1997，喀什，一次学校演出时的维吾尔族孩子
Uyghur children at a school performance, Kashgar, 1997

1984，内蒙古呼和浩特，柯雷恩和蒙古族妇女
Eric Crain with Mongolian woman, beyond Huhehot Inner Mongolia, 1984

More attractive to current entrepreneurs however are Xinjiang's rich reserves of oil and minerals. Harsh desert conditions, severe heat and lack of infrastructure pose difficulties in utilizing them. Local people struggle with filling their basic needs such as pure water and food while at the same time these new energy sources are being tapped beneath their very feet. While increased attention focuses on bringing economic reform to help people in the interior and remote regions of central and western China sometimes the modern conveniences destroy old customs in the process.

然而对今天的企业家来说，新疆最具吸引力的就是它丰富的石油矿产资源，但由于沙漠的恶劣条件、酷热和基础设施的缺乏，这些资源很难利用。虽然新能源就在他们脚下，但他们仍然在为洁净水和食物这样的基本需求而努力。近年来，人们更加关注如何推进内地和遥远的中西部的改革，使那里人民的生活也能得到改善，但有时现代化的进程是以破除旧的习俗为代价的。

When my son Eric Crain (also include his Chinese name Ke Leien) first traveled in China, age sixteen, he met with the sheepherders in the grassland of Inner Mongolia beyond Huhehot. Fortunately he learned firsthand how they protect themselves and their animals from strong winds by building walls. He listened to their predicaments about schooling their children because as nomads they must move frequently in search of fertile grass for their herds. This experience and others left a strong imprint on his mind and formed the beginning of a deep respect for the Chinese people and culture which drew him back in future years to China to study, work and live.

我的儿子柯雷恩16岁时第一次来到中国。他在内蒙古比呼和浩特更远的大草原上遇到了一队牧人，从他们那里他了解到牧人们怎样打墙防风以保护牲畜和他们自己，也了解了他们之所以不断迁徙就是为他们的牲畜寻找丰美的水草，而在这种条件下为他们的孩子提供教育是一件多么困难的事情。从这些牧人那里得到的经验使他对中国人民和中国文化开始产生了深深的敬意，从而在以后那些年里吸引他回到中国学习、工作和生活。

The highest inhabited altitude on earth presents equally harsh conditions for Tibetans living in what has been called the "Roof of the World". Most Tibetans believe in Buddhism and spin prayer wheels, shown here as thousands gathered at the Jokhang Temple in Lhasa during the sacred Saga Dawa Festival celebrating Buddha's birth and enlightenment. Pilgrims travel for hundreds of miles to offer yak butter for the lamps and circumambulate the Jokhang or other temples. Traditional prayer flags are seen on almost all Tibetans' houses. When I asked one Tibetan friend if everyone in her family believed in Buddhism, she replied, "For us it is like breathing, everybody does." The lama is considered their spiritual hero, teaching about the three principles: respect for self, respect for others, responsibility for all of your actions.

西藏一直被称为"世界屋脊",那里是地球上人类居住的最高地方,生存条件极其艰苦。大多数藏族人笃信佛教并习惯转动经筒,就像拉萨大昭寺过萨嘎达瓦节的时候那样:成千上万的人聚集在那里,庆祝佛祖的生日和神明。香客们跋涉成百上千英里去为寺庙里的灯敬上牦牛油,施行大礼。几乎在任何藏族人的家居地都可以看到传统的祈祷旗。我曾经问一位藏族朋友是否她家里的人都信奉佛教,她回答说:"对我们来说,佛教就是呼吸。所有人都信。"喇嘛是他们精神上的英雄。他们倡导三个原则:尊重自我,尊重他人,对自己的行动负责。

During a visit to Lhasa my daughter Tammy Kuypers played soccer with Tibetan students at a local school and then met with children in the Barkhor market area surrounding the Jokhang Temple. She saw how young people helped harvest the barley and sometimes carried water from the local streams and she learned about the difficulties in balancing old customs with the influx of modern ways.

访问拉萨的时候,我的女儿柯叹梅参加了一场与当地藏族学生的足球赛,接着又在大昭寺附近八角街的一个市场上会见了一群孩子。她看到本地青年怎样收割青稞,又怎样从附近的小溪取水。她还了解到他们在面对古老传统和大量涌入的现代生活方式时所遇到的困难。

Since the altitude is high and weather conditions are severe Tibetans must work extremely hard in order to survive. They rely heavily on yaks for milk, cheese, butter and sometimes meat; barley is one of the few crops that can grow in such difficult condition. Many are nomads constantly moving their herds in search of food. I watched as they labored during the harvest time and joined them for typical yak butter tea, while they sang Tibetan songs and generously shared their limited food. I admire their work ethics and strong personal beliefs.

由于海拔很高而且气候恶劣,藏族人必须拼命工作以求生存。他们非常依赖牦牛的奶、奶酪和黄油,有时还有它们的肉。青稞是少数能够在这样严酷条件下生长的作物之一。他们中的许多人是牧民,总是驱赶着畜群寻找食物。我看到过藏族人收获季节辛苦劳作的场面,并和他们共饮过典型的酥油茶。他们唱着藏族歌曲,并且慷慨地和我们分享他们有限的食物。我非常钦佩他们的工作伦理和强烈的个人信念。

The eve of the new millennium in 2000, together with my Canadian cousin and dear friend Barbara Nicholas we undertook an arduous journey in far western Tibet to Mount Kailash (Kang Rimpoche). Tibetans themselves have traditionally traveled there on foot or open trucks on hazardously steep winding roads. Such a pilgrimage for them may take weeks or months to accomplish, carrying meager supplies of food and water and sleeping under their heavy sheepskin

02 1984，西藏拉萨，大昭寺的转经人
Spinning prayer wheels at the Jokhang Temple, Lhasa Tibet, 1984

02 1986，西藏拉萨，柯叹梅和藏族孩子在八角街
Tammy Crain Kuypers with Tibetan children in the Barkhor, Lhasa Tibet, 1986

1997,西藏日喀则,收获季节的藏族妇女
Tibetan women during harvest season, beyond Shigatse Tibet, 1997

coats at night against the cold and wind. Adherents of four different religions hold that mountain, Kang Rimpoche, sacred: Buddhism, Hinduism, Jainism and the native Tibetan Bon faith. It is the source of four major rivers of Asia.

在2000年的新年之夜，我和我的加拿大表妹芭芭拉·尼古拉斯做了一次艰苦的旅行，一起去了西藏西部的冈仁波齐山。藏族人传统上步行去那里，或者坐敞篷卡车去，但那蜿蜒的山路危险陡峭。这样的朝圣要用去他们几周甚至几个月的时间，他们身背的食物和水有限，晚上就裹着羊皮大衣睡觉，以抵御寒风。冈仁波齐山被四种宗教的信徒奉为圣地，即藏传佛教、印度教、古耆那教和西藏原生宗教苯教，同时也是亚洲四条主要河流的源头。

Along this journey and to the nearby sacred Lake Manasarovar we observed the passionate dedication of the Tibetan people as they circumambulated the mountain and nearby temples, offering white silk khatas or mani stones along the way to insure safe passage across dangerous mountain passes or rushing streams, and touching their foreheads to sacred places to receive blessings. Their faces are weathered from living so close to the sun, their hands calloused from physical labor required to survive but their kindness was evident in smiles and the traditional Tibetan greeting, "Tashi delek," their way of wishing us well.

在这次旅行和前往附近神圣的玛旁雍错湖的路上，我们感受到了藏族人对信仰的虔诚。他们一路长拜前往那座圣山和附近的寺庙，沿途献上洁白的哈达和玛尼石，以求越过险峻高山和湍急河流时一路平安。他们在这些圣地前面叩头以求赐福。由于生活在离太阳很近的地方，他们的脸显得饱经风霜，他们的手也由于重体力劳动而结满老茧，但从他们的笑容和他们"（藏历）新年好"的问候中，他们的善良显而易见。

For over thirty years now individuals' stories have been the threads of an intricate embroidery in my mind. Minorities and Han, peasants and ambassadors, shopkeepers and policy planners, students and writers, heroes and ordinary citizens have woven colorful but complicated patterns. By listening to stories about their own unique situations I gained a clearer but still limited image of the total picture of the steady transformation within China.

30多年，众多的个人故事已经在我心中织成了一幅精美的图画。少数民族和汉族，农民和大使，商店老板和政策制定者，学生和作家，英雄和普通人，构成了色彩斑斓的图案。听着他们各自不同的独特故事，我得到了一幅中国在持续变化的总体画面，尽管这样的画面还不那么完整。

Section Three
第三章

Beyond Borders: Change in International Relations
国界之外：国际关系的变化

1977，北京郊区，长城上的画家
Artist on the Great Wall, beyond Beijing, 1977

Introduction
导言

For centuries the Great Wall had kept foreigners out. For decades China turned inward and maintained no official relations with the United States. As I walked along the wall in 1977 this artist caught my eye as he sat painting, nestled on the crumbling wall beyond a sign in Chinese, English and Russian that signaled "Out of bounds for visitors". To me this image seemed to symbolize the barriers long dividing China from other countries but also an opening to go beyond.

远古以来，长城都是为抵御外族而建造的。中美间曾有几十年没有外交关系。1977年，当我走在长城上时，我看到一位画家正在一段垮塌了的长城遗址上作画，他的旁边有一个警告牌，上面用汉语、英语和俄语写着：游人止步。对我来说，这个警告牌仿佛象征着长期将中国与其他国家割裂开的障碍，但我们两国新的关系也正是从那里起步。

In the following year Deng Xiaoping's new policies would pave the way for China to become increasingly involved in international relations. I want to mention a few well-known national events that occurred in subsequent years, including formal agreements with the United States and then less known exchanges that evolved on a more person-to-person level, such as the establishment of "sister-city", peasant painting exhibitions and scholarly exchanges. These examples illustrate how connections and sharing of ideas between individuals at all different levels helped break down some of the previous obstacles that divided our countries.

1978年，邓小平的新政策为中国发展国际关系铺平了道路。我想在这里提及几件接下来发生的、众所周知的国际事件，如中美建交，和一些不太为人知的、属于民间或准民间意义上的国际交流，如"姊妹城市"的建立、农民画展和学术交流等。通过这些事件，我们可以看到不同层次的联系和思想交流怎样打破了过去将我们两国隔开的障碍。

Historic Landmark Events: Changing China's Interaction with the World
标志性的历史事件：中国与世界关系的改变

The launching of the Four Modernizations in agriculture, industry, technology and defense by Deng Xiaoping in 1978 started China on the course of "reform and opening up". Economic reforms inside China became interdependent with global relationships. Several landmark events changed the course of China's interaction with the world: Nixon's visit to China and the re-establishment of Sino-American relations, Gorbachev's visit to China and Sino-Soviet relations, China's membership in the World Trade Organization and China's hosting of the 2008 Olympics.

1978年，邓小平推动的四个现代化——工业、农业、国防和科学技术现代化——使中国走上了改革开放的道路。中国的经济改革与外部世界变得息息相关。几个标志性的事件改变了中国与世界的关系：尼克松访华和中美外交关系的恢复；戈尔巴乔夫访华和中苏关系的正常化；中国加入世界贸易组织；中国主办2008年奥运会。

President Nixon's visit with Chairman Mao Zedong in 1972
1972年，毛泽东主席会见尼克松总统

President Richard Nixon's visit to China in 1972 signaled the beginning of more open relations between China and the United States, severed since 1949. When Mao Zedong and the Communist Party established the People's Republic of China the United States withheld diplomatic recognition. Nixon's visit focused on improving bilateral relations between the United States and China but also on maintaining a strategic balance of power between the United States, China and the Soviet Union.

1972年，尼克松总统的访华之旅标志着1949年以后中断的中美关系重现生机。在毛泽东和中国共产党建立中华人民共和国以后，美国撤回了它的外交使团。尼克松访华不但旨在改善中美双边关系，而且意欲保持美、中、苏间的战略平衡。

In the Shanghai Communiqué signed during his visit the United States expressed the hope of expanding cultural and economic contacts. It acknowledged the concept of the "One China Policy". Details were not worked out but the statements put forth laid the foundation for the eventual establishment of formal diplomatic relations in 1979 between the two countries. Nixon described his visit as "the week that changed the world". He said, "We have great differences... neither of us will compromise our principles. But while we cannot close the gulf between us we can try to bridge it so that we may be able to cross it."

在尼克松此行签署的"上海公报"中，美国表达了扩大两国间文化和经济交流的愿望并承认"一个中国"的立场。公报没有涉及细节但奠定了1979年中美最终建立正式外交关系的基础。尼克松把这次访问称为"改变世界的一周"。他说："我们有很大的分歧……我们双方都不会放弃原则。但是，尽管我们不能弥合我们之间的鸿沟，却可以尝试搭建桥梁去跨越它。"

Establishment of diplomatic relations between China and the United States in 1979
1979年，中美两国正式建立外交关系

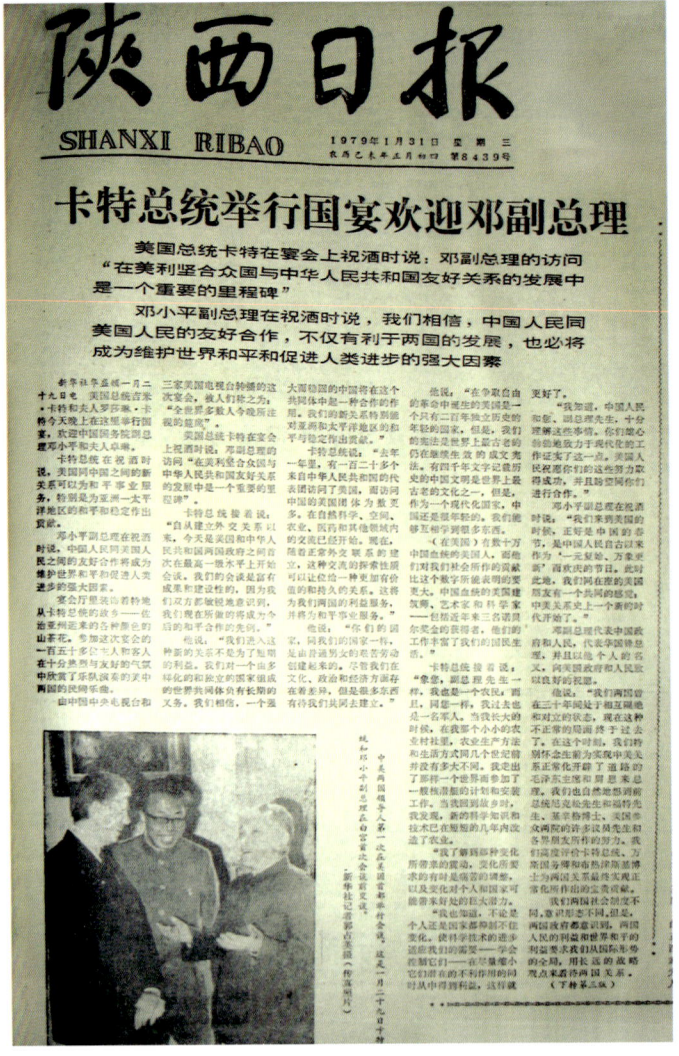

1979，《陕西日报》。邓小平在华盛顿访问时会见卡特总统
Deng Xiaoping's visit in Washington D.C. with President Carter as published in the *Shaanxi Ribao*, Xi'an, 1979

Subsequently in 1979 Deng Xiaoping, as China's Vice Premier and paramount leader, traveled to the United States to meet with President Jimmy Carter in Washington D.C. to celebrate the signing of the Joint Communiqué establishing normal diplomatic relations between the two countries. This marked the first visit of a high-ranking Chinese official to the United States since the establishment of the People's Republic of China in 1949. The Joint Communiqué, signed by both sides included the following provisions: the United States recognizes the government of the People's Republic of China as the sole legal government of China and acknowledges the Chinese position that there is but one China and Taiwan is part of China. Other agreements included plans to begin cultural, educational and scientific exchanges, which flourished in the following years.

1979年，邓小平作为中国副总理和最高领导人访美，并在华盛顿会见吉米·卡特总统，庆祝两国建交的"联合公报"的签署。这是1949年中华人民共和国成立以来中国最高领导人的首次访美。双方签署的"联合公报"包括下列条款：美国承认中华人民共和国政府是中国的唯一合法政府；承认中国方面的立场，即只有一个中国，台湾是中国的一部分。其他协议包括计划开始文化、教育和科学方面的交流。这些交流后来变得十分活跃。

Gorbachev's visit to China in 1989 and Sino-Soviet relations
戈尔巴乔夫1989年访华和中苏关系的正常化

Ten years later in the spring of 1989 the world focused on President Mikhail Gorbachev's historic visit to Beijing for the first Sino-Soviet summit since 1959, ending thirty years of strained relations between the two socialist superpowers. As I rode my bike in the packed streets in Beijing the world's news media, journalists and photographers gathered to gain information and spread reports of this concord.

在中美建交10年后的1989年春，世界的目光集中在米哈伊尔·戈尔巴乔夫总统历史性的访华之旅。这是1959年后中苏首脑的首次会面，从而结束了两个社会主义大国间长达30年的紧张关系。当我骑车穿过北京拥挤的街道时，全世界的新闻媒体、记者和摄影记者们聚集在那里，搜集信息并向全世界报道此次事件。

Similar to the historic 1972 meeting between President Nixon and Chairman Mao Zedong, Gorbachev and Deng Xiaoping discussed economlc issues and the need for opening trade relations but also centered on the power struggle involving China, the United States and the Soviet Union As Nixon's visit with Mao opened the doors for future development between China and the United States, Gorbachev's encounter with Deng Xiaoping focused on improving relations between their two countries. However, within a short time events led to the dissolution of the Soviet Union, the resignation of President Gorbachev, and declaration of independence of all fifteen of the former soviet republics. By 1991 China entered into diplomatic relations with those fifteen independent countries.

与1972年尼克松总统和毛泽东主席的会面相似，戈尔巴乔夫和邓小平讨论了经济问题并准备开放贸易，也讨论了中、美、苏之间的关系。如同尼克松与毛泽东的会见打开了中美两国关系未来发展的大门一样，戈尔巴乔夫和邓小平的会见也集中在改善两国关系上。不过，不久苏联国内又发生了一连串事件，最后导致苏联解体、戈尔巴乔夫下台和前苏联的所有15个加盟共和国宣布独立。到1991年，中国已经与这15个独立国家分别建立了外交关系。

China reflects on fifty years (1949—1999):
the 50th Anniversary of the Founding of the People's Republic of China
50年的回顾（1949—1999）：中华人民共和国建国50周年

1999，北京，天安门广场，建国50周年之夜的焰火
Fireworks on the eve of the 50th Anniversary of the Founding of P.R. of China, Tian'anmen Square, Beijing, 1999

1949—1999

On the occasion of the 50th anniversary of
the People's Republic of China
Premier Zhu Rongji of the State Council of
the People's Republic of China
requests the pleasure of your company
at a National Day Reception
in the Banquet Hall, the Great Hall of the People
On Thursday 30 September 1999 at 18:00 hours

(Your Table No. Zone)

中华人民共和国建国50周年宴会请柬
Banquet Invitation for the 50th Anniversary of the Founding of P.R. of China

The fiftieth anniversary of the founding of the People's Republic of China established by Mao Zedong and the Communist Party on October 1st 1949 was commemorated with fireworks, parades and banquets. On the eve of those National Day celebrations in 1999 Premier Zhu Rongji hosted a banquet in the Great Hall of the People, where among the guests was Ambassador Huang Hua who had accompanied Edgar Snow to interview Mao Zedong in 1936, later serving as China's Vice Premier and Foreign Minister. There were others at the banquet and parade who had obviously made contributions to their country, reflecting on their own struggles and victories.

庆祝中华人民共和国建国50周年的活动有焰火、游行和宴会。国庆前夜，朱镕基总理在人民大会堂举行了晚宴。来宾中有1936年陪伴埃德加·斯诺采访毛泽东的黄华，他后来成为中国的副总理和外交部长。晚宴和游行中的其他人也毫无疑问地为他们的国家作出了贡献；此时此刻，他们也在回顾自己的战斗与辉煌。

1999，北京，人民大会堂的国庆50周年招待会上的雪莲夫妇
50th anniversary celebration in the Great Hall of the People, Sharon and Bill Crain, Beijing, 1999

China joins the World Trade Organization, 2001
2001年，中国加入世界贸易组织

Deng Xiaoping's economic reforms internally inside China paralleled his external push to develop international trade and open China to the outside world. Beginning in the 1980's to encourage foreign investment the government set up Special Economic Zones (SEZ), granting unique privileges to entice overseas investments such as special tax incentives and preferential policies. Shenzhen was the first of five Special Economic Zones to further accelerate the economy and help China compete in the global market. Once these proved successful other areas were given similar approval, continuing China's pattern of cautious experimentation before expanding new policies.

邓小平的经济改革大大发展了国内经济，同时也加快了对外贸易开放的步伐。20世纪80年代初，为了鼓励外商投资，政府建立了经济特区，它们被给予减税和其他优惠政策以吸引外资，其中深圳是5个经济特区中的第一个。建立经济特区的目的就是要加速经济发展并增强中国在国际市场上的竞争力。一旦这些试点地区被证明是成功的，相似的政策就会推及全国。这就是先谨慎试验，再全面推广的中国模式。

During the 1990's the Shanghai Pudong New Zone played a leading role in China's economic development through enticing foreign business. Deng Xiaoping fueled the fires toward a market economy with his practical approach: "It doesn't matter if the cat is black or white as long as it catches the mouse." After years of struggle and debate China joined the World Trade Organization in 2001 and continued on its path

2001，《人民日报》，中国加入世贸组织
Announcement of China's membership in the World Trade Organization, *Renmin Ribao*, 2001

2007，北京，报道经济成就的《货币》杂志
Money Journal focusing on economic success stories, Beijing, 2007

toward becoming one of the leading manufacturing centers in the world.

在90年代，上海浦东新区扮演了鼓励外资、刺激经济的领头羊角色。邓小平用实践的方法推动着中国向市场经济发展，用他自己的话就是："不管白猫黑猫，抓到老鼠就是好猫。"在多年的谈判和辩论之后，中国终于在2001年加入了世界贸易组织，而且正在一步步成为世界最大的制造业中心之一。

Money Journal and a smiling face on the cover greeted me with stories of how to get rich when I entered my hotel room in Beijing in 2007, one of numerous publications reflecting the dominant interest of many people throughout China today. Parents often express concern that their children care only about money and are losing some of the traditional values of the past. Others who suffered years of deprivation speak proudly that their children actually have options to make money on their own.

2007年，当我在北京走进宾馆房间时，《货币》杂志和它封面上的笑脸就在欢迎我。这本杂志讲了许多如何致富的故事，也是反映今天中国人主流价值观的众多杂志之一。父母们担心他们的孩子只关心钱却丢掉了某些传统价值观。还有一些人则不同，他们过了多年的苦日子，但看到孩子们已经能够自己挣钱了，他们很自豪。

WTO and "Made in China"
世界贸易组织和"中国制造"

Facilitated by China's 2001 membership in the World Trade Organization joint ventures grew as companies came to buy or produce Chinese products. Trade centers and shopping complexes burgeoned with new investments. Reflecting back on my own travels to China during the 1970's and 1980's I realized my clothes, shoes, suitcase, and gifts I brought had all been made in the United States. Now, most of those items are "Made in China" contributing to an enormous imbalance of trade. Benefits for one country become deficits for others. While Chinese imports into the United States help satisfy an American desire for low-cost products, China currently reinvests over a trillion U.S. dollars back into U.S. Treasury Bonds.

由于中国成为世界贸易组织的成员，跨国投资和合资在中国也日益繁荣，商人们纷纷前来购买中国产品或直接设厂并将在那里生产的产品出口。随着新投资的涌入，贸易中心和购物中心不断涌现。70、80年代到中国的时候，我带去的衣服、鞋子、旅行箱以及礼物都是美国生产的。现在，绝大多数这些商品都是"中国制造"，但也由此造成了两国间巨大的贸易不平衡。此国的赢利就是彼国的赤字。不过，中国对美出口满足了美国人对廉价商品的需求，同时中国也购买了上万亿美元的美国国债，反过来投资美国。

In a steady trajectory China has risen from a backward country struggling to feed its own people to one of the world's fastest growing economies. Many companies and individuals have benefited from increased salaries and profits but widespread corruption has devastated others.

从一个挣扎在温饱线上的落后国家发展成为世界上成长最快的经济体，中国已经进入了一个稳定发展的轨道。大量的公司和个人因此受益，工资迅速增长，赢利也大幅提高，但腐败的蔓延损害了这种发展。

A friend shared with me a personal story within her family as one example: " My uncle put all his savings into building a small appliance company. After five years of hard work and sacrifice his sales increased to the point of making a profit but then my uncle lost everything when he got sick and his partner cut him out and kept all the money."

一个朋友告诉了我一个发生在她家的故事："我叔叔用尽了他的全部积蓄办了一个小公司。经过5年的惨淡经营，就在公司要开始赢利的时候，他得了一场病，结果他的合伙人背着他把所有的资产据为己有。"

2007，西安，西安国际贸易中心和金鹰国贸购物中心，律师汪大明
Xi'an International Trade Center and the Golden Eagle Guomao Shopping Center, Lawyer Wang Daming, Xi'an, 2007

In response to the need for "rule by law" both within China and internationally many people such as Wang Daming (pictured above) became lawyers, a relatively new profession in China. When my son, Eric Crain started his own business in Xi'an Wang Daming served as his lawyer for the company. They learned about law and business from each other and became close friends.

律师在中国是一个相对新型的职业。为了顺应国内外的"法治"要求，像汪大明（照片中人物）这样的律师也应运而生。我儿子柯雷恩在西安创办自己的公司时，汪大明为他的公司提供法律服务。他们各自从对方那里学到了法律和商业知识，而且成了好朋友。

China hosts the 2008 Olympics
中国主办2008年奥运会

Certainly one of the most significant events marking China's participation in the global arena was hosting the 2008 Olympics in Beijing. For many Chinese people it represented an opportunity to show pride in their country to the world. As one of my university students said, "I want to be a volunteer at the Olympics in Beijing so I can help many foreigners have a better understanding about China and make new friends." Another student who was pursuing his PhD added, "China still has a lot of problems and we have a long way to go but I am proud of the great distance my country has come since my parents were my age."

当然，使中国登上全球舞台的最重大事件之一就是主办2008年北京奥运会。对许多中国人来说，这个事件使中国有机会向世界作一次骄傲的展示。一位本科生说："我想做一个北京奥运会的志愿者，这样我就可以帮助外国人更好地了解中国，同时还可以结识许多新朋友。"一位博士生说："中国还有很多问题，我们还有很长的路要走，但是我很骄傲，因为从我父母那一代人起，我们国家已经有了很大的改变。"

2007，北京，天安门广场的倒计时钟
Count down clock in Tian'anmen Square, Beijing, 2007

2008，姚明和汶川地震的小幸存者林浩手举国旗在奥运会开幕式上——在美国看到的电视镜头
Yao Ming and young earthquake survivor Lin Hao carry the flag in the Olympic ceremony, as viewed on television in America, 2008

Although I did not attend the Olympics I watched with particular interest when China's popular basketball player, Yao Ming entered the Olympic arena on opening night along with Lin Hao, a small boy who had survived the devastating earthquake in Sichuan Province a few months before. This young nine-year old had bravely returned to a dangerous area to help rescue two of his young classmates trapped in the rubble. Later when he was asked why he had risked his own safety to go back, he replied, "I am the monitor of my class so I should do that." To me he represents a noble sense of responsibility and caring for others, which was also shown by many Olympic participants from countries throughout the world as they competed in Beijing.

虽然我没有出席奥运会，但我饶有兴趣地观看了中国最受欢迎的篮球选手姚明入场时的一幕。在开幕式之夜，姚明是和几个月前汶川地震中幸存的小孩子林浩一起入场的。在那场毁灭性的地震中，这个9岁的孩子勇敢地回到已成为废墟的教室，救出了两个埋在那里的同学。在被问到他为什么冒着生命危险回到那里时，他回答说："我是班长，我应该那样做。"对我来说，他代表了一种崇高的责任感，一种关心他人的精神，而这也正是世界各地的奥运会参与者们所表现的精神。

Sister-State and Sister-City Relationships Reap Benefits
省际和城际的国际交流

Beyond the spectacular events of official agreements between countries and international occasions such as the Olympics, quiet exchanges took place between cities, states, provinces and schools to share information and create projects for mutual benefit.

除了像奥运会那样的大型国际交流以外，在城市间、州与省之间、学校之间也有着平静的交流，大家通过交流增进了解，也达成一些互惠的项目。

China's "opening-up policy" led to establishing hundreds of sister-state and sister-city relationships between people in the United States and also with other countries. These connections facilitated individual and group exchanges and made it easier to obtain permission for activities or secure visas from both sides. Since the majority of my thirty years of involvement in China has taken place in Shaanxi Province I want to focus my lens on a few exchanges within that province, which provide glimpses of the impact that individual exchanges can have on broadening the horizons of international relations.

在改革开放的政策下，中国已经同美国及其他国家建立了数以百计的姊妹省

（州）和姊妹城市关系。这些关系使得个人和团体间的交流更加顺畅，也更容易得到官方的许可和签证。由于我在中国的30年大都待在陕西，所以想将注意力主要集中在这个省的对外交往上，这些交往实际上拓宽了我们对国际关系的理解。

Shaanxi and Minnesota become "sister-state", 1982
1982年，陕西省与明尼苏达州

One example of a sister-state relationship is between Shaanxi Province and the State of Minnesota in the United States. Minnesota is proud of its strong connections with China dating back to the late 1800's. It currently has one of the largest concentrations of Chinese faculty and students in North America. After establishing official ties in 1982 both sides enthusiastically entered into academic partnerships, business agreements and cultural exchanges.

这方面的一个范例是陕西省和明尼苏达州之间的姊妹关系。明尼苏达州与中国的紧密联系可以追溯到19世纪晚期，它很为此而自豪。现在它是北美中国学生和中国教授最集中的地方之一。1982年建立了官方关系之后，双方的交往都很积极，并进入到学术、商业和文化交流等领域。

One of those exchanges involved Global Volunteers, headquartered in Minnesota. It became the first Non-government Organization (NGO) to be invited to send volunteer teachers to China, which took place in Shaanxi Province and later involved hundreds of Americans. Then Global Volunteers became the first NGO invited to participate in work projects in China, which resulted in building a new school in An Shang together with local villagers.

这些交往包括总部设在明尼苏达州的环球志愿者组织。它现在已成为第一个被邀请派志愿教师去中国的非政府组织，支教的目的地都在陕西，涉及的美国志愿者陆续有几百名。环球志愿者也是第一个受邀参与中国具体工程的非政府组织，这个工程就是在安上村由志愿者和本地村民一起建立的一个新学校。

When Shaanxi Governor Yu Mingtao and Lt. Governor Li Lianbi came to the United States to meet with Minnesota leaders they first visited New York City where Mayor Edward Koch welcomed them. He told them he tried to set up bike lanes on busy New York City streets similar to those he had seen during his visit to Xi'an the previous year. Together they talked about some of the problems facing government officials in both countries.

在陕西省省长于明涛、副省长李连壁前往美国会见明尼苏达州领导人的途中，

1982，纽约市，陕西省省长于明涛、副省长李连璧与纽约市市长爱德华·科赫和雪莲等的合影
Shaanxi Governor Yu Mingtao and Lt. Governor Li Lianbi with New York City Mayor Ed Koch, Sharon Crain and others, New York City, 1982

他们首先访问了纽约市并受到爱德华·科赫市长的欢迎。爱德华·科赫市长告诉他们他正尝试着在纽约繁忙的大街上设立自行车道，就像他一年前访问西安时看到的那样。他们还谈到了各自面临的其他问题。

Xi'an and Kansas City: a "sister-city" strengthens old bridges
西安和堪萨斯市：加固友谊之桥的"姊妹城市"

Eventually lots of cities in China established official sister-city relationships with cities throughout the world, which enabled interested citizens to learn the history and cultural heritage of each other.

许多中国城市与世界各国的城市建立了姊妹城市关系，这样就使得有兴趣的市民可以学习彼此的历史和文化遗产。

One such relationship between Xi'an and Kansas City was formed because of previous strong bridges of friendship. Xi'an, China's ancient capital is situated in Shaanxi Province; exactly halfway around the world in the middle of the "bread-basket" of the United States is Kansas City, the hometown of Edgar Snow where he lived and studied journalism before going to China in 1927. On his treacherous journey to northern Shaanxi Province to interview Mao Zedong in 1936 he was helped along the way by the people of Xi'an. Then much later in Kansas City an Edgar Snow Memorial Fund

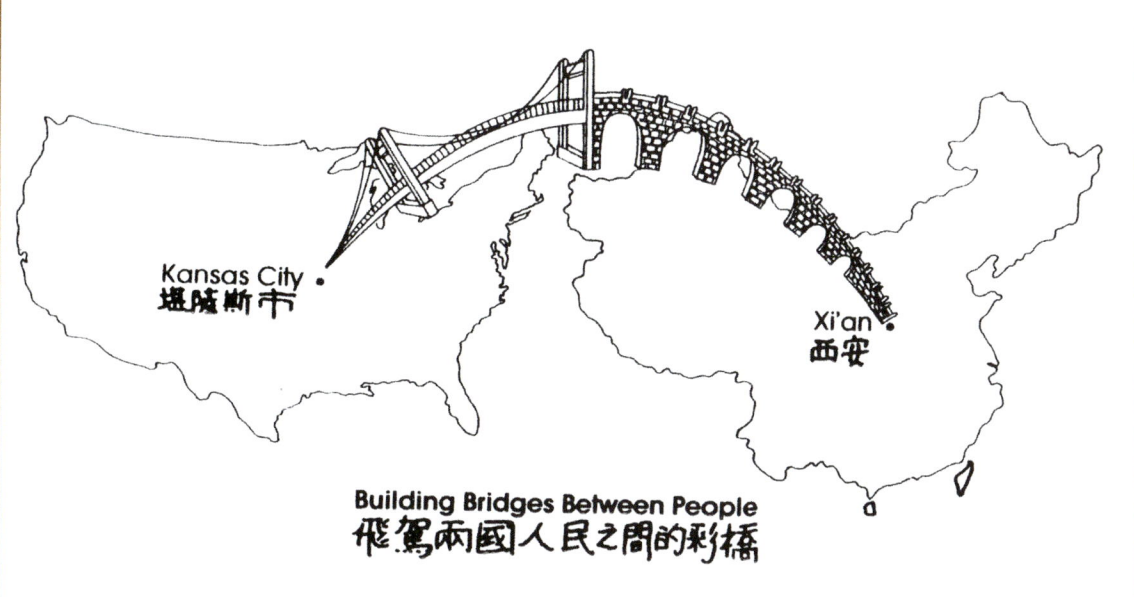

1989，"飞架两国人民之间的彩桥"是堪萨斯市和西安姊妹城市的标志语
Building Bridges Between People as seen on the Kansas City-Xi'an Sister-City logo, 1989

1989，西安，西安和堪萨斯市建立姊妹城市的签署仪式（从右至左，西安市市长袁正中，堪萨斯市市长理查德·伯克利，亨利·密切尔，鲍勃·钱和雪莲）
Signing the sister-city relationship between Xi'an and Kansas City Missouri, Xi'an, 1989（R to L, Xi'an Mayor Yuan Zhengzhong, Kansas City Mayor Richard Berkeley, Henry Mitchell, Bob Qian and Sharon Crain）

was established by Mary and Grey Dimond to carry on his legacy of promoting understanding between China and America. All of these links proved important in leading to this sister-city relationship.

西安市和堪萨斯市建立姊妹城市就是由于它们以前的友谊。西安市位于陕西省，是中国的古都；堪萨斯市则恰恰在地球的那端，在美国的中部，是美国的"面包篮子"，也是埃德加·斯诺的故乡。1927年去中国前，埃德加·斯诺一直在那里生活，并学习新闻。1936年，在西安人民的帮助下，他克服了重重险阻去陕北采访了毛泽东。很多年后，玛丽和格雷·戴蒙德在堪萨斯市建立了"埃德加·斯诺基金会"，以此来延续他的精神，增进中美两国之间的理解。所有这些联系都在建立两座城市姊妹关系的过程中发挥了重要作用。

Primarily because of Edgar Snow's personal connection to both cities as well as the efforts of many people in each place, a Sister-City accord was signed in 1989. At that time I was living in Kansas City, was deeply involved in Xi'an, and had been working with Helen Snow for many years. As Chairman of the Kansas City-Xi'an Sister-City Organization, I was fortunate to accompany Kansas City's Mayor and a delegation to Xi'an for the official signing of our relationship.

西安市与堪萨斯市姊妹关系的最终建立仰赖于埃德加·斯诺与西安的个人情谊和众多有关人士的努力。正式的协议是1989年签署的，那时我生活在堪萨斯市，并且已经对西安有了很深的了解，还与海伦·斯诺一起工作了很多年。作为堪萨斯市-西安姊妹城市协会的主席，我有幸陪同堪萨斯市长及由他率领的堪萨斯市代表团访问了西安，并参加了姊妹城市的官方签字仪式。

Peasant-painters build new bridges
农民画家搭建新的友谊之桥

Soon after forging the Kansas City-Xi'an connection in April of 1989, Sino-American relations spiraled downward to a new low. However, people in both sister-city believed in promoting individual friendships in the same spirit pioneered by Helen and Edgar Snow decades before.

1989年4月堪萨斯市与西安市建立姊妹城市关系之后不久，中美关系很快就下降到空前的低点。不过，两市人民始终坚信由斯诺夫妇数十年前开创的友谊应该得到继承。

Together both sides started planning the first event, which was to be a major exhibition of over two hundred peasant-paintings from Huxian County, a rural area near Xi'an. Local peasants in that area had originally been utilized by Mao Zedong to promote revolutionary goals during the Great Leap Forward in 1958, having been given brushes and directives to illustrate China's push forward through their paintings and posters. Years later peasants continued to paint on their own, capturing the essence of their everyday lives in vivid colors: harvesting bright red sorghum, herding white sheep or weaving brilliant yellow baskets in the courtyard.

Sunday, September 23, 1990 The Kansas City Star

'Red Sorghum,' by Zhang Xuan-Zhang, from an exhibit this week of Chinese peasant paintings.

Chinese paintings to visit Kansas City

Art work by peasants from Xi'an area will go on display during Edgar Snow Symposium.

By LAURA CARUSO
Art Critic

For the next several weeks it will be possible to see rural China without leaving Kansas City.

A program sponsored by the Kansas City-Xi'an Sister City Committee is bringing 200 peasant paintings from Xi'an and the surrounding agricultural area, Huxian County, to various sites around town. The majority of the vividly colored, stylized paintings on paper are on display at Halls Plaza store (through Oct. 7). Smaller groupings are at the Nelson Gallery (also through Oct. 7) and Johnson County Community College (starting Oct. 4). About 25 Plaza area merchants also have agreed to hang the works.

Kansas City's sister city relationship with Xi'an, China's ancient capital, was struck in April 1989, but the connections between the two cities can be traced to the 1930s and Kansas City journalist Edgar Snow. Snow was so fond of Xi'an — the word means "western peace" — that he gave this name to his only daughter, says Sharon Crain, who heads the Sister City Committee.

"Everybody there expressed concern about the events, and we started talking about what we could do to keep the sister cities program going, and we decided on the idea of a peasant painting exhibit," Crain says. Huxian County had been designated in 1987 as the "Home of Modern Chinese Folk Art" by the Chinese Ministry of Culture, and 2,000 practicing folk artists live in the region. Although peasant paintings from that area have been shown before in other countries, Crain says that, to her knowledge, this is the first time they have been exhibited in the United States.

The paintings show scenes of everyday life — herding livestock, harvesting sorghum — and although styles vary, they are generally flat and outlined like pages from a coloring book. They were brought to Kansas City in May by local businessman Huang Zheng, who is the son of Edgar Snow's former interpreter in China, Huang Hua.

The peasant painting exhibition coincides with the fourth biennial Edgar Snow Symposium. It will be held Monday and Tuesday at UMKC's White Recital Hall and will bring numerous U.S. and Chinese journalists and professors to Kansas City. The White Recital Hall lobby also is the site for an exhibition of photographs of Snow and his first wife, Helen, taken during their years in China, through Oct. 7.

A gala benefit reception is scheduled for 6-8 p.m. Thursday at Halls Plaza store, with music, slides and a chance to view and purchase the peasant paintings. One painter, Fan Zhi Hua, will demonstrate his techniques. He will repeat the demonstration at 1:30 p.m. Friday, just inside the Nelson's main entrance, and at 1:30 p.m. Oct. 3 at Maple Woods Community College.

Tickets for the gala cost $25. To make a reservation or for more information, call 274-3222.

那时双方都已经开始筹备第一个活动，即户县农民画展，参展的农民画有200多幅。户县临近西安市，1958年的大跃进中，当地农民被动员用他们的画笔来描绘革命理想，将中国推向前进。革命高潮过去后，农民继续描绘他们自己的生活，以生动的笔墨捕捉他们日常生活的真谛：收获火红的高粱，照看白色的羊群，在农家院落里编织黄色的竹篮。

1990，密苏里州堪萨斯市，邀请中国农民办画展
The invitation for the Chinese Peasant Painting Exhibition, Kansas City, Missouri, 1990

Style

TUESDAY, October 2, 1990 — THE KANSAS CITY STAR

Photos by KEVIN J. MIYAZAKI/The Star
Fan Zhi-hua and one of the 230 paintings by Chinese peasant artists he brought to Kansas City

A PEASANT PAINTER COMES TO KANSAS CITY

Goodwill ambassador shares artwork illustrating simple lives of Chinese farmers.

By LIZ SEATON
Special to The Star

When Fan Zhi-hua left home, he packed the cloth shoes his wife had made for him. By wearing them, she said, he would remember her message: "No matter how far you go, I'll always be with you."

From Huxian County, China, to Kansas City is 6,510 miles as the crow flies. This was a distance Fan could hardly imagine. He had never been in a plane before.

He is here through Thursday to initiate the first cultural exchange between Kansas City and its sister city, Xi'an, an industrial and commercial center about 25 miles northeast of his home. The sister city, like Kansas City, is surrounded by farmland. (See related story on Page E-5.)

Fan left the autumn crop of corn still to be harvested. Members of his extended family and villagers volunteered to help with his harvest while he traveled in the United States.

He came as an envoy of good feeling, bringing more than 200 folk paintings made by him and other peasants in his county.

He came as a representative of his people, the insular, hard-working peasants who make up about 75 percent of China's population. More specifically, he came to demonstrate to Kansas Citians what he has been doing in his "spare time" for more than 31 years. And he came to show them what other farmers in his territory also have been creating during "fallow" seasons.

Huxian County is the home of more than 2,000 peasant painters. China's minister of culture recently designated it the "home of Chinese modern folk art."

Fan was chosen for the trip from many artists by the Huxian County Farmer Painters Association because he was a member of the original group of these artists. The communist government began to recruit Chinese peasants to paint

See **CHINESE**, E-5, Col. 3

Fan Zhi-hua paints a colorful scene during a demonstration at Halls Plaza.

Fan Zhihua was selected by his fellow peasant-painters to go to Kansas City to represent all of them. His paintbrush and smile earned him the reputation of Ambassador of Goodwill. The activities and paintings of this first sister-city event seemed to open new bridges of understanding and friendship and led to further cultural, educational and business exchanges in the following years.

樊志华被选为农民画家的代表来到堪萨斯市。他的画笔和微笑为他赢得了"亲善大使"的美誉。这对姊妹城市的第一次活动和樊的画作架设了理解和友谊的新桥梁，开启了随后的文化、教育和商业交流。

Other cities and provinces set up their own connections linking people and ideas together through creative thinking and visionary action to overcome misconceptions based on lack of contact. Sometimes it was top leaders such as the compassionate Lt. Governor Li Lianbi or the globally minded school principals Gao Hongjian and Dr. Sandi Mond, or very young students who provided the necessary stimulus to move beyond past obstacles and expand the horizons of those involved.

其他省市也建立了它们自己的联系，通过创造性的思维和有想象力的活动克服了那些由于缺乏接触导致的误解，使人们之间得以沟通。参与这些活动的有热心的高层领导，如副省长李连璧，或者具有国际视野的教育工作者，如陕西师大附小的高红健校长及康涅狄格州公园路小学的校长森蒂·蒙德博士，甚至还有那些小学生。他们超越了过去的阻碍，扩大了交往的范围，为这些交流提供了必要的动力。

Student and School Exchanges: Open Minds and Expand Learning
学生交换和学校互访：打开心灵、学习新知

There are no barriers in the eyes of children
孩子眼中没有障碍

This young boy stared at me as a foreigner in his city while I stared back in surprise at his "I love N.Y." button in the early 1980's. There were limited knowledge between China and the United States at that time but keen curiosity existed on both sides.

这个小男孩儿正盯着我看，因为我是一个外国人，而我也惊奇地盯着他那个"我爱纽约"的纪念章。那是80年代早期，中美双方对彼此都缺乏了解，但又充满好奇。

1982，西安，戴着"我爱纽约"纪念章的小男孩儿
Young boy with I love N.Y. button, Xi'an, 1982

Exchange of scholars between China and the United States
中美交换学者

1979，北京，北京大学校长周培源教授欢迎中美建交后第一批由美国官方派出的学者（照片由美国学者舒衡哲提供）
The first group of official scholars from the United States to China after establishment of diplomatic relations, welcomed by Zhou Peiyuan President of Beijing University at that time, Beijing, 1979 (Photo courtesy of Professor Vera Schwarcz, one of the American scholars)

Soon after the 1979 establishment of formal diplomatic relations between the People's Republic of China and the United States a small group of American scholars was selected by the U.S. State Department to go to China to begin to open up educational doors. (Organized by the National Committee on US-China Relations as mandated by the State Department.) Likewise a small official group of Chinese Scholars and then other students started coming to universities in the United States as well as to other countries. In 1980, I met with many of these Chinese students to help set up a Scholars' Program at China Institute in New York City, which remains as the oldest organization in America to focus solely on teaching about Chinese history and culture.

中美建交后不久，一小批经过挑选的美国学者被美国国务院派往中国（由美国国务院主管、美中关系全国委员会组织实施），开始打开双方教育往来之门。同样，为数不多的中国学者和学生开始陆续到美国和其他国家的大学留学。1980年，我见过许多这样的中国学生，并协助纽约华美协进社创立了一个"中国学者计划"。华美协进社是美国历史最悠久的教授中国历史和文化的组织。

China Institute became their "home away from home" and a place to meet other scholars or professionals in their field of study, as well as a place to learn about America at a time when few Chinese students were in the U.S. Often they gathered at our nearby home in Madison, Connecticut

1980，康涅狄格州麦迪逊，中美建交后的第一批中国赴美学者在雪莲家中
Some of the first Chinese students in the U.S after establishment of diplomatic relations, Crain's house in Madison, Connecticut, 1980

where they learned about America's past in one of its oldest towns, first settled in 1641 at the time of the Ming Dynasty.

那时在美国的中国学生极少，华美协进社就成了中国学者的"海外之家"。在那里，他们可以接触到相关领域的学者和专业人士，也可以进一步了解美国。他们经常聚集在我康涅狄格州麦迪逊的家里，了解美国的过去。麦迪逊是美国最早的移民点之一。第一批移民是在1641年到达这里的，那时还是中国的明代。

Many students stayed in America for years of undergraduate and postgraduate study and then for further work experience. At first many hesitated to return to China. "I am waiting to see what happens with Deng Xiaoping's policies." They waited, they studied, they learned.

很多中国学生在美国完成本科和研究生的学习，并且在那里工作，一待就是很多年。起初，许多人对回国犹豫不决。一个学生告诉我说："不知道邓小平的政策会给中国带来什么变化，我要等等看。"他们在美国等待、学习，并且深入地了解。

Currently there are thousands of students studying in the U.S. In recent years many have been returning to China because of better job opportunities, better salaries and more security than the China they left years before. They are returning with graduate degrees and valuable work experiences, which have broadened their knowledge in practical ways. Many return to leadership positions in business, government, research institutes or universities in China and are well equipped to interact in cooperative projects between Chinese and Americans. Two former professors from the university where I teach in Xi'an have taken leadership positions in American universities and are engaged in fulltime China-related teaching and educational exchanges with China.

目前有成千上万的中国留学生在美国学习。近些年，由于国内有更好的就业机会、更高的工资和更安全的环境，很多学生回到了中国。他们有美国的学位和工作经历，这使他们有了更丰富的知识，同时也更有竞争力。他们中的很多人在商界、政府部门、研究机构和大学担任了领导职务，能够在中美两国的合作项目中更好地互动。有两名我在西安任教过的大学的教授，目前在美国的大学担任一定的领导职务，教授与中国有关的课程，并从事与中国相关的教育交流工作。

Elementary and high schools become "sister-school"
结成"姊妹学校"的中小学

Attempts to create more people-to-people experimental exchanges led to "sister-school" agreements that developed between China and other countries. One example was the sister-school agreement between Fu Xiao Elementary School in Xi'an and Parkway Elementary School in Madison, Connecticut. Fu Xiao is directly affiliated with Shaanxi Normal University in Xi'an. This relationship typifies the fruitful exchanges between students, teachers, principals and parents who shared educational methods while exploring cultural differences.

中外"姊妹学校"的发展说明了对更多人与人交流的渴望。陕西师大附小和康涅狄格州麦迪逊市公园路小学结成"姊妹学校"就是一个例子。这种关系的特点就是学生、教师、校长和家长之间富有成果的交流，他们不但分享各自的教育理念和方法，而且也探究他们之间的文化差异。

2004，康涅狄格州麦迪逊，雪莲家中，陕西师大附小和公园路小学的学生、老师和校长
Students, teachers and principals of ShiDa Fu Xiao and Parkway School, Crain's house, Madison, Connecticut, 2004

2004，康涅狄格州格林威治市公园路小学欢迎师大附小师生到访
Ceremony to welcome the Fuxiao students and teachers to the Parkway School, Greenwich connecticut, 2004

Chinese villagers and Global Volunteers build a school in An Shang
中国村民和环球志愿者共建学校

From an earlier "sister-state" relationship (Shaanxi Province and Minnesota 1982) developed a meaningful educational project. For three years local peasants in Shaanxi's An Shang village worked together with Americans from Minnesota's Global Volunteers to build a school (2005) which rises out of the cornfields.

时光流逝，早期的"姊妹州省"关系（陕西和明尼苏达）已经发展成为具有重大意义的教育工程。2005年，经过3年的建设，陕西安上村的村民们和来自美国明尼苏达州的环球志愿者一起在昔日的玉米地里建起了一所学校。

安危和雪莲在学校前，背后是飘扬着的中美两国国旗
An Wei and Sharon Crain in front of the school overlooking corn fields with flags of the U.S. and China

2004，安上，中国村民和环球志愿者共同努力建立安上村学校
Chinese villagers and Global Volunteers working together to build a school, An Shang, 2004

Before the work began no foreigners had ever been to An Shang. Now the flags of both countries fly equally over the school. An Wei, elected by the local people to coordinate the project, had grown up in this remote rural village. He was one of the few to break the cycle of poverty and receive a university education. In recent years he returned to work with local people and American volunteers to further improve the lives of local people.

在这项工程开工以前，安上村从来没有来过外国人，而现在中美两国的国旗同时飘扬在学校上空。安危就在这个偏僻的村子里长大，现在被村里人选为工程的协调人。他是村里为数寥寥的能够摆脱世代贫穷接受大学教育的人之一。这些年他回到家乡，同当地人民和美国志愿者们一起，进一步改变当地人民的生活状况。

Americans to China
到访中国的美国人

1984，纽约，雪莲率领的美国代表团和梁于藩大使
American delegation led by Sharon Crain with Ambassador Liang Yufan, New York, 1984

A surge of Americans began traveling to China in the 1980's and 1990's when I organized several delegations of individuals who were eager to learn firsthand just as China was opening and who were willing to share their expertise and become more involved.

20世纪80年代到90年代，美国曾有一个去中国旅游的热潮。很多人渴望得到关于中国改革开放的第一手信息，也渴望和那里的人们分享他们的专业知识，并且更深入地感受中国、了解中国。因此，我曾组织过几个代表团来到中国。

On two occasions we set up management-training sessions in Xi'an for some of the first groups of Chinese managers who were being exposed to the ideas of private ownership and individual management under Deng Xiaoping's new policies. However in the 1980's and even in the 1990's most had never heard of a company having a Board of Directors and knew little about management's supply and demand charts. Previously, almost all major decisions had been made by the government in state-run industries.

得益于邓小平的新政策，我们曾经在西安举办过两期企业管理培训班，第一次对中国的管理者进行培训，使他们有了民营和个体管理的概念。不过，在80年代，甚至90年代，大多数人还从未听说公司还有个"董事会"，对经济管理中的供求关系图表也知之甚少。以前，国有企业几乎所有的重大决定都是由政府作出。

One question repeatedly asked of the United States businessmen who ran the session in 1984 was "How much money does it cost to buy a machine for fast foods?" The new managers were ready to move forward quickly! Now questions frequently come from businessmen in the United States concerning how to deal with the imbalance of trade and keep China's investment in the U.S. treasury as the Chinese economy flourishes.

1984年，负责培训班的美国商人不断被问到一个同样的问题："一部生产快餐的机器需要多少钱？"这意味着新的管理者们已经做好了快速发展的准备！现在，随着中国经济的蓬勃发展，经常提问的一方轮到了美国人。他们的问题是，怎样才能应对两国贸易的不平衡，怎样使中国继续投资美国债券。

Two members of another delegation to China were Virginia Young, Director of the World Library Federation, and Ambassador Rosemary Ginn, owner of a publishing company. Together they started a program of sending thousands of reference books and textbooks in English to several libraries in Xi'an and to Shaanxi Normal University in the 1990's.

在另一个代表团里，有两个值得提起的美国人，一个是世界图书馆联盟的主席维吉尼亚·杨，另一个是一家出版社的业主罗斯玛丽·金大使。90年代他们共同发起了一个给西安的几家图书馆以及陕西师范大学赠送英文参考书和教科书的计划。

At that time many libraries in China were filled with books in Russian, but after the disintegration of Sino-Soviet relations, beginning in the 1960's, fewer people had continued with the language. Moreover many books in English had been destroyed during the Cultural Revolution years, leaving empty shelves so that new shipments of books were invaluable. These delegations proved beneficial for both sides to learn about each other and to promote further friendship and understanding within their own communities and organizations.

那时，中国的许多图书馆有很多俄文书籍，但自60年代中苏关系破裂后，通晓俄语的人已经越来越少。"文革"期间，很多英文书籍被毁，书架上空空如也。所以，那时新到的英文书很有价值。所以这些代表团对双方来说都是有益的，可以在自己的领域和组织里彼此学习，增进友谊和理解。

Personal Reflections: Looking Back and Looking Forward
个人的反思：回顾与展望

While attending the 50th anniversary celebration in Beijing, my husband Bill Crain stood beneath a giant poster of Deng Xiaoping with video camera in hand as he recorded the National Day events and reflected on his first visit to China in 1976 when Deng Xiaoping was briefly denounced as following the "road to capitalism". Crain later returned to do business in a China transformed by Deng Xiaoping's bold economic reforms.

在北京参加建国50周年庆祝活动的时候，我丈夫威廉·柯雷站在有邓小平形象的巨幅宣传画下，用摄像机记录了国庆的活动，并且还回忆了1976年他第一次访问中国时的情形，那时邓小平还被短暂地打为"走资派"。在后来邓小平的大胆经济政策改变中国时，威廉·柯雷还不断地回到那里继续他的商业之旅。

1999年10月1日，北京、天安门广场，建国50周年的庆祝游行。威廉·柯雷手持摄像机站在有邓小平形象的巨幅宣传画下
50th Anniversary parade, Bill Crain with video camera just beneath the large poster of Deng Xiaoping, Tian'anmen Square, Beijing, Oct 1st, 1999

Yukong moves the mountain
愚公移山

"Yukong moves the mountain" is a well-known Chinese folk tale about how a foolish old man digs, shovel-by-shovelful, to open a path to the other side of a mountain, which obstructed his village. When others laughed that it couldn't be done, Yukong replied he would begin and then his sons would take up the shovel and continue the task and so on to his sons' sons until the task was completed, never giving up.

愚公移山在中国是一个家喻户晓的民间传说，是说一位愚笨的老人想要从挡住他们村民去路的大山中开出一条道路。当别人嘲笑他说这种做法行不通时，愚公回答说，他的工作只是一个开始，他的子子孙孙会继续下去的，直到任务完成，否则绝不放弃。

My husband's and two sons' involvement with China over the last thirty years share Yukong's positive long view and willingness to continue even to overcome obstacles. Their personal experiences parallel the evolutionary development of doing business in China after Mao to now.

从70年代末到现在，我丈夫和两个儿子与中国交往时秉承的观点和意愿同愚公一样，即克服困难、坚持不懈。在这风风雨雨的30年中，他们的这种经验始终伴随着他们事业的发展。

Bill Crain
威廉·柯雷

In 1976 Mao Zedong was still living. There were only a few Americans in China when my husband, Bill Crain attended the Guangzhou Trade Fair that year. Speeches praised Mao Zedong thought and denounced capitalism. He was then President of Child Guidance Toys and met with people in the Light Industry Bureau concerning the possibility of producing toys in China which were popular in America: *Sesame Street* hand-puppets, (characters from a U.S. educational-television program) and wooden Tinker Toys (another well-liked toy made in the U.S. for decades).

我的丈夫威廉·柯雷1976年就参加了广交会，是最早参加广交会的极少数美国人之一。那时毛泽东还在世，舆论推崇毛泽东思想，严厉抨击走资派。威廉·柯雷当时是一家玩具公司（Child Guidance Toys）的总裁，他与轻工业局的人士会面，讨论在中国生产美国畅销玩具"芝麻街"手动木偶（美国教育电视台电视节目中的角色）和木制汀克尔玩具（一种在美国风行了数十年的玩具）的可能性。

The idea of making a product according to U.S. specifications was totally unheard-of in China at that time, but the Bureau offered a similar wooden product with Chinese packaging, which they suggested he could sell in the United States and help Americans learn Chinese. My husband tried to clarify that he would be competing against his own products and that most people in the United States did not read Chinese nor was it the role of a business manager to teach them a new language through packaging.

在那个年代，根据美国的要求生产产品在中国是闻所未闻的事情。但是，那些官员愿意在使用中国包装的前提下生产类似的产品，并建议在美国出售这些产品，从而使美国人了解中国人。我丈夫试图解释说他不能生产同自己竞争的产品，同时多数美国人也不懂中文，而且企业经理的职责不可能是向顾客讲授产品商标上的陌生语言。

The Chinese rejected making the *Sesame Street* puppets by saying many of them, such as "Cookie Monster" or "Oscar the Grouch" were too scary looking and factory workers would not want to work on them. He returned to the Trade Fairs the following two years hoping to develop business but received similar explanations of why it was not possible.

轻工业局的人士表示，他们不会生产"芝麻街"中的角色，因为其中像"甜怪饼"、"奥斯卡"等形象很恐怖，工人们不愿意制造这样的玩具。以后的两年里，他都参加了广交会，希望能做成这样的生意，但收到的答复都是一样的。

By the mid 1980's as President of Lee Apparel Company Crain returned to do business in a China that had dramatically changed. He negotiated contracts with Chinese companies for making products to exact specifications to import to United States. Continuing in the 1990's Crain returned to oversee

1976，广州，广州贸易交易会
Guangzhou Trade Fair, Guangzhou, 1976

production of raincoats and jackets for the London Fog Company with excellent workmanship, according to exact requirements.

80年代中期，威廉·柯雷以Lee服装公司总裁的身份再次来到中国，此时中国的状况已经大为改观。他与中方签订了协议，在中国制造那些能出口美国、而技术要求和美国一样的产品。90年代，威廉·柯雷继续来到中国为伦敦富格公司监督生产那些做工精美的雨衣和便服，而质量要求与国外是完全一样的。

In recent years he has again been lured to China as a consultant for a U.S. company, which has been expanding its products to a growing consumer market within China as trade has developed in a two-way street as the American company now exports products to the Chinese market. Even the educational TV programs of *Sesame Street*, along with the main character "Big Bird" finally entered the Chinese market.

2006，辽宁丹东，威廉·柯雷和儿子柯雷恩合影，后面是毛泽东塑像和柯雷恩居住的现代化公寓楼

Photo of Bill Crain and son Eric Crain(Ke Leien) with statue of Mao Zedong and the modern apartment building where Eric now lives, Dan Dong, Liaoning Province, 2006

近些年来，他又以一家美国公司顾问的身份回到中国，在迅速成长的中国市场上推销他们的产品。这时双方的贸易已经成为双向的了，美国公司也向中国市场出口产品，甚至教育电视台的节目"芝麻街"也随着主角"大鸟"一起终于进入了中国市场。

Eric Crain
柯雷恩

Carrying on the China interests, our youngest son, Eric Crain (Ke Leien) began by studying Chinese at Shaanxi Normal University in 1986 after high school. He continued his Chinese studies at Duke University in the U.S. before returning to Xi'an to establish his own business called Eco Dragon. His factories in Shaanxi and neighboring Gansu Province often employed peasant women who could work in their homes and make extra money, and handicapped workers who were given new training to work in his factories. China's harsh conditions in the interior provided Eric with the opportunity to

20世纪90年代，甘肃。柯雷恩工厂里的工人
Workers in one of Eric Crain's factories, Gansu Province where Eric had factories 1990's

拿着铁锹的柯雷恩在华盛顿中国大使新馆的奠基仪式上，他的新公司参与了大使馆的建设
Eric Crain with shovel at the ground breaking ceremony of the Chinese Embassy in Washington D.C. which his new company helped construct

learn from local peasants. For a while he lived in a one-room apartment near the factory with his small coal-burning stove, which provided minimal heat but abundant smoke during the long cold winters. In the beginning he struggled with quality control and export regulations, but then enjoyed considerable success manufacturing hemp shoes and apparel.

怀着对中国的兴趣，我们的小儿子柯雷恩1986年中学毕业后先后到陕西师范大学和美国杜克大学学习中文，然后又回到中国，在西安创办了自己的公司埃克龙。他设在陕西及其邻省甘肃的工厂经常雇佣当地的农村妇女，她们可以在家里工作，赚些外快。他还雇佣一些残疾人，这些人在他的工厂上岗前都要接受培训。他从当地农民身上受益良多，同时也在中国的内陆省份经历了艰苦的生活。有一段时间他住在工厂附近的一间房里。在漫长寒冷的冬季，他的房间只有一个小煤炉，提供的热量有限，却释放出大量呛人的煤烟。一开始，柯雷恩很不熟悉质量管理和出口条例，但是慢慢地他成功了，生产出了以麻类纤维为原料的鞋子和服装。

Eric Crain has joined a Chinese company that epitomizes privatization and entrepreneurialism in China. The owner grew up as a coal miner. Now his company owns and operates the former state-run paper mill, several construction companies, real-estate firms and the port at the Yalu River bordering North Korea. Eric divides his time living in the Untied States and in Dan Dong, Liao Ning Province. He lives in a beautiful high-rise apartment (not heated by a coal stove) and enjoys the benefits of China's progress.

柯雷恩现在在一家中国私营企业工作。这家公司可以说是中国民营经济和企业家精神的一个缩影。公司老板原来是个挖煤的矿工，现在他的公司拥有一家前国营造纸厂、几家建筑公司和房地产公司，以及中朝边境鸭绿江边上的一个港口。柯雷恩现在将他的时间分为两半：一半在美国，一半在中国辽宁省丹东市。他在丹东住在一幢漂亮的高层公寓里，冬天用不着再用煤炉取暖了，也享受到了中国进步带来的实惠。

Wes Crain
巍斯·柯雷

Our oldest son Wes Crain joined with his brother to help manage Eco Dragon and promote sales from the United States side, as they built the business together with Chinese colleagues and hundreds of workers and peasants in China. Wes had gained personal understanding of China from living and teaching at Shaanxi Normal University in Xi'an in 1989. Wes Crain is now a partner in a health food company in the United States that imports products from China.

1989，西安，巍斯·柯雷在陕西师大教书时与学生在一起
Wes Crain with his students while teaching at Shaanxi Normal University, Xi'an, 1989

我们的大儿子巍斯·柯雷后来也加入了弟弟的事业，参与了埃克龙公司的管理，并负责公司产品在美国的销售。他们的公司有很多中国同事及几百名中国工人和农民。巍斯1989年曾在陕西师范大学教过书，对中国有一些切身的经验。目前他是美国一家健康食品公司的合伙人，这家公司从中国进口产品。

Yukong, the foolish old man of the mountain, never gave up!

愚公，这位憨厚的老山民，绝不放弃！

Navigating a viable course for the future
破浪前行

Yi Fan Feng Shun, "One Sail with Favorable Winds", is a common Chinese expression to wish someone success in their journey. As relations have developed and trade expanded between China, the U.S. and other countries, it has not always been "smooth sailing" or easy negotiations or satisfactory results. Quality control, corruption, late shipments, and infringement of property rights have plagued businessmen and manufacturers for years. Some years have proven to be more treacherous and dangerous than others, as both sides work to make a profit and keep trade and relations in balance. Disparity of trade, the Taiwan situation, and other sensitive issues have frequently escalated tension and conflict between our countries.

"一帆风顺"是中国人常说的一句话，期待一个人旅途顺利。然而，随着中外贸易活动的扩展，经贸领域想要一帆风顺绝非易事。轻松的谈判，令人满意的结果，都不是轻而易举的。质量监控、商业腐败、推迟到货以及侵犯知识产权等很多问题都困扰了生产商和贸易商多年。一些年份贸易关系显得非常紧张而缺乏信任，因为双方都想获得利润同时保持贸易平衡。贸易不平等、台湾局势和其他敏感问题会经常加剧中美两国的紧张关系和摩擦。

1984，桂林，漓江上驾着小船的渔民
A fisherman navigating his boat on the Li River, Guilin, 1984

Precariously balanced
不稳定的平衡

Amidst strong currents, spiraling downturns in the economy, or international uncertainty charting a proper course for future relations requires patience and vision to maintain the necessary balance, which will most certainly affect the lives of millions within China and the world. Now, the focus is on commanding economic power, which directly impacts the greater balance of power in the world. The stakes are high. With the steady flow of trade, international conferences, research, and travel there is an increasing interaction and interdependency that can be mutually beneficial or potentially destructive.

在各种力量形成的权力争斗、经济下滑及不确定的国际形势下，对未来关系发展的合理规划需要耐心和想象力，从而保持一种必要的平衡。这种对未来的预期和规划肯定会影响中国和世界千百万人民的生活。现在的焦点则是掌握经济实力，这种实力能给世界政治的平衡带来直接影响。情况依然诡谲：稳定发展的贸易、世界性的会议、跨国的研究和旅行，各国经济的互动性和相互依赖性与日俱增，但它又是一把双刃剑——既可以给双方带来利益，也是潜在的破坏性因素。

Section Four
第四章

Shaanxi Normal University: A Microcosm of Change in Chinese Education
陕西师范大学：中国教育变化的缩影

2007，西安，陕西师范大学图书馆
Libraries of Shaanxi Normal University, Xi'an, 2007

"All who have meditated on the art of governing mankind have been convinced that the fate of empires depends on the education of its youth."

Aristotle

"所有对管理术有过深思熟虑的人都会承认，国家的命运系于对年轻人的教育。"

——亚里士多德

Introduction
导言

Current educational reforms could revolutionize China's future as dramatically as the economic reforms did in the recent past. During my teaching in China, spanning nearly thirty years, Shaanxi Normal University has provided a window for me to view these changes in one of the places where the seeds of transformation were launched and are being cultivated.

像这些年经济改革的巨变一样，目前的教育改革对中国的将来会有革命性的意义。我在中国教学已将近30年，陕西师范大学为我提供了一个可以观察变化的窗口，在那里我看到了改革的种子怎样发芽和成长。

Shaanxi Normal University (herein referred to as ShiDa) has been a teacher-training university since its founding in 1944. Located in the ancient capital of Xi'an, which is considered the cradle of Chinese civilization, ShiDa is praised as the "cradle of teachers" in Northwest China. It is one of the six key teacher-training (normal) universities directly under the National Ministry of Education.

陕西师范大学（SNNU）自1944年建校以来一直是一所师范类的学校。它坐落在被视为中华文明摇篮的古城西安，而且被誉为中国西北地区的"教师摇篮"，也是教育部直属的六所师范大学之一。

Throughout centuries of Chinese history education has been highly prized, influenced by Confucian ideas. Dating back to ancient times an imperial examination system was established for selection to hold office and then a rigorous examination to enter university studies was instituted, which were based on merit. Educated elite became respected advisors bringing honor to their families and their country. However no segment of Chinese society has reversed its role as drastically in the last thirty years as have intellectuals. Now intellectuals are considered the key to guiding China's economic growth. Students once sent to the countryside to do menial labor are being trained to be innovators of the future and leaders within the global community.

由于孔子思想的影响，在中国漫长的历史中，教育始终享有很高的地位。中国很早的时候就建立了科举取士的制度，莘莘学子从此可以一跃龙门，光宗耀祖，成为国家栋梁。建国后严格的全国大学入学考试遵循的也是这样的路子。不过，在过去30年中，中国社会没有哪个领域像知识分子这样彻底改变了它的社会角色。现在，知识分子被看做是引导中国经济成长的关键。曾经被送往农村从事体力劳动的学生们现在正在被培养成未来的开创者和世界的领导者。

Revering the role of intellectuals
尊重知识和人才

Worker Peasant Soldier
工农兵

These huge Worker Peasant Soldier images represented the three predominant categories in China during the Cultural Revolution years when the former National University Entrance Examination, based on academics, was discarded. The foremost way a person could progress (or enter the limited schools when Mao Zedong began to reopen them) was to be recommended for outstanding ideological fervor and proper political and family background. The dominant focus was following Mao Zedong thought as a good worker, soldier or peasant. One scholar who had been sent to the countryside for several years told me, "I buried banned textbooks and English books in a hole in the dirt floor under my bed but managed to secretly read them at night to keep on learning."

"文革"期间，知识分子被送往农村，学术机构实际上被关闭，工农兵代表了当时中国占主导地位的形象。高考制度被废弃了，人们深造的唯一机会就是对工农兵形象的意识形态性认同，从而被推荐上大学。一位朋友告诉我他下乡时为了汲取知识，怎样将一些禁书和英文书埋在床下的一个小洞里，晚上拿出来偷偷地阅读。

In contrast, it was an exhilarating, historic event when the Entrance Examination was re-introduced in 1977 and millions of young people throughout China were allowed to participate in the exam with the hope of attending a university again after years of working in rural areas with little or no substantive education. This one examination, administered simultaneously throughout the country, became the sole criterion for admission to the university or college level. Students were selected according to their marks, based on academic qualifications. The government then paid tuition for those who received a qualifying score. After graduation, jobs were guaranteed and assigned according to the needs of the country. This marked an important new beginning that would place intellectuals at the forefront of China's economic reforms.

1977年高考的恢复是一个令人欢欣鼓舞的历史事件。在农村耽误了多年之后，数百万年轻人被允许参加高考，从而有机会进大学学习。这次全国各地同时举行的高考成为学生是否能够进入大学的唯一依据。学生选拔是根据他们的分数进行的。政府为这些合格的学生付学费。毕业后，他们根据国家的需要被分配工作。这是一个非常重要的开端，它将知识分子推到了中国经济改革的前沿。

1977，广州，绘有工农兵形象的革命宣传画
Revolutionary posters with Worker Soldier Peasant images, Guangzhou, 1977

Professor PhD Entrepreneur
教授·博士·企业家

2007，西安，吴进副教授，王晓凌博士，企业家苗妮娅
Associate Professor Wu Jin, Dr. Wang Xiaoling, Manager Miao Niya, Xi'an, 2007

These three people were among the first group of students admitted to universities in 1977 with the re-instatement of the examination system. Now, instead of the Worker, Soldier, Peasant categories of the past they currently hold positions of Associate Professor of Chinese Literature, PhD and Vice Dean of the International College of Chinese Studies, and entrepreneur and manager of several companies. They reflect some of the options and opportunities available to those who received their education after 1977. In late 1980's they were all young teachers at Shaanxi Normal University and attended my classes. Today, the competition and pressure to score high marks on this national examination is extremely intense because it is the decisive factor for admission to higher education, which holds the key to their future.

这三个人都是1977年高考恢复后进入大学的第一批学生。"文革"期间的大学生被称为"工农兵学员"，体现了当时一种制度化的意识形态倾向。而现在他们是中国文学副教授、博士和国际汉学院副院长、企业家和几个公司的管理者。对1977年之后上大学的学生来说，现在有了更多的机会和选择。80年代后期，他们都是陕西师范大学的年轻教师，都曾在我的英语班上学习。今天在高考中获得高分的竞争和压力空前激烈，因为那是进入大学的决定性因素，而只有进入大学才算拿到了迈向未来成功的钥匙。

Because of teachers such as these and hundreds of young students through the years, Shaanxi Normal University became the prime location from which I was privileged to sharpen my focus on the dramatic reshaping of education within China. Through the prism of one school and the daily details of student and faculty life I observed closely differences in housing, courses offered, selection of majors, projected goals and shifts in priorities for training teachers. I listened to the students' concerns when their jobs were assigned by the government in the 1980's and then compared their worries and intense pressure now, when they are given the choice and responsibility of securing their own jobs.

这些年来，由于有了如上所说的一些教师和大批的年轻学生，我才将陕西师范大学作为我的主要基地，从那里我可以更清楚地观察到中国教育的巨大变化。通过这个学校及其师生的日常生活，我近距离地看到在住房、课程设置、专业选择、规划目标、师范优先性质的转移等各方面的变化。我也注意到学生对毕业之后工作的关切，并且比较了这些年来在这方面的不同。80年代时，学生的工作是由政府分配的，而现在他们在这方面有了自己的选择，但这也让他们感觉到巨大的责任和压力。

Through the years I compared the assignments turned in for classes by undergraduate students and later those pursuing a master's or doctoral degree; and also noted the words and thoughts expressed by faculty and administrators. By returning to teach in the same place and strengthen relationships with the same people I witnessed both continuity and transformation at one university, as ShiDa became my constant barometer for measuring the effects of nation-wide policies on individual lives for several decades.

执教这些年来，我比较了本科生和后来的硕士及博士生交来的作业，也注意到了教师以及行政人员在思想表达方面的变化。由于不断回到同一个地方教学并加强与同一人群的联系，我成为了一个大学发展演变的目击者。陕西师大一直是我的晴雨表，通过它我可以看到几十年来国家政策如何在个人身上得以体现。

Beneath the surface
透视

"Seeing the flowers from a galloping horse" before dismounting
走马观花：下马之前

"Seeing the flowers from a galloping horse" is a Chinese expression for seeing things from a distance in a fast-paced surface glance. In wide-open grasslands in the far northwestern Xinjiang Uyghur Autonomous Region I watched, then rode with local Kazakh horsemen as the ground and flowers blurred beneath our horses' hoofs. Another time on horseback I searched for the beautiful

1986，新疆，哈萨克族牧民的赛马
Kazakh horsemen racing in the fields while participating in local games, Xinjiang, 1986

flowers called "xue lian", a snow lotus growing in harsh climates just along the frost line in areas such as Xinjiang and Tibet (Xue Lian is my Chinese name). For years I had explored China from a distance: studying Chinese history in the United States and then in China at a surface level.

"走马观花"是中国的成语，意指从远处很快地、表面地看一个事物。我曾在遥远西北的新疆维吾尔自治区的辽阔草原上看赛马，然后和哈萨克族牧民一起骑马驰骋，大地和鲜花在奔腾的马蹄下变得模糊不清。另一次是我骑着马寻找美丽的雪莲。雪莲沿着高寒地区——诸如新疆和西藏——一带的雪线生长，那里气候严酷。雪莲也是我的中国名字。多少年我都是在遥远的美国学习中国历史，接着就是去中国走马观花。

However, at Shaanxi Normal University in 1982 I dismounted from that symbolic horse: I began in earnest to explore beneath the surface and sink my roots deep into teaching and learning in a place that would become my second home as I returned repeatedly for decades.

然而，1982年，在陕西师范大学，我从"马"上下来了，开始认真地探求表面下的真实，扎根在那里，教书和学习。那里是我的第二故乡。在以后的几十年里，我一次次地回到那里。

Shaanxi Normal University became my microcosm for change in education. I observed in vivid detail a remarkable evolution from the end of the Cultural Revolution and beginning of the "reform

1982，古代的石雕马和雪莲
Ancient stone-carved horse statue and Sharon Crain, 1982

and opening up" period to the unfolding of bold new educational policies in 2004, which forecast a shift in educational training for the next generation.

陕西师范大学是中国教育变革的缩影。从"文革"结束和改革开放开始到2004年有开拓意义的新教育政策的展开，我在那里看到了这种变革的生动细节，看到了它的长足发展，它预示着下一代师资教育方面的深刻转变。

Threads of connections and the varied meanings of "connections"
"关系"的含义

In Chinese one very important word for connections is "guanxi" which can refer to the relationship between individuals: such as a significant relationship between friends, parent and child or student with teacher. However it can also mean more than this common usage. It can imply getting in through the back door by having the "guanxi" or personal connections with people who have the power to help you get what you want. Some people's rise to a leadership position was expedited by having "guanxi" in high places. If a parent wanted their child to be admitted to a prestigious key school that was already filled they tried to rely on "guanxi" or connections to overrule. For years in the 1980's and 1990's I saw how people benefited or lost because of their "guanxi" or lack of it. Now, people have more opportunity to succeed because of their own skills, training and experience. However it often still takes "guanxi", plus money (the new power) to make things happen.

中文里有一个重要的词："关系"。它可以指个人间的关系，如朋友、父母与子女、师生的关系，但也可能指比这种普通含义更多的意义。比方说，它也暗示"走后门"，即与一些手中握有权力的人有私人关系，他们能够帮你得到你想要的东西。如果一个人有高层"关系"，他就可能被提拔到领导岗位；如果家长想让子女上已经录满的重点学校，他们也要依赖"关系"。在80和90年代，我看到人们怎样受益于"关系"或由于缺乏关系而失败。现在，人们则有了更多的机会凭着他们的技能、才干和经验去取得成功。不过，人们还是要经常通过"关系"或者金钱（新的权力）去解决问题。

Yet another word for connections is the so-called "thread of connections" that I mentioned in my initial introduction. This word literally means the thread that holds fabric together but also expresses an old belief that we are often connected by a special thread, one to another. And so I began my years of teaching and learning at ShiDa weaving patterns of connections in my quest to understand China. I share some of what I discovered in hopes of presenting a view of what was happening at the time and a glimpse into the future.

不过，表达关系还有另外一个词，即"线"，那是我在本书序言中提到的。就字面而言，"线"意味着"将织物连缀在一起"，但它也反映了一种古老的观念，即有一根特殊的线将我们联系在一起。所以，当我开始在陕西师大教书和学习时，我就在编织一张关系网，从而可以更好地理解中国。这里我将与你们分享我的发现，也希望你们能了解在这段时间发生了什么，并对未来有所预测。

Why I came to ShiDa
我为什么来师大

My first connection to ShiDa originates from my friendship with Helen Snow. As mentioned, Helen and Edgar Snow had lived in China in the 1930's and had been given assistance by the people in Xi'an on their dangerous journeys to interview Mao Zedong and others in the northern part of Shaanxi Province. They were witnesses to the beginning of the communist revolution, which led to the founding of the People's Republic of China in 1949, documented in their classic books *Red Star over China* and *Inside Red China*. Their first-hand information was secretly circulated throughout China, when word of mouth was the main form of communication for the common people, and when very little was known about Mao Zedong and other young leaders. Helen and Edgar Snow continue to be highly respected by the Chinese people for their lifetime efforts to build bridges of understanding between China and America.

我和陕西师范大学的最初联系是由于与海伦·斯诺的友谊。正如我提到的，海伦和埃德加·斯诺在20世纪30年代生活在中国，而且在前往陕北采访毛泽东和其他中共领导人的艰难路途中，得到了西安人民的帮助。他们是共产主义革命初期的见证者，这场革命最终使中华人民共和国得以建立。这些都记录在他们的著作《西行漫记》和《续西行漫记》中。那时口口相传是中国老百姓的主要沟通方式，大家对毛泽东和其他年轻的中共领导人的情况都知之甚少，他们书中的第一手信息在中国秘密地传播。由于他们花费毕生精力搭建中美之间的理解之桥，斯诺夫妇一直受到中国人民的高度尊敬。

Beginning in 1979 Helen Snow and I became good friends in Madison, Connecticut where we both lived at that time. She explained how she escaped one night in 1937 through the window of a Xi'an guesthouse past Kuomingtang soldiers and barricades with the help of brave people in Xi'an to reach Yen'an and Mao Zedong. The Snows never forgot their friendship with people in Xi'an and in Beijing where they lived and became actively involved for over ten years.

我在1979年与海伦·斯诺结为好友，那时我们都住在康涅狄格州的麦迪逊。她给我讲述了1937年的一天晚上，她怎样在勇敢的西安人的帮助下跳出旅馆的窗子，冲破国民党的层层封锁到达延安，并见到了毛泽东。斯诺夫妇从来没有忘记他们和西安人民的友谊——当然也没有忘记与北京人民的友谊，他们在那里生活并积极投入现代中国的历史进程长达十余年。

Helen was eager for me to meet her good friend An Wei from Xi'an who had served as her interpreter when she returned to China for a visit in 1976. She entrusted An Wei with the task of translating many of her books into Chinese; he now serves as the Director of the Helen and Edgar Snow Center in Xi'an. Helen had already made the meaningful connection for me with her old friend Madame Soong Qingling.

海伦急于让我会见她从西安来的好友安危。在她1976年重返中国时，安危是她的翻译。她委托安危将她的许多著作译成中文。安危现在是西安斯诺夫妇研究会的会长。海伦那时已经为我与她的老朋友宋庆龄女士建立了重要的联系。

With encouragement from Helen Snow and because of An Wei's connections with Shaanxi Normal University, I was granted an opportunity to present lectures about Sino-American relations at ShiDa in the spring of 1982 when only a small number of foreign teachers and students were in China. At that time information was tightly controlled, people's lives were carefully restricted, foreigners were often looked upon with suspicion and Chinese people were warned not to reveal anything to people from other countries. However, because of my friendships with Helen Snow and Soong Qingling I was considered "less of a risk" for students or teachers who met with me and slowly they began coming to my room after classes. I started recording their stories in my mind and my journals but never publishing or revealing to others what they personally shared of their struggles, fears and hopes.

由于海伦·斯诺的鼓励和安危先生与陕西师范大学的关系，我有机会于1982年春到陕西师大教授中美关系课。那时中国的外国老师和学生很少，信息被高度控制，人们的生活也受到严格限制。外国人经常遭到怀疑，中国人也被警告不要向外国人透露任何消息。但是，由于和海伦及宋庆龄的友谊，我被认为是"安全"的，可以会见学生和老师。慢慢地，他们也可以在课后来我的房间。我开始在心中和日记中记录这些人的故事，但从未将他们私下告诉我的那些矛盾、恐惧和希望公开发表过或透露给其他人。

Sometimes I would turn on a small tape-recorder with classical music to muffle our words when we spoke of sensitive issues. In the early days almost anything could be considered a sensitive issue or "giving secrets to the foreigners", such as how many students were unable to afford to go to school in a rural area, or how little food was available in certain regions, or what people really thought of leading officials.

在谈论敏感话题的时候，有时我会打开一个小录音机，放上一段古典音乐，盖住我们的声音。在那个时候，任何事都有可能成为"敏感问题"或"向外国人泄密"，比方说有多少农村的孩子上不起学、一些地方的粮食如何短缺，或人们对领导人的真实想法等。

From the beginning I lived on campus unlike some foreign teachers who were separated from their students and kept at a distance from personal contacts. During the 1980's and 1990's foreign students studying at ShiDa were housed in separate buildings and took courses in separate classrooms. Chinese students were expected to avoid mingling with foreigners for fear that the young people would be corrupted by Western influences.

不像别的与学生隔离或缺乏个人接触的外国老师，我从一开始就住在校园里。在80和90年代，陕西师大的外国留学生都住在一个独立的小楼里，在不同的教室里上课。校方希望中国学生不要和外国人接触，因为担心年轻人会被西方的影响毒害。

1982，陕西师范大学，雪莲的第一堂课
The first lecture on campus by Sharon Crain, Shaanxi Normal University, 1982

Curiosity filled the room: first lecture
第一堂课：充满好奇的教室

Nearly a thousand students attended my first big lecture in 1982. They filled every seat in the room, sat in the aisles, stood in the back and peered through windows from outside with curiosity and eagerness to learn. For most of them it was their first time ever to meet a foreigner or to hear a native speaker of English. Prior to computers and power point presentations I used large photographs of snow-covered trees to symbolize the cold relations between China and the United States during the previous years without diplomatic relations, while blossoming trees symbolized new developments in Sino-American relations after 1979.

1982年，我在陕西师大的第一堂大课大约有上千名学生。教室里座无虚席。带着好奇和了解的渴望，人们甚至坐在走道里，站在教室后面，还有人从窗户外面往里看。对绝大多数学生来说，这是他们第一次见到外国人，或者第一次听到以英文为母语的人讲话。那个时候没有电脑，不能用PPT展示，我就用了一张枝头带雪的树的大图片，说明在没有外交关系的年代里中美两国间的冷淡局面；而另一张图片中枝叶茂盛的树则象征着1979年后两国关系的新发展。

As was then customary, a monitor in a Mao jacket sat in the front row of my lecture series and in my regular classes. He was the monitor for the class and as I later learned also monitored what I was saying. I was never told what to say or what not to say but I did have some difficult questions from students, which required careful thought to answer. Students rarely spoke openly in front of others but with encouragement during classes they slowly began submitting written questions without their names.

在我举行系列讲座或者上课的时候，一个穿着毛式服装的班长总是坐在前排。他是这个班的管理人，后来我才知道，他也负责监督我都说了些什么。从没有人告诉过我应该说什么或不应该说什么，但我也碰到过一些困难的问题，需要仔细考虑才能回答。学生们很少在大庭广众之下公开发表意见，但在我的鼓励之下，他们慢慢开始给我递纸条，但没有署名。

"Why did the U.S. sell F16 fighter planes to Taiwan?"

"为什么美国把F16战机卖给台湾？"

"Do the young people in your country have lofty ideals and what are they?"

"你们国家的年轻人有崇高的理想吗？如果有的话，是什么样的理想？"

"The U.S. is very young compared to the long history of China but your country is very successful economically and we are so backward. What are the reasons?"

"和中国比起来，美国非常年轻，但你们在经济上很成功，而我们却很落后，为什么？"

Planting seeds of friendship
播撒友谊的种子

My students and teacher friends gathered around the tree we planted during my first year of teaching, symbolizing the cultivation of Sino-American relations. Helen and Edgar Snow along with many others had planted seeds of friendship long ago; now was our chance to build on that foundation. For the most part they all dressed alike and spoke alike in class but in private they began to open up and share their own opinions and describe what was happening in their individual lives.

在我教学的第一年，我的学生和一些教师朋友聚集在我们栽的树旁，这棵树象征着中美关系。海伦和埃德加·斯诺很久以前就和很多人一起播下了友谊的种子，现在轮到我们在他们的基础上添砖加瓦了。那时大多数人穿着同样的服装，说着同样的话，但私下里他们已经开始开放了，开始表达他们的看法，并将他们的故事讲给我听。

1982，陕西师大老校区，雪莲和学生及教职工在她为中美关系栽种的第一棵树旁边
Crain with students and faculty gathered around the first tree she planted for U.S.–China relations at ShiDa's old campus, 1982

Observations while Teaching and Learning during Five Presidents at ShiDa
教书学习之余的观察：历经陕西师范大学的五位校长

Badges and the beginning
校徽和开端

1982，陕西师大，（从右至左）陈立人校长、胥超、雪莲、李绵校长、杨春元、李吟西
(R to L) President Chen Liren, Xu Chao, Sharon Crain, President Li Mian, Yang Chunyuan, Li Yinxi, ShiDa, 1982

I have had the privilege of teaching at Shaanxi Normal University during the leadership of five presidents while I closely observed the educational shifts from year to year. Li Mian was president of the university during my first year teaching and greeted me when I arrived on campus in 1982, along with Xu Chao the Director of the President's Office. Later I learned how Li Mian had been humiliated during the anti-intellectual and anti-Western extremes of the Cultural Revolution but was deeply admired by professors for his courage and dignity during those difficult years. He had given them hope through his actions. I was impressed that he was willing to warmly welcome me as a foreigner to give lectures to his students during the very beginning of the re-opening with the West.

我在陕西师大教学时有幸历经了五位校长，同时我也近距离地观察了教育改革的实际进程。我在陕西师大的教学从1982年开始，那时的校长是李绵。我到达陕西师大时是他亲自迎接的我，还有校办主任胥超。后来我知道在"文革"那种反知识分子和反西方的极端情况下，李绵曾受过怎样的凌辱，但他在那些困难日子里表现出来的勇气和尊严让学校的教授们钦佩，并给了他们希望。在与西方交往的最初时期，他对我这样一个外籍教师的热烈欢迎让我印象深刻。

In the 1980's when I first arrived at ShiDa almost all teachers and students still wore the so-called "Mao jackets" and had a small red or white metal badge as identification. Everyone at the time belonged to a "danwei" or unit, such as a school or factory. The place where a person worked was directly responsible for his or her actions and controlled almost all decisions in that person's life. The badge had a number, which identified the person along with his particular danwei; everyone had one and usually wore it at all times. University leaders had difficulty understanding that I was on my own as an individual without a "danwei". This represented an extremely basic difference between our countries at that time.

80年代我第一次到陕西师大时，几乎所有的教师和学生都穿着毛式服装，带着红的或白的校徽。当时每个人都属于某个"单位"，比方说学校或工厂，而这个单位直接对它职工的行为负责并为他们生活中的几乎一切作决定。校徽上有号码，它可以显示出此人属于哪个单位。每个人都有校徽，而且总是戴着它。学校领导很难理解我是一个没有"单位"的个人。这可以说是那时我们两国间的一个根本差别。

During the leadership of President Li Mian and then the next President Chen Liren, ShiDa (and all teacher-training universities) were solely entrusted with the responsibility for training students to become teachers or educational administrators. A certain number of students throughout China were required to attend one of these universities to become teachers. After graduation students were assigned by the government to teaching positions, according to wherever they were needed in the country.

在李绵校长和继任的陈立人校长的任期内，陕西师大（以及所有师范院校）的唯一责任就是将学生培养为教师或教育管理人员。全国有一定比例的考生进入这类学校，最后成为教师，毕业后由政府根据国家需要分配到相应的教学岗位上去。

While Chen Liren was president my son Eric Crain (after graduating from high school in 1986) became a student at ShiDa to learn the Chinese language and culture.

His experiences as a student provided further insights into everyday life on a university campus and the uniqueness of being a foreign student at that time. According to government requirements Eric lived in a dorm separate from Chinese students. In an effort to learn more directly from the people he often attended classes to acquire basic language skills and then would take off by train, public bus or even horse-drawn carts into remote areas to practice his Chinese and learn from local people in areas that were often officially closed to foreigners.

我的儿子柯雷恩(1986年高中毕业)是在陈立人校长任期内到陕西师大学习中国语言文化的。他的学生经验使他深入了解了大学校园的日常生活，也了解了那时一个外国学生的特殊性。根据学校的要求，柯雷恩住在一个与中国学生隔离的宿舍里。为了直接从实际生活中学习汉语，在学习了一段汉语的基本语言技巧后，他就离开了校园，乘火车、坐汽车，甚至马车，到那些偏远地区练习中文，也向当地人学习，而那常常是官方向外国人封锁的。

In one small village over a hundred people gathered around to talk with him in the courtyard and listen to a tall Westerner with reddish blond hair speak halting Chinese. One lady told him, "We have never had a foreigner in our village."

在一个小村子里，有一百多人围在院子里跟他聊天，听这个高个的、有着金黄色头发的西方人在讲一口结结巴巴的中文。一位女士告诉他："我们村从来没来过外国人。"

Honored by my second home
来自第二故乡的荣誉

During the leadership of President Wang Guojun (the third president during my teaching) international relations were expanded. As a noted mathematician he was selected to become President of the University for his academic achievements at ShiDa and abroad. He attended the 1999 ceremony when I was granted the honor of becoming the university's first honorary visiting professor. The idea of having foreigners more directly involved was still a new concept in China. Now there are several professors from other countries who have joined as visiting professors, and students and educators from around the world come to study and teach. I was very proud to call Shaanxi Normal University "my university" officially. After many years of returning to teach and learn it has become my second home.

在王国俊校长（我在陕西师大任教时的第三任校长）任期内，陕西师大的国际关系扩展了。他是一个卓有成就的数学家，而且由于他的学术成就和广泛的学术影响被选为校长。1999年，当我成为他们学校第一位客座教授时，他参加了仪式。让外国人直接介入学校教学当时在中国还是一个新概念，现在有来自不同国家的一些外籍教授在师大做访问教授，还有来自世界各地的教师和学生在师大教学和学习。我很骄傲地把陕西师大称为"我的大学"。多年在那里教学和学习后，陕西师大已经成了我的"第二故乡"。

1999，陕西师大，雪莲成为陕西师大客座教授时，前任校长王国俊参加了仪式
President Wang Guojun attending the ceremony when Sharon Crain became an honorary professor at ShiDa, 1999

2002，陕西师大，赵世超校长和张建祥副校长给雪莲介绍新校区的规划
President Zhao Shichao and Vice President Zhang Jianxiang show Sharon Crain the plans for the new campus, ShiDa, 2002

Plans to expand
扩建的计划

Throughout the country, particularly in the 1990's, national directives had encouraged rapid expansion of university enrollment. (The number of students in higher education increased over tenfold from 400,000 in 1978 to 4.5 million by 2004; and the number of postgraduates increased over thirty times in the same period.) Exciting new plans for ShiDa's new campus to accommodate these increased undergraduate and graduate students were presented to me in drawings and discussions with my fourth President, Zhao Shichao, and Vice President Zhang Jianxiang who also serves as Director of International Affairs. They shared images for this second campus, which would be built in 2004 in the countryside.

90年代，国家鼓励全国高校扩大招生规模（1978年到2004年，高校的学生数从40万增加到450万；研究生的数量在这一时期增长了30多倍）。陕西师大有了一个令人激动的新校区建设计划，它能够容纳数目急剧增加的本科生和研究生。我在师大教学期间的第四任校长赵世超和负责对外事务的张建祥副校长向我介绍了这个计划和有关部门的设想。这个新校区计划于2004年建成，地点选在郊区的农村。

Academic partnerships offer new opportunities
学术合作关系提供新的机会

Academic partnerships, including collaborative research, along with student and faculty exchanges have been greatly strengthened during the leadership and global vision of President Fang Yu, the fifth president during my teaching. One such example of substantive exchange involved a delegation of educators headed by Sara McCalpin, President of China Institute in America, which has developed several programs for sending students and educators to ShiDa, in coordination with the International Programs Office. China Institute is the oldest organization in the United States focused solely on teaching about Chinese culture and history. In 2009 an intensive five-week course was held at ShiDa entitled, *Xi'an: From Ancient Capital to Modern Metropolis* organized by China Institute, with the support of the National Endowment of Humanities in the United States and China Institute.

房喻校长是我在陕西师大任教期间的第五任校长，具有国际视野。在他的领导下，陕西师大的国际交流合作扩大了，这包括合作研究和学生及老师的互相交换等。由美国华美协进社社长江芷若率领的美国教育代表团的到访就是这方面的一个实例。华美协进社与陕西师大外事处合作成

2007，陕西师大，房喻校长（左起第五人），华美协进社社长江芷若（左起第三人），雪莲
President Fang Yu(fifth L), Sara McCalpin President of China Institute(third L), and Sharon Crain, ShiDa, 2007

功地举办了几个项目,由华美协进社派出学生和教育工作者到陕西师大。在美国,华美协进社是专门教授中国文化和历史的时间最长的机构。2009年,由华美协进社举办的一个被称为"从古都长安到现代西安"的五星期课程在师大开设,这门课程得到了美国人文科学资助项目和华美协进社的支持。

Currently hundreds of students from many countries come to learn Chinese language and culture at ShiDa's International College of Chinese Studies as partnerships continue to be developed with other universities throughout the world. ShiDa currently has more than 60 sister school relations with U.S.A., Britain, France, Germany, Japan, Australia, Canada, Korea, Vietnam, Hong Kong and other countries and regions. ShiDa has trained more than 3,000 foreign students.

目前,有数百名不同国家的留学生到陕西师大汉学院学习汉语和中国文化。陕西师大与世界各地很多大学的校际关系也在发展,目前已与美国、英国、法国、德国、日本、澳大利亚、加拿大、韩国、越南、香港等国家和地区的60多所学校建立了校际友好与合作交流关系,培养留学生3000余人。

Teacher training and academic excellence are key priorities as the university moves forward. As one of six key teacher-training universities directly under the national Ministry of Education, ShiDa is considered the number one normal university for the vast northwestern region of China. Setting an example, President Fang Yu is highly respected for his academic research and teaching in the field of chemistry.

师资培训和出色的学术研究是陕西师范大学继续发展的关键优势。作为教育部直属的6所师范大学之一,陕西师范大学被认为是中国西北地区最好的师范大学。房喻校长本人因为其在化学领域的研究和教学受到了高度尊重。

As China's economy flourished in the 1990's and demand for highly trained professionals increased ShiDa (like other normal universities) expanded to become a comprehensive university and now offers a broad variety of courses and majors in addition to retaining its primary responsibility for teacher training. While the majority of students still enter the teaching profession after graduation, a rising number are selecting from among diverse majors and graduate work such as gene-therapy research, environmental science, international business or psychology preparing them for careers that did not even exist a few years ago. Reflective of a national emphasis on graduate training of professors, over 68 percent of the faculty holds either their master's or PhD degree.

由于90年代中国经济的飞速发展和对高水平人才的需求,像其他师范大学一样,陕西师范大学已经成为一所综合性大学。除了培养师资的主要任务外,学校还开设了广泛的专业和课程。虽然大多数学生毕业后仍然从事教学工作,其他专业的学生和研究生的数量也在上升,比如基因工程、环境科学、国际贸易、心理学等一些不久前学校还没有的学科,从而为学生未来的就业做好准备。鉴于国家强调教授们的研究生学历，陕西师范大学已经有超过68%的教师拥有硕士或博士学位。

ShiDa's impressive libraries rank as the largest collection in the northwestern region, one of the largest in China. Prestigious elementary and secondary schools are directly affiliated with the university, such as the Fu Xiao Elementary School which subsequently became a place where I watched creative experimentation in early education and learned about concrete results of international exchanges among young students.

陕西师大图书馆令人印象深刻，它是西北地区最大的图书馆，也是全国最大的图书馆之一。大学还附设颇有声望的中学和小学。陕西师范大学附小在早期教育方面有创造性的实验，而且开展了学生间的国际交流活动。

Threads of connection
扯不断的线

In every way I was drawn back to ShiDa: by the openness of students, who were willing to teach me while I was teaching them; by the eagerness of new friends who wanted to learn more about life in the United States and Sino-American relations; by the honesty of young and old professors who were willing to engage in meaningful discussions about policies that radically affected their lives and their families, and by those who wanted to work together to build positive connections for the future.

我回到陕西师大的原因太多了：学生们的坦率——在我教他们的同时他们也愿意教我；新朋友们求知的强烈——他们想更多地了解美国人的生活和中美关系；还有年轻和年长教授们的真诚——他们愿意跟我讨论那些极大影响他们生活和家庭的政策，也想共同努力建立未来的积极联系。

Slowly I also became familiar with people outside the campus in the market places where I shopped and in open-air restaurants along the streets across from the university where I often ate. I became friends with shopkeepers around the ancient Drum Tower in the center of Xi'an where I rode my bike to buy old embroideries, woven with threads from the past. Each person had a story that became a chapter in my mind as I gained information beyond textbooks. Personal stories and friendships with those on campus and beyond lured me back to uncover more. A web of connections led me from one person to another.

慢慢地，我与校园外面的人们也熟悉了，因为我时常要去市场上购物，以及到沿街的露天摊档去吃饭。我和市中心鼓楼下的小店老板成了朋友，我常骑车去那里买一些旧的刺绣，它们是用古老的丝"线"绣成的。每个人的故事都留在我的心中，成为我书中的一节，而这些故事是在教科书上看不到的。与校园内外人们的友谊以及他们的故事吸引我回来并发现更多。这样的关系网络使我从一个人走向另一个。

Beloved professor and mentor
亲爱的教授和挚友

One of the main reasons I was drawn back to ShiDa was Professor Jiang Binghua. He was Dean of the Foreign Language Department and loved by his students for his compassion and humor, his command of English and his interesting classes on British and American poetry. My teaching began with classes for students in his department but then for nearly thirty years he continued as my mentor and friend. Frequently, he would come to the Foreign Expert Building where I lived (which had heat) and we would share long discussions as he taught me about China's history through stories of his own experiences: growing up in the countryside, later working in the capital at the powerful Radio Beijing (which controlled almost all communications at the time) and holding on during the many ups and downs of political campaigns, often utilizing poetry as a source of strength.

我回到陕西师大的主要原因之一是江冰华教授。江教授是外语系主任，他的幽默、对学生的关照、对英文的掌握和他关于英美诗歌引人入胜的课程都为他赢得了学生的热爱。我在师大的教学是从他的系上开始的，以后的30年他成了我的良师益友。由于我的房间有暖气，他经常来到我住的外国专家楼，有时一谈就是几个小时。从他自己的故事中，我了解到一段不同的中国历史。他是在农村长大的，后来到中央人民广播电台工作，那是当时一个权力很大的部门，它几乎控制了所有的消息。他在各种政治运动中经历了多次的沉浮，但经常从诗歌中汲取力量。

Once in the 1970's he was asked to serve as the translator for Mao Zedong in a meeting with the President of Tanzania. At the time, it was widely circulated that Mao was learning English. After the hour-long meeting finished, Mao Zedong asked Jiang Binghua, "What language was the President of Tanzania speaking?" When Jiang replied, " English," Mao then asked, "What language did you speak to him?" Again Jiang replied, "English." Professor Jiang smiled as he told me that Mao had not understood a word of English, only his Chinese translation.

江教授告诉我，70年代时，有一次毛泽东会见坦桑尼亚总统，他被请去做翻译。那时毛泽东学英文的事情广为人知。在一个小时的会见结束后，毛泽东问江冰华："坦桑尼亚总统说的哪种语言？"江回答说："英语。"毛又问："你跟他说的哪种语言？"他接着回答："英语。"江说着笑了。他告诉我，毛泽东除了他的中文翻译外，一句英文也不懂。

1982，陕西师大，江冰华教授在外国专家楼
Professor Jiang Binghua at the foreign expert building, ShiDa, 1982

1983，纽约，江冰华教授在曼哈顿维利学院作访问学者
Professor Jiang as a visiting Professor at Manhattanville College in New York, 1983

2007，陕西师大，江冰华的儿子、孙女和重外孙出席图片展
Jiang Binghua's son, granddaughter and great grandson attending the photo exhibition, ShiDa, 2007

Jiang Binghua was one of the first professors to go abroad soon after the reestablishment of Sino-American relations; he was invited to become a visiting Professor of Chinese Language and Culture at Manhattanville College in the United States in 1983 and 1984. He taught very cautiously. He was respected by his American students and was an excellent representative of Shaanxi Normal University in those early years of exchange.

江冰华是中美建交后第一批出国的中国教授之一。1983和1984年，他作为中国语言文化教授应邀前往美国的曼哈顿维利学院。他教学严谨，深受美国学生的尊敬。在早期的中美文化交流中，他是来自陕西师范大学的杰出代表。

Professor Jiang Binghua's son, granddaughter and great grandson attended my photo exhibition about changes in China in 2007 (with images of Professor Jiang in the background). Through the years I observed the changes in the lives of four generations of the Jiang family. Compared to his father, the son's apartment is greatly expanded with heat, refrigerator, television and many modern appliances. He enjoys abundant food without standing in lines with coupon books for a rationed allotment as his father did in the 1970's and 1980's. However, he and his wife had to retire early to open new jobs for younger people. Because of China's large population sometimes regulations mandate that people retire when they are in their fifties or even their forties, often at the peak of their skills and experience.

2007年，江冰华教授的儿子、孙女和重外孙出席了我在陕西师大举办的图片展，并在他的照片前合影。在与他家的多年交往中，我见证了江家四代生活中发生的巨大变化。比起江冰华，他的儿子拥有更宽敞的房子，以及暖气、冰箱、电视和更多的家用电器。家里食品充足，无需像他父亲当年那样拿着票证去排队购买配给的食品。但是，他和妻子却不得不提早退休，给年轻人腾出位置。由于中国的庞大人口，企业会要求人们在50多岁，甚至40多岁时就退休，虽然那常常是他们最年富力强的时候。

Jiang Binghua's granddaughter Jiang Nan graduated from the university and became a teacher in Xi'an before pursuing her master's degree in Australia, taking advantage of other policies in a positive way. In the traditional fashion her parents took care of her son while she worked and studied. She has grown up during a time of peace, without the political struggles of the Anti-Rightist Campaign, The Great Leap Forward and the Cultural Revolution experienced by her grandfather, which resulted in turmoil, confusion and personal suffering.

江冰华的孙女江楠从大学毕业之后，在西安当了一段教师，接着利用国家的优惠政策，去澳大利亚攻读硕士。像传统的中国家庭一样，她的儿子由她父母带着。她成长在和平时期，不像她的爷爷，经历了反右、大跃进和"文革"等政治运动，以及由这些运动带来的混乱、迷惑和痛苦。

As I began a pattern of returning to teach, to learn and to participate in educational exchanges I witnessed the breathtakingly rapid succession of changes. Sometimes I was struck by the jarring contrast from just a few months before, not only from year to year or decade to decade. First there were the obvious physical alterations on campus.

回到中国成为我的一种模式，我去那里教书、学习、参加国际教育交流项目，与此同时，我也看到了一系列令人惊讶的巨大变化。有时我会为看到的快速变化而震惊，因为用以衡量变化的时间单位不是十年，也不是年，而是几个月。首先是校园中那些明显的外在变化。

Physical Changes Reflect the Reshaping of University Life
天翻地覆的大学生活：硬件变化

Faculty housing...then
早期的教职工住房

This narrow congested hallway on the second floor of one of the cold concrete buildings for faculty housing was always filled with charcoal, woks, teapots and cooking utensils. Cardboard boxes stored bottles of soy sauce, salt and black vinegar along with a few metal plates and cups. In Chinese these halls were called the "long dark tunnel", and served as kitchens outside their one-room apartments where food was cooked over fires with total disregard for any safety precautions. Downstairs on the first floor were the bathrooms, often overflowing with water; showers could be taken only at certain hours in another building when there was hot water.

这是教师"单身"宿舍楼的第二层，狭窄拥挤的楼道里挤满了做饭用的盆盆罐罐，纸箱子里装满了酱油醋瓶子以及盘子和杯子。在中文里这种楼被叫做"筒子楼"，楼道成为宿舍外面的厨房，没有人顾及做饭的火炉可能的隐患。楼下是卫生间，经常到处是水；洗澡只能去学校的公共浴室，而那里的热水定时供给。

After class I often went with teacher friends to make jiaozi (dumplings) together in the crowded space where heat and smoke funneled down the hallway. We then gathered with husband, wife and child in their one designated room; with a bed against each wall and a small desk at one end piled high with books. Placing a wooden board across the two single beds

1989，陕西师范大学，教师单身宿舍外的楼道厨房
Hallway kitchen outside university teacher's one room apartment, Shaanxi Normal University, 1989

became our table, leaving barely enough room to sit but plenty of time to laugh and listen to stories of how their parents and grandparents had also struggled with harsh living conditions in the past when food was scarce and regulations were oppressive. In contrast to their parents and certainly to their grandparents they felt their life was much better.

课后我经常和一个教师朋友一起去他们的"筒子楼"包饺子，那时热气和烟就使楼道成了大烟囱。屋子里两张床分别挨着墙根放着，一张小小的写字台放在房子的最里面，上面摆满了书。我就跟他们一家三口聚在这小屋里。一块板担在两床之间当餐桌，剩下的地方刚刚够大家坐下来，但我们说说笑笑很开心。我也听到了他们的父母和祖父母的故事。那时食品短缺，各种规定又都是强迫性的，日子过得很艰苦。比较起他们的老人，他们觉得自己的日子还是好得多了。

And now: hallway kitchen to private home
现在：从"筒子楼"到私人住宅

One snowy day just five years later I went with the same teacher friend with whom I had cooked in the dark hallway kitchen shown above to her two-story home near a golf course outside of Xi'an. As we drove in her own car I flashed back in my mind to when all she had was a black bicycle with vegetables tied on the back. Now in her new spacious living room we watched programs on her big screen television and listened to modern music on her stereo: bedrooms and bathrooms were upstairs and down. But we shared the joy of making and eating dumplings just as we had done in the 1980's and 1990's when teachers lived in the old faculty building and cooked in the narrow halls. Taking advantage of the government shift toward privatization she

2004，西安郊区，苗妮娅与丈夫和朋友在他们的屋前
Miao Niya with her husband and friends at her home, suburb of Xi'an, 2004

had become the owner of a large printing company and then manager and owner of two hotels. Not everyone has taken such a giant step in a short time but she represents some of the new options reshaping China's landscape.

一个下雪天，只不过是和我的教师朋友在她的"筒子楼"里做饭后的五年，还是同一个人，她就带我去看了她在西安郊外一个高尔夫球场附近的新家——一栋两层小楼。当我们坐进她的私人汽车时，我想起她骑着自行车，后面带着蔬菜的样子。在她宽敞的新客厅里，我们看大屏幕的电视，听音响里面的现代音乐，而且他们新居的楼上楼下都有卧室和卫生间——一种完全不同的生活。但我们依旧包饺子、吃饺子，分享着快乐，就像我们80和90年代在"筒子楼"里那样。她赶上了政府鼓励私人创业的政策，成为一家大印刷公司的老板，而且还拥有两家旅馆。当然不是所有人都能在如此短的时间里有这样大的变化，但她代表了某种新的机遇，这种机遇重新塑造了中国。

New faculty housing towers over the old
旧楼旁的新塔楼

Some of teachers who taught with Miao Niya now live in new multi-roomed apartments on campus rising above the old concrete faculty buildings. For many of them it was the first time to live in their own apartment with a refrigerator, a bathroom and shower, hot water and heat all right there for their convenience. Yet others remain in small crowded spaces and cook in tiny outside balconies overlooking the modern high rise apartments next to them. China's large population and rapidly rising demands for modern conveniences has created an urgent need for new energy sources. No longer totally subsidized by the government or by one's work unit as in the past many teachers face a rising fear of how to pay for the new cost of living: in the 1990's the financial burden was shifted from the government to individuals who were required to buy their own apartment. Initially it was almost impossible to get loans from the bank and teachers' salaries are low so many people had to borrow from relatives and extended-family members, creating hardships for many while depleting valuable savings for the future.

现在，很多曾和苗妮娅一起教学的教师已经住进了新建成的塔楼。新楼比旧的教职工宿舍楼高，每个单元的房间也多多了。他们中的许多人都是生平第一次住在有冰箱、洗澡间、热水和暖气的公寓里。不过，还有人依旧住在拥挤的小房子里，在外面狭小的阳台上做饭，而紧挨他们的就是现代化的高层住宅楼。由于中国的庞大人口和对现代便利生活急速增长的需求，对能源供给的压力越来越大，国家和单位已不像过去那样全额买单了。人们开始担心怎样才能承担这种新的居住成本。从90年代起，购房的财政负担就从政府肩上转移到了个人身上。一开始，由于从银行贷款几乎不可能，而教师的工资又太低，很多人只好向亲戚朋友借钱，结果他们的积蓄都被花光，很多人因此产生了新的困难。

2004，陕西师大．旧楼旁新起的教工宿舍楼
New faculty apartments rise over the old, ShiDa, 2004

Student housing and student life
学生住房和学生生活

The dorms...then
那时的宿舍

While a teacher shared one room with family members, students were often allotted one room for seven or eight people in the old dorm buildings. The crammed space had just enough area for eight beds (four double-decked beds). Almost all students at ShiDa and other universities in the 1980's and 1990's were crammed into similar spaces. Clothes, books and personal belongings were stuffed under the beds or hanging over the side, with sometimes one empty bed supporting suitcases filled with the possessions of all seven students. The other beds piled high with heavy quilts filled the room, with no heat during the long cold winters, no desks to study, no closets, no running water and only one dim light bulb hanging from the ceiling by a cord. On sunny days colorful quilts were aired on branches of trees outside the dorms. Students wore paddled winter jackets in their rooms and in campus buildings during the long winter months. When my son was a student at ShiDa and living in his separate dorm for foreigners one item on his wish list was a pair of gloves to warm his hands in class but with flexibility to take notes. What he feared most however were the loose electrical wires near the water on the floors of the communal showers.

1989. 陕西师大，校园里的学生宿舍
Student dorm rooms on campus, ShiDa, 1989

1989，陕西师大，校园里的学生宿舍
Student dorm rooms on campus, ShiDa, 1989

　　在80年代和90年代，教师与家人同挤一间屋，而学生的住宿条件则更差，大概7至8个人才能在老旧的宿舍楼里分得一间房，勉强塞进去4个架子床。其他学校的学生住得差不多都是这个样子。他们的衣服、书籍和个人用品都塞在床下或者放在一边。有时有一张空床，7个学生便把装着他们"家当"的箱子都放在上面。床上的被褥很厚，因为那里冬天很长，而且没有暖气。房间里也没有书桌，没有储藏室，室内没有自来水，只有天花板上吊着的昏暗灯泡。一到大晴天，宿舍外的树枝上就晒满了五颜六色的被子。在漫长的冬季，学生们在宿舍和教室里都穿着厚厚的冬衣。我儿子在陕西师大学习的时候，在留学生宿舍住了一学期，他最想要的就是一副既保暖又不影响记笔记的手套，而最害怕的就是公共浴室地板上松弛的电线，而地板上又都是水。

New student dorms...now
现在的学生宿舍

Student life is different now in most universities. Dorm rooms are heated, well lit and certainly more spacious with only four students. Each person has a desk, bookshelves, a closet, a bed and usually a cell phone. Many have their own computers. This student is from the countryside and was the first in her family to attend a university. Jobs are no longer assigned so she will have many opportunities to choose from but worries about getting a good job because of keen competition from a huge population and rapidly increasing numbers of university graduates in recent years. Since tuition is now the responsibility of individuals rather than the government heavy burdens have been placed on their families. With progress have come new challenges.

2007，西安，李瑞在她邮电学院的宿舍里
Li Rui in her dorm room at the Post and Telecommunication University, Xi'an, 2007

在大多数大学里，现在的学生生活已经完全不同了。学生宿舍大了很多，而且通常只有4个人，还有了暖气，光线也好多了。每人都有自己的书桌、书架、储柜、床，以及手机。许多学生还有自己的电脑。这个学生来自农村，是她家第一个大学生。国家不包分配了，她有了更多选择的机会，但她也担心找不到一份好工作，因为这些年来毕业生那么多，竞争又是如此激烈。学费也要自己交，这加重了家里的负担。生活在进步，但也有新的挑战。

Eating on campus...then
吃在校园：过去

Imagine taking your own enamel bowl or metal box and your one pair of chopsticks and racing across campus the instant the bell rang at 12 noon or 5 pm as thousands of students converge on one small building and push each other to receive a scoop of rice, a few vegetables and two large steamed buns.

想象一下中午12点或者下午5点，下课铃一响，你就拿着搪瓷碗或者铝饭盒，还有筷子，疾步走过校园，和数千学生一起涌进不大的食堂，拥挤着去拿到自己那一份菜、一份米饭或者两个馒头。

While teaching at ShiDa in the 1980's and 1990's this was the common scene every day as

1986，陕西师大，学生一边穿过校园，一边吃午饭
Students eating lunch while crossing the campus, ShiDa, 1986

students rushed out of class and raced across campus to get their allotment and then slowly walked back across campus eating their limited food without a place to sit and enjoy it. The building had inadequate seating and there were no tables or chairs in their dorms. It behooved me to end my noontime classes on time so they were not delayed for the rush. Sometimes students shared the campus with horse-drawn carts bringing in vegetables and supplies for the day.

80和90年代我在陕西师大教学的时候，这是司空见惯的场面。学生们冲出教室，穿过校园，涌进食堂，买到饭后再慢慢地一边吃饭，一边再次穿过校园。饭是定量的，食堂里也没有地方坐，更谈不上享受了。中午时分，我不得不按时下课，这样学生们就不致太匆忙。有时校园里还可以见到运送供给的马车。

1982，陕西师大，校园里运送蔬菜的马车
Horse carts bringing vegetables from the countryside to the campus, ShiDa, 1982

...and now
现在

Multi-storied multi-roomed cafeterias now offer a variety of foods for students and teachers to make their own selections during many hours of the day and evening. Students enjoy increased choices but struggle with rising costs of food.

现在，为师生服务的多层和多空间的食堂可以提供更多的时段供应品种丰富的菜肴。学生们就餐的选择多了，但也要为上涨的饭菜价格而犯愁。

2004，陕西师大，校园里的一座食堂
One of many cafeterias on campus, ShiDa, 2004

2007，陕西师大，丰富的饭菜供学生挑选
A wide variety of food is available for students to select, ShiDa, 2007

Pressure...then and now
压力：过去和今天

New dormitories, modern classrooms, beautiful sculptures and flowers all adorn the campus and unquestionably have reshaped the living standards of the students. However, one element remains constant: pressure. First there is the pressure beginning in primary school to study and be prepared for the one national examination (zhong kao) to be selected for high school and then the one examination (gao kao) to enter a university and then pressure to secure a job after graduation. It consumes their daily thoughts and behavior.

新的宿舍，现代化的教室，美丽的雕塑和鲜花，所有这些都装饰着校园，同时毫无疑问也提高了学生的生活水平。不过，有一个因素依然存在，即压力。学生们在小学时就有压力，上了中学又要努力学习准备"中考"，上一个好的高中；接着还要准备"高考"，进入大学学习；大学毕业后还要努力找工作。这些压力都在耗尽着他们的精力，甚至影响到他们的行为。

Back in the 1980's my students told me that quite frequently they did not want to study the major that had been selected for them by the government. Just weeks before classes began they received a notice informing them what school they would attend and what major they would study. They had no choice. The students with the highest marks attended the best universities. Students were placed in a department for training according to what professions and what jobs were needed in the country at that particular time. Once selected the student lived for the next four years in the same dormitory room with the same seven or eight students who had the same major with courses narrowly focused within that major. After graduation they were assigned jobs by the government. Almost all ShiDa students were trained to become teachers, many to be sent back to their hometowns in rural areas.

80年代时，我的学生们常常告诉我他们并不喜欢被分配的专业。学生们接到录取通知书并得知他们的专业时距离开学只有几个星期了，他们没有选择。得到最高分数的学生可以上最好的大学，至于去哪个专业，要看特定时期国家的需要。而当学校和专业都选定之后，接下来的四年他们要和同样的七位或八位同专业同学住在同一间宿舍里。他们都在本专业内狭小的范围里选择课程。毕业时，根据国家的需要，他们由政府分配工作。几乎所有陕西师大的大学生接受的都是成为教师的训练，许多人被分配回他们在农村的故乡。

"I don't want to take that job in such a backward area and be there forever. I worked so hard to get to the university and now I must go back," one senior told me when she received her assignment to a position and a place where the government decided she was needed. "I might refuse once but if I refuse a second time then no one else will take me and I won't get another job anywhere."

"我不想做那个工作，那个地方太落后了，我不想在那里待一辈子。我那样努力进了大学，可是现在我还得回去。"一个毕业生在接到通知，得知她已被分配了一个政府认为是合适的工作时，这样对我说，"我可以拒绝一次，但不能两次，要是那样的话，我就不会再得到一份工作了。"

Now the situation has reversed as students are no longer assigned jobs by the government and can freely choose their own careers. However their intense fear is that they may not find a job suitable for their qualifications or any job at all, as the huge number of highly educated graduates creates extreme competition.

现在已经完全不同了。国家不包分配了，大学生们可以自由选择自己的工作。当然他们也担心找不到一份好工作，或者干脆就找不到工作。因为大学毕业生那么多，竞争又是如此激烈。

New buildings, new possibilities
新的建筑，新的可能性

In the 1980's I frequently lectured in large old buildings that had no heat, no equipment and no bright lighting. During my first few years of teaching I brought tiny (two inch) canisters from America, each one filled with a long strip of film than had to be hand-turned through a small metal projector to show images on a blank wall. One by one during class we looked at photos of historic events, famous leaders or authors from the United States or China as a backdrop to discussions on Sino-American relations.

80年代，我经常在一座大而旧的教学楼里上课。那里没有暖气，没有教学设备，灯光暗淡。在陕西师范大学教书的最初几年里，我总是拿着一个从美国带来的小型幻灯机，里面装进比手动机器长的一组胶片，然后通过一个投影仪把图像投放在一堵空墙上。我们一张张地看着这些胶片，它们有的是历史事件，有的是中美两国的著名领导人或作家，他们成为我们的中美关系课堂讨论的背景。

On other occasions students shared small paperback translations of Ernest Hemingway's *Old Man and the Sea* in class and compared his message of man's struggle against nature with the difficulties faced by their own families, such as: the famines in the 1960's, the Cultural Revolution and other difficult times. To improve their English-writing skills they practiced Hemingway's literary style of using simple words to portray complicated conflicts. From their writings I learned more about China's past difficulties.

另外一次，学生们在课上交流阅读海明威的《老人与海》的体会，并将老人与自然的斗争与他们的家庭所面临的困难相比：如60年代的饥馑，"文革"和其他困难时期。为了提高他们的英文水平，他们练习海明威的写作技巧，即用简单的文字去描写复杂的冲突。从他们的写作中，我了解到许多中国过去的艰难日子。

In subsequent years modern buildings replaced the old with first-class equipment to facilitate

2000，陕西师大，配有先进设备的逸夫音乐楼
The Yifu Music Building with sophisticated equipment, ShiDa, 2000

2009，陕西师大，新建成的崇鋈楼
The newly-built Chongwu Building, ShiDa, 2009

power-point presentations and simultaneous translation during international symposia. Several modern Buildings on campus were partly funded through the generosity of Chinese in Hong Kong. International scholars attended conferences at ShiDa to share intercultural ideas or to present lectures open to students from different disciplines. Students now take elective courses or attend special lectures to broaden their knowledge beyond their own chosen majors, representing a major deviation from the past.

后来，现代化的大楼取代了那座旧的教学楼。新大楼里有一流的设备，能在开国际研讨会时使用PPT（图文演示系统）和同声翻译系统。这几栋现代化建筑是由几位香港人分别捐资兴建的。出席在陕西师范大学召开的国际会议的外国学者也会做一些跨文化的交流，或者就不同的课题做一些公开的演讲。学生们也会上一些选修课，或听一些特殊的讲座，目的是想在专业之外扩大自己的视野。这是一种与以往不同的主要变化。

Fountains and fish are allowed
喷泉和鲤鱼被允许存在了

2007，陕西师大，一个学生下课后躺在喷泉附近的长椅上
A student lying on the bench near the fountain after class, ShiDa, 2007

  Fountains with sculptured fish (and live ones) now beautify the campus. Red azaleas and evergreen trees create a lovely setting, in sharp contrast to the Cultural Revolution years when Red Guards crushed flowers and destroyed children's gold fish as being decadent, bourgeois and unnecessary to the development of China. Students today are far removed from those tumultuous years of the Cultural Revolution (1966—1976) and often relax, as does this student on the bench, after courses in computer science and international economics. ShiDa received an award of "National Advanced University in the Building of Spiritual Civilization", from the Central Civilization Committee (CPC) in 1999 for creating a beautiful environment on campus as an important element of student life.

  喷泉、鲤鱼雕塑和池中的鲤鱼美化了校园，红杜鹃和柏树烘托出了可爱的环境，这一切都和"文革"时期形成了鲜明的对比。那时红卫兵践踏鲜花，毁掉孩子们的鲤鱼，因为对他们来说，这些都是颓废的、资产阶级的、对中国的发展无益的。今天的学生已经远离了动荡的"文革"年代。就像这个躺在长椅上的学生一样，他们可以在电脑科学和国际经济等课程的重压下小憩一下，喘一口气。陕西师大曾在1999年被中央文明委首批授予"全国精神文明建设先进单位"荣誉称号，美化校园是校园生活中的一个重要因素。

Old tools advance to multiple choices
鸟枪换炮

Hand-set typewriter...then
过去：手动打字机

1984，陕西师大图书馆，手工打字机和打字员
A hand-set typewriter and operator in ShiDa's library, 1984

The system for writing a document or printing was a laborious process of hand selecting and lifting to put into place each character from among thousands of possibilities. I watched this staff worker in the library at ShiDa select from many boxes and drawers filled with characters as she explained that each person operating the typewriter had her own system of remembering their location. Foreign newspapers or publications were almost non-existent. Paper was scarce.

过去，用打字机写作和印刷是一个耗时耗力的过程，因为得从成千个字模里面选字，再把选好的字模排版。我在陕西师大图书馆见过一位工作人员从很多装满字模的抽屉里选字。她说每个打字员都有自己的字模排列系统，只有他（她）知道该用的字模在哪里。那时几乎没有外国报纸和出版物；纸张极其缺乏。

Options in hand...now
现在：任由选择

The current generation has its hands on many new sources for gaining facts and ideas from around the world. Professor Wang Xiaoling accessed instant information from a hand held device to share with me while we had lunch during a break between classes.

目前的一代人可以利用多种资源在世界范围内方便地获取各种信息。王晓凌教授在我们课间吃午饭时就可以用手头的设备告诉我

2004，陕西师大，王晓凌教授与电子设备
Professor Wang Xiaoling with battery operated device, ShiDa, 2004

一些即时的信息。

Technological breakthroughs of course have facilitated the easy spread of information as economic reforms facilitated the spread of knowledge with a steady flow of businessmen, educators and scholars from other countries.

技术上的突破使得信息的传播越来越容易，这就像经济改革一样，由于国外的商人、教育家和学者不断地涌入，知识的传播越来越容易。

When I first started taking American delegations to China in the 1980's and working on several educational projects it would often take three months for letters to be sent back and forth. Part of the time was for mailing, and part was for bureaucratic decisions and approval from leaders in Beijing and leaders in Shaanxi Province. At that time even small decisions needed approval from top levels of leadership. Today I can send details for a project via email in the evening and when I awaken the next morning the answer is often already in my computer.

80年代，当我第一次带领美国的代表团来中国并且同时在几个教育项目上工作时，一封信来回大约得3个月，其中部分时间花在邮寄途中，部分则是等待中央或省上领导的官方决定或批准。那时即使一个小小的决定也需要高层的批准。今天我可以在晚上通过电子邮件发出项目的细节，等我次日早晨醒来时，回复就已经在我电脑里了。

Renting books outside...then
过去：户外租书

In the 1980's it was common for students to gather when books were set up in open areas and could be rented for a few cents. The number of books and information available was extremely limited, often just comic book style. One of the young teachers, however, nostalgically remembered, "When I was young, we were really poor but I would go with a friend on a warm day and sit for hours outside and read books. That's all we had."

80年代，学生们去那些露天的书摊花几分钱租书看是一件很平常的事。那时能得到的书籍和信息很有限，而且经常只是连环画。一位年轻教师很怀念那个时期："小的时候，我们都没钱，但我喜欢和小朋友在天气暖和的时候一起到外边（的书摊上）看书，一看就是几个小时。那就是我们所有的快乐。"

1982,陕西农村,租书的年轻学生们
Young children gather to rent books, Shaanxi village, 1982

Using computers inside now
现在：在室内使用电脑

Students today enter the library at the university or open computers in their elementary school classrooms to gain knowledge at their fingertips. Personal ownership of computers for students and in private households is rapidly expanding. One university student told me, "I remember the day when I was six years old and my family got our first electric light, but now I have had my own computer for six years." She was still amazed at the progress within her lifetime.

今天从大学图书馆到小学教室到处都是电脑，学生们动动手指，就能得到他们想要的信息。学生和私人家里拥有的电脑数量正在急剧上升。一个大学生告诉我："我记得当我六岁的时候家里才有了第一盏电灯。但是六年前我就有个人电脑了。"她仍然为她生活中的进步而感到惊奇。

2007，陕西师大，图书馆电脑前的学生
University students with computer screens in the library, ShiDa, 2007

2002，陕西师大附小，教室里的小学生在用电脑
Elementary students in classroom using computers, Fu Xiao School of ShiDa, 2002

Breaking new ground: a second ShiDa campus
新的突破：师大新校区

When I returned in 2004 for the sixtieth anniversary of the founding of Shaanxi Normal University they had completed the rudiment of the construction of the second campus. Ten other universities were being constructed in the same surrounding area in the southern part of Xi'an. A "city of students" was rising from fields where peasants had raised their crops, as universities built second campuses to accommodate enormous increases in numbers of students.

2004年，我为了60周年校庆而重返陕西师大时，他们的新校区已经初具规模；与此同时，在西安南郊毗邻地区有十座别的大学也在大兴土木。一座大学城从过去的农田里拔地而起。众多新校区的建设使这些学校接收学生的能力大大提高。

The reason for ShiDa's second campus was to respond to the emphasis of expanding university education since the end of the 1990's. A nationwide surge resulted in phenomenal 30% to 35% increases per year in university student enrollment for several years in a row. ShiDa is now composed of two separate campuses with more than 60,000 students, including a rising number of those pursuing master's and doctoral degree work. Nearly 40,000 of those students are registered for part time, non-degree, adult education or distance-learning programs, which are relatively new programs for China to meet new demands.

建设陕西师大新校区是为了回应90年代末以来高校扩建的浪潮。这个全国性的浪潮导致连续几年的大学招生人数都以高达30%至35%的惊人速度上升。陕西师大现在有了两个校区，超过6万名学生，包括那些数字不断上升的硕士生和博士生，其中近4万名学生是业余的、非学位的、成人的和远距离教育的学生，这些都属于为了满足新的需要而建立的新的教育项目。

The library on the second campus captures the grandeur of the Tang Dynasty, considered China's golden era. It ranks as one of the largest in China with advanced equipment and 2.8 million books and publications. The fountain at the entrance to the university displays shooting water, which seems to dance to the Mozart or classical Chinese music with multi-colored lights surrounded by flowers and trees: a totally different scene from what I remember of my early teaching years.

唐代风格的新校区图书馆是中国最大的图书馆之一，拥有先进设备，藏书达280万册。学校大门内的喷泉经常应和着莫扎特或中国古典音乐的旋律及多彩

2007，陕西师大，新校区建成的唐代风格的图书馆
The library on the new campus built in classic Tang Dynasty style, ShiDa, 2007

的灯光，变幻出一片绚丽的水晶世界。校园内林木葱茏，百花盛开，气象万千——一幅与我早年在这里教学时完全不同的景象。

During the celebrations for the 60th Anniversary students in Western dress sang traditional and contemporary songs in sharp contrast to uniformed blue Mao jackets and the eight controlled

2004，陕西师大，雪莲在60周年校庆上
Sharon Crain attending the sixtieth anniversary ceremony, ShiDa, 2004

2004，陕西师大，陕西师大60周年校庆
60th Anniversary Celebration of Shaanxi Normal University, ShiDa, 2004

revolutionary operas allowed during the late 1960's and 1970's. Watching students singing in tuxedos and long gowns I reflected on my first overnight train ride to Xi'an in the spring of 1982 when I was awakened by the loud speaker adjacent to my head on the top bed in a hard-sleeper compartment playing an American Christmas song, *Jingle Bells*. One of the Chinese ladies in the same section whispered to me, "That's real progress. In the past Western music was banned." She looked similar to all the others on the train who wore blue jackets but she had noticed the beginning of something different.

在陕西师大举行60周年校庆时，学生们身着西式服装，唱着传统歌曲和当代歌曲，与60、70年代的人们穿着千篇一律的蓝色毛式服装、唱着单调的八个样板戏的场面形成鲜明的对比。看着这些穿着华丽的演出服、忘情歌唱的学生们，我想起了1982年在前往西安的火车卧铺上，我被设在头顶上的大喇叭吵醒了，喇叭里放的是美国圣诞歌曲《铃儿响叮当》。同车厢的一位中国妇女悄悄对我说："这就是进步。过去西方音乐都是被禁止的。"像列车上的其他人一样，她也穿着毛式服装，但她注意到情况开始变化。

Scenes on campus reflect seeds of economic change
校园里破土而出的经济改革幼苗

A private job
个体劳动者

My first introduction to private enterprise on campus was in the late 1980's watching a shoe repairman who set up his tools in a busy section of the school. He worked long hours in the same place every day; he was good. He charged a small fee and kept the profit, unlike all the state-run jobs at the time where people received a fixed government wage, regardless of how hard they worked. Previously he himself had held a position in the physical education department at the university on a fixed salary but because of Deng Xiaoping's economic reforms and popular slogan "to get rich is glorious" he decided to "go private" and was able to make more money. Over the next several years each time I returned to ShiDa he was still repairing shoes at the same spot on campus. He was experimenting with the new market economy and it seemed to be working for him.

我要介绍的第一个校园个体户是一个修鞋匠。那是80年代末，他在校园里的一个繁忙路段摆起了他的修鞋摊。他每天都去那个地方，工作时间很长，手艺不错。和那时国家的"铁饭碗"不同，不像那个时代领取国家固定工资、却不管工作努力程度的国家职工，他收费不高，但能挣钱。他曾是学校体育系的一名员工，拿着一份旱涝保收的国家工资。不过，邓小平的经济改革和"致富光荣"的口号使他下决心"干个体"，而且挣了更多的钱。以后的几年里我每次回到师大，他都还在那里修鞋。他在尝试新的市场经济，而那对他似乎很有效。

1986，陕西师大，校园修鞋工
Repairing shoes on campus, ShiDa, 1986

A radio repairman just next to him built a tiny enclosure around himself using a few big boards with just enough room to sit and work during the day, securing the large and small radios at night with a big padlock. Once I walked past with a teacher friend who looked over at him with alarm and said, "Can you believe he can make more money than a professor or maybe even more than the president of this entire university?" It was so new in China that people were shocked when they learned about the benefits of a system with individual profits.

在修鞋匠旁边还有一个收音机修理工。他用一些大木板建了一个仅能容身的小木房，白天坐在那里工作，晚上用一把大锁把那些大大小小的收音机锁在里面。一天我和一位教师朋友路过那个摊，朋友看到他，带着一种不愿相信的口气对我说："你能相信他挣的钱比教授，甚至比校长都多吗？"在中国这样的故事是这样新奇：当知道市场的"利润"时，人们被震惊了。

Another teacher friend at the same time told me, "My father wants to start his own business but I told him to wait and see if the policies change again." China was cautiously proceeding down a new road and evidence of success was surfacing on campus and elsewhere.

另一个教师朋友对我说："我的父亲想做生意，但我告诉他还是等等看政策是否会变。"中国正在谨慎地走上一条新路，但是成功的事例到处都有。

Fluffing quilts or painting photos for a fee
弹棉花、绘彩照

Another example of the entrepreneurial spirit was evident just outside the campus' front gates as I watched the "fluffing of quilts" as young men and boys refurbished cotton-filled quilts for families or students and gained a profit, according to what the market would bear.

另外一个企业家精神的例子是在学校大门外，我看到一些年轻人和男孩子在做他们的生意——弹棉花，即将做被子用的棉絮翻新，供家庭和学生们继续使用，而他们自己也能因此挣得一份收入。

On sunny days in the botanical park near the back gate of the campus this man climbed up a ladder to take a black and white photo for others. It was long before digital photos and very few people owned their own cameras. Another person carefully hand painted color on top of black and white photos and smiled at the profit he made.

1986，陕西师大附近，弹棉花的工人
Workers fluffing the quilts for a fee, near ShiDa, 1986

1985，陕西师大附近，在梯子上照相
Climbing the ladder for a better shot, botanical park near ShiDa, 1985

1985，陕西师大附近，给黑白照加彩
Painting color on top of black and white photos, near ShiDa, 1985

　　天气好的时候，在陕西师大后门附近的植物园，这个人正爬上梯子为别人照一张黑白照片。那时离数码相机的出现还早，也很少有人有照相机。另外一个人很认真地把照片绘成彩色，对自己的劳动所得很开心。

　　These were early seeds of a new idea planted with Deng Xiaoping's economic reform that would soon take hold and spread across China like a rushing stream downhill. These individuals probably did not know the meaning of "market economy" or realize that China's economic system was being reshaped starting with people like them.

　　这些人可以说是邓小平的经济改革思想播下的早期种子，他们的所为很快就会像奔腾而下的江河，在全国激荡，虽然作为个人他们也许并不知道什么是"市场经济"，也没有意识到中国的经济体制正在被像他们这样的人重新塑造。

Outside the university's front gate: then and now
校园大门外：今与昔

Chang'an Road near the front gate of Shaanxi Normal University, 1982
1982年，陕西师范大学大门前的长安路

During my early years of teaching at ShiDa I often shared the bumpy muddy roads with horse or mule-drawn carts bringing vegetables from the nearby countryside into the city each morning as in this scene just outside the front gate of my university. Neither private cars nor taxis existed; all buses were old, crowded and infrequent. Often the roads were totally filled with bikes and people pulling heavy loads while trucks from behind honked loudly to warn of their approach. However, only when the blaring horn was loud enough to realize the truck was very close did people move to the edge, before returning quickly to the middle of the road for space to carry their heavy loads. At night trucks or government cars often drove without their lights on (or quickly turned them on and off to see what was ahead) so as not to temporarily blind the vision of so many bikers who filled the dark streets. This actually added to hazardous conditions.

刚在陕西师大教学时，我经常在校门前那条泥泞又凹凸不平的道路上骑车。那条路上还挤着每天早上从附近农村给城里运送蔬菜的马车或驴车。那时没有私人汽车或出租车，公共汽车间隔时间很长，而且又旧又挤。路上经常挤满了自行车和人力车。卡车在后面大声地按着喇叭，但人们只是在觉得它真的靠近时才会躲到一边给它让路，等车过后又迅速回到路中间。夜晚，卡车和政府的汽车行驶时经常不开灯（或者只是很快地开关一下看看前面有什么），因为担心会让那些在黑暗中挤满街道的骑车人晃了眼睛。但实际上这使情况更危险。

1982，西安，长安路，运菜的马车和骑自行车的雪莲
Horse carts bringing in vegetables from the countryside share the road with Sharon Crain on her bike, Chang'an Road, Xi'an, 1982

Chang'an Road near the front gate of Shaanxi Normal University, 2002
2002年，陕西师范大学大门前的长安路

Now the exact place outside the front gate is a different scene on Chang'an Road with buses, taxis and private cars providing many conveniences for transportation but creating new congestion and a major energy crisis. I no longer need a bicycle but sometimes it takes longer.

现在，长安路上的同样地方出现了完全不同的景观。公交车、出租车和私人汽车使得交通更加方便，但也制造了新的拥挤，还出现了能源紧张的问题。我不再需要自行车了，经常坐汽车，但有时用的时间更长。

2002，西安，长安路，小汽车、公交车和出租车与行人在同一地点挤做一团
Cars, buses and taxis converge with pedestrians at the same place, Xi'an, 2002

Restructuring Education: Old Methods Merge with New Approaches
教育改革：新旧方法的融合

A major national educational reform entitled *The Action Plan for Rejuvenating Education* was just announced when I returned to teach in 2004. It was beginning to break new ground in the way teachers were to teach and interact with students, introducing Western methodology and reversing many traditional practices. If fully implemented these policies initiated by China's President Hu Jintao and Premier Wen Jiabao and endorsed by all of the nation's top eleven ministries could redirect China's future as dramatically as did the economic reforms of Deng Xiaoping. The ideas put forth in this plan merit very careful scrutiny as a forecast for the future.

2004年，当我再次回到陕西师大任教时，中国刚刚宣布了一个重大的全国性教改计划，名为"教育振兴行动计划"。它在教师教学和与学生互动方面开始了一个重大的突破：西方的教育理念被介绍进来，许多传统的习惯被质疑和颠覆。这些新政策是在胡锦涛主席和温家宝总理领导下推行的，得到国家11个部委的全力支持。如果完全落实的话，中国的未来就会有巨大的变化，像是邓小平的经济改革所做的那样。作为未来的蓝图，这个计划中的思想值得仔细的考察。

The goals set forth in the new education plan
新教育计划中设定的目标

*Encourage creativity

*Promote individual student participation

*Develop positive teacher-student relationships

*Change single-subject orientations to integration of broader courses

*Strengthen the connection between course content and students' lives

*Encourage critical analysis through independent investigation

*Introduce specific techniques for student involvement

*Allow for regional differences in textbooks

*Focus on the process of learning and how to study rather than on rote-memorization of facts

*鼓励创造性

*提升个人参与能力

*发展积极的师生关系

*将单科学习转变为跨学科学习

*加强课程内容与学生生活的联系

*鼓励经过独立调查而作出的批评分析

*引入可调动学生参与的技巧

*允许教科书中的地区差异

*注重学习过程，即学习的有效性，而非死记硬背

Traditions from the past reflect core values
作为核心价值观的传统

On the surface these goals seemed admirable but if put into action within China's historic educational framework it would require a radical departure from century-old practices. As Western methodology was being infused into Chinese traditions I was frequently asked, "What is the difference between students in China and students in the United States?" One basic example is illustrated in the two different ways we teach our children to put on their jackets or smocks at a very early age.

表面上看，这些目标似乎都是被肯定的，但要将它们落实在行动上，就需要相当程度地偏离千百年来中国传统的教育体系。当西方的方法被融入中国传统时，我经常被问到这样的问题："什么是中美学生之间的不同？"在这方面有一个很好的例子，即看一下教小孩子穿衣服的两种不同方法。

I have watched in primary schools in China as children gather in a circle and help the child in front of them fasten their smock, which ties in the back. It is one of the first lessons a child receives about the importance of working together in a group.

我在中国的小学看到一个活动：孩子们围成一个圈，然后帮助前面的孩子从后面系上衣服。这就是孩子们学到的第一课，即"集体"的重要性。

In contrast, one of the first lessons children learn at a similar age in the United States is how to put on their jackets all by themselves. Just before going outside the teacher or parent shows the child how to place their jacket on the floor in front of them, upside down, and then wiggle their arms into the sleeves and flip it over their head so they can do it "all by themselves".

相反，同年龄美国孩子学到的第一课是怎样完全靠自己穿上衣服。外出前，老师或父母会给孩子做示范，怎么把衣服摆在前面，翻过来，把胳膊伸到袖子里，然后套头，这样孩子们就完全能靠自己做这件事了。

One student learns the importance of communal and inter-dependent efforts, while the other learns the importance of individualism and independent effort. These two approaches represent two fundamentally different philosophies reflecting core values taught for centuries in our two different culture. Now this is changing in China as new curriculum, revised textbooks and teacher-training programs introduce methods with increased emphasis on individualism and participation, incorporating elements of Western methodology.

这两种方法代表了完全不同的哲学观点：一个学到的是共同努力和相互依存的重要性，另一个学到的是个人主义和独立操作的重要性。两种方法在各自的文化里沿袭了很久。但现在中国的情况有了变化，因为新的课程、修改了的教科书以及师资培训计划都引进了新的方法，强调个性和参与，从而融进了西方的方法。

I began to hear conflicting opinions of these new reforms. To find out more I started meeting with a small seminar group in the Education Department. They were teachers, principals, professors and administrators from many provinces who had come to ShiDa to pursue a master's degree in education and had years of teaching experience but expressed concern as to how the new policies could be effectively implemented. In their particular schools, they had encountered various obstacles: reluctance by teachers to let go of old customs, difficulty maintaining discipline in classrooms of fifty or sixty students, parental pressure to prepare students for the national examination.

我开始听到关于这些新方法的不同意见。为了发现更多的材料，我在教育系开始建立了一个研究小组，成员有教师、校长、教授和行政管理人员，他们来自不同省份，在陕西师大攻读教育硕士。他们都有多年的教学经验，但却对新政策如何能有效地被落实非常关切。在他们各自的学校里，他们会碰到不同的障碍：老师不愿意摒弃旧习惯，在有50到60名学生的班上很难维持纪律，应对来自家长的让学生准备全国统考的压力，等等。

On the other hand many of the same teachers and school principals in this group expressed excitement and welcomed the idea of greater student participation and having textbooks reflect regional diversity. Many questions surfaced: "How could new teachers be trained? How could the older teachers be won over? How could parental support be elicited?" Most of them expressed the belief that the young students would eagerly embrace the chance to be more involved but it would take considerable time to go beyond the patterns of the past.

2007，西安，在陕西师大幼儿园王老师的班里，学生们正在互相帮助穿衣服
Young students helping each other put on smocks in teacher Wang's class, ShiDa Kindergarten, Xi'an, 2007

2009，佛蒙特，美国的学龄前儿童皮特·奎珀斯在穿衣服
American preschooler Peter Kuypers putting on his own jacket, Vermont, 2009

另一方面，许多有类似问题的老师又为新政策感到激动，赞同鼓励学生更多地参与并让教科书反映地方的多样性。许多问题被提了出来："怎样培训新教师？老教师怎样才能体现自己的价值？怎样赢得家长的支持？"大多数人相信学生会积极把握机会，投入到课堂学习过程中去，但是要超越过去的模式还要走更长的路。

From memorizing Mao to marking ballots
从背诵语录到清点选票

For decades students like this high school freshman were hesitant to express their own ideas or to deviate from the political influences of the past, while portraits of Mao Zedong, Sun Yat-sen, Lenin, Engels and Marx looked over their shoulders. For generations they were trained to sit quietly and listen to the undisputed words of their teacher, to memorize and recite. No one ever asked them, "What do you think?"

几十年来，像这个高一学生一样，在毛泽东、孙中山、列宁、恩格斯和马克思画像的注视下，学生们在表达自己思想和偏离过去的政治影响时都很犹豫。一代代的学生被要求静静地坐在那里听讲，去理解教师的话，去背诵和默诵。没有人问过他们："你们怎么看？"

A dissimilar scene appeared one day in 2007 when my class was cancelled as the buzzer sounded and all the students filed outside to vote. They examined their pink ballots and waited to mark their

1988，陕西，在马克思、列宁、恩格斯、孙中山和毛泽东的像下，中学生在班上背诵
High school student reciting information in class with photos of Marx, Lenin, Engles, Sun Yat-sen and Mao Zedong, on the wall, Shaanxi Province, 1988

choice for the university representative to the district. One girl told me, "I have no idea who the candidates are." Another spoke up, "I am voting for my professor because he is really smart and honest and can express his ideas to others." I watched them vote as an example of grassroots democracy and the first in their family to experience democratic participation. These elections on campus opened up many subsequent discussions in class about the meaning of democracy in China right now as they stood up and spoke out.

2007年，不同的场景出现了。有一天，上课铃响起时我的课被取消，因为所有的学生都去参加选举了。他们检查手中粉色的选票，等着选出这个选区的代表。一个女生告诉我："我不知道那个代表师大的候选人是谁。"另一个学生说："我选了我的教授，因为他很聪明又诚实，并且善于向他人表达自己的想法。"我把学生们的选举看做基层民主的一个范例，而且首先在他们的社区里体验民主参与。校园里的选举活动在学生中引发了一系列关于当今中国民主的讨论。他们各抒己见，畅所欲言。

One said, "I think democracy is coming. Great changes have taken place in recent years. Many people can vote for their village head instead of having someone appointed. But I don't think the real democracy will come easily. Democracy is not just the democratic system but also the viewpoints embedded in people's mind in building democracy. I believe the waking up in the people's mind is the most important thing. Chinese people haven't realized all the rights they own; they think politics is none of their business. Although this is changing, it will be a long process through more education."

一个学生说："我觉得民主正在到来。这些年来，巨变已经发生。在农村，村民选举已经取代了领导任命成为村干部产生的方式。但是，在我看来，要获得真正意义上的民主绝非易事。民主不只是一种政治制度，而且是植根于民众心里的观念，而民众民主思想的觉醒才是实现民主的关键。中国人还没有意识到他们所应拥有的全部权利，对政治漠不关心。尽管情况在变化，但还需要加强对民众的教育，还有很长的路要走。"

Another student said, "Democracy means people have rights to be safe, to have food and clothes and shoes. That is first. Then democracy means everyone can voice his desires and views."

另一个学生说："所谓民主，首先要保障民众的安全及衣食住行等基本权利。这是第一位的。接下来民主才意味着每个人都能表达自己的愿望和观点。"

A PhD candidate who said he hopes to play an important role in China's future expressed these thoughts to the class, "On the last day of the Party Congress Premier

2007，陕西师大，大学生在投票选举
University students gathering to vote at ShiDa, 2007

Wen Jiabao mentioned two key words which repeatedly flew into the ears of every common person who watched in front of the TV. One word was 'democracy' and the other was 'the well-being of the people'. I think there can be no well-being without democracy." This student like others throughout the country is paying close attention to the words as well as the actions of China's top leaders.

一个声言希望将来在中国扮演更重要角色的博士生面对全班表达了这样的想法："在中共十七大的最后一天，温家宝总理提到了两个关键词，每个新闻记者或电视机前的观众都会听到。一个词是'民主'，第二个是'民生'。我认为没有'民主'，'民生'就无从谈起。"和其他人一样，他密切关注着中国领导人的一言一行。

Another student expressed her feelings openly to the class. "I think Deng Xiaoping led us down the right path that is integrating China with the world, embracing globalization, entrepreneurship and all the useful economic theories that will help China to prosper. I believe in my lifetime we will see China having the biggest GDP (gross domestic product) of any country. China is on a speedway to becoming an economic world power."

另一个学生公开向全班表达了她的看法："我认为邓小平带领我们走上了一条正确的道路。他将中国融入世界、接受全球化、企业家精神和所有有用的经济理论，这样就推动中国走向了繁荣。我相信在我的一生中中国将拥有世界上最高的GDP。中国正在加速成为世界上最大的经济体。"

Teacher training and new textbooks
教师培训和新教科书

To spread the educational reform policies and to introduce new methods, training classes were first set up in experimental regions such as Xi'an before expanding to other areas. I attended one of these sessions at a large high school in Xi'an where students were being asked to think creatively and teachers were being trained to interact with students and encourage participation. Powerpoint presentations on a large screen gave students a topic as the teacher encouraged them to discuss ideas with fellow students and then present their own individual ideas or solutions by standing up in front of the class. Other teachers from the school attended these model sessions, taking notes on practical suggestions.

在推广教育改革的政策和引进新的教学理念和方法之前，西安等试点地区先举办了教师培训班。我在西安一所较大规模的高中参加了一次培训班。在那里学生被要求创造性地思考，教师则被要求要与学生互动，并鼓励学生积极参与。大屏幕上展示的课件给学生一个题目，教师则鼓励学生讨论，然后在全班面前陈述自己的观点或解决办法。学校的老师都参加了这些示范课，并记下自己的心得，提出一些实际的建议。

2007，西安，借助教师的PPT的文字，参加教师培训的中学生正在学习新方法
High school students participating in teacher training sessions to learn new methods, with words from the teacher's powerpoint presentation, Xi'an, 2007

These new directives are very different from the traditional norms embedded since Confucian times when the Emperor ruled with the Mandate of Heaven, the father ruled in the household and the teacher's words were memorized but never questioned.

这些新政策与渗透着儒学观念的传统标准不同。在帝制时代，皇帝的君权来自上天，父亲在家里的权力至高无上，先生的话也要熟记——他们的话向来是一言九鼎，不能质疑。

By 2005 new textbooks utilizing revised curriculum were introduced into Grade One in experimental areas, further expanded the following year and by 2007 reached all districts at all grade levels throughout the country. This represented an enormous endeavor in a country of China's size and population.

到了2005年，修改了现行课程的新教材开始在一年级使用，接着再推及剩下的年级。到2007年，全国所有地方和所有的年级都使用了新教材。就中国的幅员和人口而言，这是一个巨大的进步。

When I stayed with peasant friends in the countryside in Shaanxi Province I saw their new high school textbooks that had been rewritten for students that year. Some sections now reflect local customs and regional differences, non-existent before when one textbook was published by the central government for all regions. Now local educators and many publishers are involved in selecting materials, which encourage student participation and are more specific to that area. Both excitement and resistance to this approach by teachers and students were expressed: One teacher told me, "I don't believe it is an efficient way when many classes have fifty students. How can we keep control in chaotic and noisy classrooms resulting from so many students talking?" A student in the same school said, "Now the textbooks are so colorful and much more interesting and talk about things we care about in our everyday life."

住在陕西农民朋友家里的时候，我看到了那一年为全国学生重新编写的新中学教材。教材的一些单元反映了地方风俗和地区差异，而这在以前的全国统编教材中是没有的。现在一些教育机构和出版社也参与了遴选更适合本地区教材的工作，这样的教材鼓励学生的参与，并更有地方的针对性。在学生和教师中，欢迎和批评两种意见都有。一位教师告诉我："当大多数班有五六十个学生时，这不是一个有效的方法。这么多学生都在讲话，我们怎样控制这种混乱和嘈杂的局面？"一个来自同一所学校的学生说："现在的教材内容丰富，更有意思，谈的都是我们日常生活中的事。"

Still, both students and teachers feel constant pressure, to prepare for the exams required for placement into high schools (zhong kao) and for entrance to a university (gao kao) since a student's score on these exams holds the key to his or her future. If too much freedom is allowed in the classroom when students discuss and debate ideas parents often become critical of the teacher and the new teaching methods. Consequently they put demands on the teachers to teach what is required so their children will score well on the exam and secure a coveted position at the next level.

不过，学生和老师依然感到持续的压力。即要准备"中考"，以便根据学生的分数决定他（她）上哪所高中。然后学生们又要面对"高考"，他们的未来就取决于他们参加这些考试的成绩。如果学生在课堂讨论时被给予太多的自由，家长们就开始批评教师和新的教学方法，结果他们就让老师教考试所需要的东西，这样他们的孩子就能在考试中得高分，在下一轮考试中占得先机。

Most people agree it is hard to change old ways as long as the exams hold so much power. In discussions with teachers, parents and students the vast majority, however, continues to believe that the entrance examination is a valid way to measure students' qualifications fairly by allowing anyone throughout the entire country to compete based on academics. Without this universal exam there is a fear that entrance can become too dependent on a person's personal connections (guanxi) or money. It will take years to train the teachers to teach in a new way and for students to feel comfortable to speak openly in a society where authority from above has held total control.

大多数人都同意只要高考对学生们的命运还是这么重要，要改变过去的教学方法就非常困难。在与许多师生的讨论中，我发现仍有不少人认为这些考试是衡量学生素质的一个公平合理的办法。人们担心如果没有这些考试，学生是否能被大学录取就靠关系和钱了。让教师熟悉新的教学方法需要时间。在一个行政当局掌握所有权力的社会里，要让学生没有压力地畅所欲言也需要时间。

Education and happiness
教育与幸福

A groundbreaking conference called *Education and Happiness* was held at Shaanxi Normal University in 2007. Scholars and educators discussed happiness as a key priority on the teaching agenda, a topic not traditionally discussed within China's educational goals. As I walked across campus I explored this idea with one of my students who responded, "When I was young, if I didn't know the answer, I was beaten by the teacher. But it worked. It made me go home and study harder." This was the accepted practice in China for generations. Now conferences and teacher training sessions promote positive interaction between teachers and students and explore how to add happiness to students' learning while still preparing for the necessary examinations.

2007，陕西师大，中国教育学会学术年会"教育与幸福"的会议现场和一位参会者
One of the participants at a national educational conference entitled *Education and Happiness*, held at Shaanxi Normal University, 2007

2007年，一次具有强烈创新意义的教育研讨会在陕西师范大学举行，会议的主题是："教育与幸福"。与会的学者和教育家们讨论一个问题，即是否把幸福作为教学的优先因素。这是一个在传统的中国教育目标中不予关注的问题。在校园里散步时，我和一个学生谈起这个问题，他说："我小时候，如果回答不上问题，就会被老师打。但这种方法很有效。它能让我回家后更努力地学习。"在中国人们一直是这么做的，是一种可以接受的做法。而现在，在中国的一些研讨会或教师培训活动中，人们开始关注新型的师生关系，并探讨如何在备考的同时增加学生的学习乐趣。

One student planning to become a teacher said, "The education system of China has always stressed teaching but ignored the student's ideas. I hope I can learn a different way of thinking and teaching and at the same time let my students gain knowledge."

一个将来准备当老师的学生说："中国的教育体制重视教师的教学，但往往忽视学生自己的想法。我希望让学生学到知识，但也希望学会不同的教学方式、从不同的角度思考问题。"

Learning English, one aim of the reform
学习英语：改革的目标之一

New directives call for increased emphasis on teaching English beginning at the primary school level in an effort to prepare the next generation with bilingual language skills to compete in a global economy and become more proficient with advanced technology. English has been taught in secondary schools for years and every university student (regardless of their major) must pass an English proficiency exam before graduation.

新的教育改革进一步强调英语教学。英语教学将从小学就开始，从而使下一代具备良好的双语能力，适应未来全球化经济的竞争，而且在掌握先进技术方面更有效率。英语在中国的中学已经被教授了很多年，所有的大学生——不论他们学什么专业——都必须在毕业前通过一种英语水平考试。

Students consider learning English a necessity (not a luxury) to provide a competitive edge to open doors for better job opportunities, learn directly from primary source material, utilize information available through computers and communicate directly with English-speaking people to develop an understanding of other countries.

在学生们看来，学习英语为他们提供了一种竞争的利器，对未来的求职大有裨益，所以是必要的，绝非中看不中用的花活。不过要达到这样的目的，就要直接学习第一手资料，利用电脑上的相关信息，并与以英文为母语者直接对话，最后建立起对其他国家的理解。

An English club and leadership skills in one university
一个英语俱乐部和大学生活中的领导技巧

2007，陕西师大，房喻校长在出席雪莲英语俱乐部成立10周年庆典时与雪莲合影
President Fangyu attended the celebration for the 10th anniversary of the English Club with Sharon Crain, ShiDa, 2007

"How can we improve our English skills?" was a serious question asked by one of my students at ShiDa after class in 1997. Fu Wenjun was an undergraduate in the history department struggling to perfect his English. Together with Chu Guofei and a few other students they decided to established an English Club which was one of the very first student organizations allowed on ShiDa's campus. Students had no clubs at that time and no experience in organizing and running an organization on their own so this provided a way to improve skills and practice leadership responsibilities. Most students had never had these opportunities while growing up.

1997，陕西师大老校区，英语俱乐部的成员和第一任主席付文军（右起第一人）
Members of the English Club and first president Fu Wenjun (top R), established in 1997, old campus ShiDa

    1997年，一次课后，一位学生问了我一个严肃的问题："我们怎样才能提高英语水平？"付文军是历史系的本科生，正在努力提高英语水平。他和诸国飞及别的同学一起决定建立一个英文俱乐部，这是师大校园里被允许存在的第一个学生社团。那时在学生中没有这种自发的俱乐部，学生们自己在组织和管理社团方面也完全没有经验。这样英语俱乐部的建立就给学生们提供了一种实践并且提高领导技能和责任感的途径。大多数学生在他们成长的年代里没有这样的机会。

    At the beginning a small number of students met in a dimly lit building in a cold classroom to talk about how to set up a club. They began planning creative programs and innovative ways to practice and improve their English: writing and performing their own dramas and holding literary and speaking contests. They gained support from university leaders and were actually forerunners of policies later stressed in *The Action Plan for Rejuvenating Education*. Illustrating the eagerness on the part of other students to learn English it has grown to become the largest club at the university, reaching nearly 1,500 members on both campuses.

    一开始，来的学生不多，地点是在一栋昏暗大楼里的一间寒冷的教室里。大家谈论建立俱乐部的事情，计划一些实践和提高英语的创造性方法，比方说创作和表演话剧、举行写作和演讲比赛等。他们得到了学校领导的支持，而且实际上成了"教育振兴行动计划"的先驱者。俱乐部成长的本身也说明学生们学习英语的热情：现在它已成为学校最大的学生社团，两个校区的成员总数差不多有1500人。

In a similar fashion over a hundred different clubs have been founded at ShiDa by students as examples of their interest in more active participation and creative expression: fiction writing, photography, martial arts and even a club for break-dancing and one called YOB (your own beauty) to express individual ideas as student involvement flourished. Opportunities to hold leadership positions in these clubs provided new ways for students to assert responsibility and practice making decisions. They set up departments to plan activities, raise funds from local merchants and write newsletters. One officer in the English Club was even called the minister of their Department of Ideas to solicit new ideas. A small library maintained by club volunteers was established in 1998 to help expand their knowledge base while practicing reading skills with over a thousand books in English donated by Americans.

在雪莲英语俱乐部影响之下，陕西师大也相继成立了一百多个学生俱乐部，如创作、摄影、武术，甚至还有霹雳舞和"自我美"的俱乐部，这些都是学生基于兴趣而建立的组织，在那里他们的自我得到表达，成为校园里日益积极的学生参与的例子。学生们有机会在俱乐部里担任领导职务，使他们有可能用新的方式去担负责任和作出决策。他们在俱乐部里建立不同部门去规划活动、筹集资金和编写简报。英语俱乐部的一位同学甚至建立了一个"策划部"去征集新鲜的想法。1998年，一个由俱乐部志愿者管理的小小图书馆建立起来了，它被用来扩大成员们的知识积累，也用美国人捐赠的一千多本英文书来提高他们的英文阅读水平。

Follow your dreams
追随你的梦想

Another vivid example of promoting student participation was the creation of Dream-Maker Awards, initiated to recognize those who followed their dreams and worked hard for the benefit of others. To be encouraged to "follow your dreams" was a significant departure for students who had been accustomed to always following directions from parents, teachers and leaders.

另一个增加学生参与的生动例证是追梦奖的创立，以奖励那些追寻自己梦想、刻苦工作、有益于他人的人。过去，父母、老师、领导发出指示，学生只是执行，而追梦则意味着与这种昔日的模式决裂。

These two students received awards at the ceremony when the English Club planted a tree dedicated to Dream-Makers at the University. Their stories show how some students have been pursuing their own dreams in recent years. After graduation Chu Guofei went on to receive her master's and PhD degrees at Nanjing University, in collaborative work at Harvard University in the United States and became an editor of an academic publication in Beijing. Fu Wenjun received his

1999，陕西师大，付文军（左）和褚国飞都是追梦奖的获得者
Fu Wenjun (L) and Chu Guofei were two recipients of Dream Maker Awards, ShiDa, 1999

master's and is pursuing a PhD in Chinese History at FuDan University and serves on a commission to preserve historic sites in China. They are following their dreams. Not all students are experiencing these students' incredible success but when I first taught at ShiDa in the old buildings on campus not one of my students had a hint of any of these options.

在这两个学生被授予追梦奖时，雪莲英语俱乐部也在授奖仪式上种下了一棵献给得奖者的树。他们的故事表明这些年来学生们怎样追寻自己的梦想。从陕西师大毕业后，褚国飞又在南京大学拿到了硕士学位，还在那里拿到了与哈佛大学合作培养的博士学位。现在她在北京的一家学术刊物任编辑。付文军也拿到了他的硕士学位，现在复旦大学历史系攻读博士，并在一个历史遗址保护的委员会任职。他们都在追寻自己的梦。不是所有学生都像他们一样成功，但是当我第一次在陕西师大的旧教学楼里上课的时候，没人有这样的机会。

At the 10th Anniversary Celebration of Sharon English Club people gathered for creative performances; as a sign of the times the president of the university, Fang Yu, spoke in perfect English without a need for translation to an audience of a thousand students.

在雪莲英语俱乐部成立10周年的庆祝活动上，大家欢聚一堂，表演了富有创意的节目。作为一个时代的代表，房喻校长还用流利的英文为在场的一千名学生作了演讲。

2007，陕西师大，房喻校长在庆祝雪莲英语俱乐部成立10周年活动中与学生的合影
President Fang Yu joins the students in the tenth anniversary celebration of Sharon English Club, ShiDa, 2007

Pushing educational reforms to rural areas
将教育改革推向农村

From key schools to countryside
从重点学校到农村

2006，安上，拿着新书的孩子们走在泥泞的路上
Peasant children with new books along muddy roads in An Shang, 2006

The vast majority of China's huge population is still living in the countryside. Educational reforms advocate educating the masses by improving basic education in the rural and interior regions, which have been neglected while the key schools in big cities and coastal areas developed first.

中国人口的大多数还是农民。目前的教育改革强调通过改善农村和内地基础教育的方法来普及大众教育。由于以前奉行大城市和沿海地区重点学校优先发展的战略，农村教育被忽视了。

Young students (like these in An Shang village) received newly published books when revised curriculum reforms were extended to the countryside. In 1986 China enacted the nine-year compulsory education plan but it has taken time to implement in many poor regions where there have never been local schools beyond the primary school level. For many years the financial burden for education has been the responsibility of local regions and individual peasants, inflicting financial hardship. Recently tuition for primary and secondary schools was waived in the rural areas to help make it possible for children to afford to attend.

随着教育改革向农村的深入，这个名叫"安上"的小村子的小学生们得到了新书。1986年，中国开始实施九年义务教育，但对很多没有能力开设小学以上水平学校的贫困地区来说，义务教育的真正落实尚需时日。多年来教育开支已经成为地方政府和农民的经济负担，使他们的经济状况雪上加霜。最近，农村地区中小学生的学费已经取消，那里的孩子们不再为筹措学费而犯愁。

Following dreams along mountain roads
从山路上走来的追梦者

Listening to the specific dreams of young students in another rural area throws open a window to enter their world for a moment. Nestled at the foot of the Qin Ling mountain range is a tiny elementary school of Han Jiaping with only 263 students and a handful of teachers, one of the poorest in Shaanxi Province. Their hopes are vastly different from students just mentioned at Shaanxi Normal University.

听着这些农村孩子的特殊梦想，我仿佛找到了进入他们世界的窗户。韩家坪小学位于秦岭山脉，只有263名学生，教师也不多，属于陕西最为贫困的地区之一。他们的希望同上面提到的陕西师范大学的学生们大不相同。

When I asked these young students about their dreams in 2000, on the eve of the new millennium, these were some of their replies.

在进入2000年的前夜，我曾问过这些学生他们在新一年中的梦想是什么。他们这样回答：

"My dream is just to be able to attend school," this young boy said. He has difficulty walking, but wants to learn. A neighbor student helps him along the dangerous mountain road to school, two miles from his home. They also must walk home for lunch and back again, as there are no facilities for eating at the school.

"我的梦想就是能够上学。"这个小男孩说。他走路有困难,可是真的想学习。在一个朋友的帮助下,他每天徒步两英里,沿着一条曲折而危险的山路来到学校。因为学校无法提供午餐,他们中午还要回家吃饭,然后再回学校上下午的课。

One child said, "Many students have no money to go to school, no clothes to wear, even no food to eat. I dream of building a stronger school."

一个孩子说:"很多学生没钱上学,没衣服穿甚至没饭吃。我希望有一天能建一所更好的学校。"

Another ten-year old girl explained: "When I go home from school every day I practice with my older sister and brother. We don't have chalk or a blackboard or a brush, but we use a rag and the yellow earth and write on the door. We want to overcome hard things to learn."

还有一个10岁的小女孩说:"每天从学校回到家里,我都会和哥哥姐姐一起做练习。我们没有粉笔、黑板和毛笔,但可以用抹布或黄土块在门上写字。为了学习,我们什么困难都能克服。"

A shy little boy whispered, "I will tell you softly, I want to be an ordinary teacher. Some people say it is so hard. Can you bear it? I read in a book that we made development in China, but we are behind other countries. In our village there are still many students that have to give up schooling for poverty. My dad told me our country has a plan to help the interior of China, like us. I want to be a teacher and help them. Teachers have a poor life but devote their learning to their pupils. I want to be like the story of the silk worm that gives its life to make something beautiful."

一个比较内向的男孩子说:"我想跟你说一句悄悄话:我要当一名普通教师。人们说:那份工作很艰苦,你受得了吗?我在一本书里读过,中国有了很大的进步,但跟其他国家相比,我们还很落后。在我们村子里,还有很多学生因为家贫而上不起学。爸爸告诉我国家已经有了计划,要帮助那些和我们一样的内地孩子们。所以,我想当一名老师,为这项工作出一份力。教师的生活虽然苦,但他们把知识给了学生。我想像春蚕一样,把一生献给那些美好的事物。"

When I first visited the school in 2000 they had only a few bare classrooms and no library, in fact almost no books. Dedicated teachers lived in a space with just enough room for a small bed. Both rain and cold seeped in. In a cooperative effort with the school, local villagers and people in the United States a small library and several classrooms were built and dedicated at this ceremony in 2002; all the students, teachers and many parents attended. This was accomplished with the great efforts a

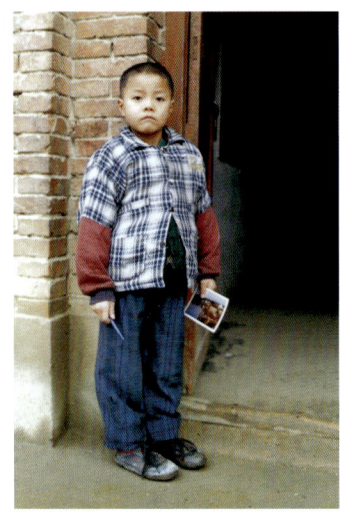 

2000，韩家坪学校的小学生　　2002，韩家坪学校的捐赠仪式
Young student at Han Jiaping School, 2000　　Dedication ceremony at Han Jiaping School, 2002

Chinese-American, Bob Chien, Chairman of the Kansas City-Xi'an Sister City Association in the United States. An Wei, Helen Snow's old friend, coordinated the project as the threads of connection continued.

2000年，当我第一次到那个学校的时候，看到的只是一些空荡荡的教室，没有图书馆，而且几乎没有书。富有奉献精神的老师住的地方刚刚够放一张小床，还到处透风。在学校、村民和一些美国友人的共同努力下，一个小图书馆和几间教室建了起来，并在2002年举行了捐赠仪式。学校的全体学生和老师及部分家长参加了仪式。美国堪萨斯-西安友好协会主席（成员）、美籍华人鲍勃·陈促成了这项善举。安危是这项善举的协调人。

China's ambitious education reforms are attempting to reach places like Han Jiaping to cultivate the potential of students who are waiting. In recent years Chinese individuals from another region donated some computers to Han Jiaping but the school lacked electricity and phone lines to utilize them. If successfully connected this could be a powerful link to knowledge beyond their remote location. Sometimes university students at ShiDa do their practice teaching or volunteer in their summer break to help students at Han Jiaping or other rural areas where they in turn learn from these young children.

中国雄心勃勃的教育改革正在试图深入到像韩家坪这样的偏远地方，使那里渴望学习的孩子们能够得到正规教育。近些年来，其他地方的中国人给这所学校捐献了电脑，可是学校不通电，也没有电话线上网。也许网络是把这些偏远山区与现代知识联结起来的有力手段。有时候陕西师范大学的学生利用暑假去韩家坪和其他山村，以志愿者或教学实习等方式来帮助那里的孩子们，同时也从山区的孩子身上学到他们在大学学不到的东西。

From famine to Fudan
从极度贫困到复旦学子

One story of another peasant shows the extraordinary changes in education within one lifetime. Liang Lijun grew up in a distressed rural area in Gansu Province. Only two or three students from his entire district of thousands of people had ever attended a university when he entered. He majored in history at Shaanxi Normal University but had a strong desire to make his own contribution in the field of economics, especially for rural areas. In 2004 he proudly earned his doctoral degree in economics from Fudan University, one of China's most outstanding schools. He went on to become a Professor of International Economics in Guangdong Province where he shares ideas with his students. Even today only a few peasants earn their PhD's but in the past this was completely impossible.

另一个农民的故事显示了一个人一生中受到教育后的巨大变化。梁立俊在贫困的甘肃农村长大。他考上大学时，他所在的数万人的地区只有两三个人读过大学。梁立俊在陕西师范大学读历史，但他渴望能在经济领域，特别是农村地区的发展方面有所贡献。2004年，他在中国一流的复旦大学获得了经济学博士学位。然后他去了广东省成为一名国际经济学专业的教授。即使今天，也只有很少的农民子弟能够获得博士学位；而在过去，这种事情绝无可能。

To help alleviate the financial burden for peasants who want to attend universities and to raise the educational level of teachers in remote and rural areas a new policy was announced in 2007. It provides for free university tuition, housing and a stipend for some students from poor areas who make a commitment to continue teaching for ten years with at least the initial two years in rural areas. Shaanxi Normal University was selected by the Ministry of Education to serve as one of six teacher-training universities in the country to implement this program. One aim of this program is to lessen the imbalance of qualified teachers in the middle and western regions of China. However one disadvantage for the students is

2000，上海，梁立俊在复旦大学
Liang Lijun at Fudan University, Shanghai, 2000

they are not allowed to pursue a Master's program, which helps insure they continue as teachers rather than selecting other careers.

  为了进一步减轻农民子弟上大学的经济负担和增加农村和边远山区教师的职业水平，2007年国家出台了一项新政策。这项政策规定，只要学生在入学前签订协议书，承诺大学毕业后连续从事教师职业十年并且至少在最初的两年里在农村地区从事教学工作，国家将为其免费提供上大学期间的学费、住房和津贴。陕西师范大学被教育部选为实施这一计划的六个师资培训大学之一。这项计划的目的之一是，降低中西部地区合格教师的不平衡状况。但是这项政策规定这些学生不能连续攻读硕士学位，目的是为了确保他们继续做教师，而不是选择其他职业。

Rising above the cornfields
农村建校

Rising above the cornfields this school offers students new options to advance beyond previous limitations in the countryside. It is the first school to go beyond the primary level in the history of An Shang village. It will take a long time for schools such as this to reach across China's vast country but unquestionably in rural and urban areas seeds are being planted in education with hopes of an exceptionally abundant harvest.

这所在农田上兴建的学校可以让本地学生就地升学。这是安上村历史上第一所中学。要使这样的学校遍及中国的广大地区还需要很长时间，但毫无疑问希望的种子正在播种。

2004，扶风县安上村，村子里的新学校
A new school for the village, An Shang village, Fu Feng County, 2004

Shifting the focus from professional to vocational
焦点转移：从正规教育到职业培训

In addition to expanding education to a broader mass of people in rural and interior areas the recent educational reforms have shifted the focus from producing a huge core of university graduates and postgraduates to addressing the urgent demand for skilled and semi-skilled workers. Simultaneous with China's economic boom peasants have been displaced when their land is used for development projects; massive numbers of workers have been laid off as inefficient state-run industries closed, and millions of migrates float into cities searching for work. Most of these individuals lack skills.

除了将教育扩大到农村和内地的广大人群外，近年来的教育改革也将重点从培养大规模的本科生和研究生转移到满足对熟练和半熟练技术工人的大量需求。由于中国经济的迅猛发展，农民的土地被大量征用，很多农民涌入城市寻找工作，而且由于很多国有企业不景气，大量工人下岗，但他们中的大多数人缺乏技术，很难找到好工作。

After years of emphasis in the 1990's on increasing the number of scholars and trained professionals the concentration now is on practical vocational and semi-skilled training programs. There exists a shortage of qualified personnel in the service industries as well as high technology jobs. China's Ministry of Education and other officials call for more government and private training programs, university adult education programs, distant learning courses and the establishment of more vocational colleges and institutes, offering on-line and on-site training. China is still lacking in social services to provide a safety needed for millions who are unemployed.

从90年代末大学的本科和研究生扩招以来，中国教育改革也开始注意职业技能和准职业技能的培训。在第三产业及高科技产业存在着对合格工作人员的大量需求。教育部和其他有关部委倡导更多的由政府或私人举办的培训计划，包括大学的成人教育、远程教育，以及建立更多的职业培训机构，提供各种各样的网上或在校培训。中国仍然缺乏为千百万失业者提供安全保障的社会服务。

One example of the dual benefits of retraining is that of Xiao Dang who fled poverty in the countryside to seek a factory job in the city to gain a small amount of money to send back to her mother far away. She worked long hours seven days a week, slept in a crowded room lined with beds and many workers but never complained for fear of losing that job and having to return to the countryside with no other options.

就业培训双方获利的一个例子是小党。小党离开了贫穷的乡村，想到城市的工厂里找一份工作，从而能够给远方的母亲寄些钱回去。她每周工作7天，每天工作很长时间，晚上就和其他工人睡在塞满一排排床的拥挤不堪的房间里，但她从不抱怨，因为她害怕丢掉工作，那样她就只好再回到农村。

A local hotel manager needed more workers, hired her and then started providing further on-site training. Realizing Xiao Dang's potential the manager invested in accounting courses for her at a vocational college and now both benefit from her new skills. She has become a valuable employee, entrusted with increased responsibility. Xiao Dang earns enough to send money to her mother and recently settled into her own apartment with her husband, whom she met in her new classes. Of course on the other hand are those who continue to be mired in miserable situations in both cities and countryside.

一个需要更多工人的旅馆经理雇佣了她，并给她提供了进一步在校培训的机会。经理认识到小党的潜力，资助她到一家职业培训学校学习会计课程，现在双方都因为她的新技能而获益。她已经成为一个被倚重的雇员，得到了信任，责任也更多了。现在小党的工资高多了，可以给母亲寄更多的钱，还在培训班上遇见了她现在的丈夫。最近两人买了房，正式安顿了下来。当然不论城市还是农村都还有很多人仍然身处逆境。

Beyond the Classroom, Learning from Other Countries
走出教室：向国外学习

Another vital element of the educational reform has been international interaction and learning from other countries.

教育改革的另一个关键因素是国际交往和向国外学习。

When I first taught at ShiDa in the 1980's it was indeed a rare occasion that a teacher was allowed to study abroad. It required considerable effort: years of patience to be recommended within their department, great difficulty to secure permission from the provincial and national government officials to attain a passport and usually a lot of "guanxi" (special connection) to make it all happen. Almost never did any of my students study in other countries, although everyone wanted to. Frequently if given the chance to leave they did not return.

80年代，我第一次在陕西师大教学时，教师被允许到海外学习是很少见的。要做到这一点要有相当的努力：首先要耐心苦熬多年，等待系上的推荐；还要克服极多困难去得到省及国家有关部门的批准，才能拿到护照；通常还要动用很多关系才能完成这一切。

虽然每个人都想出国学习，但那时我的学生中几乎没有一个人有海外学习的经历。如果有机会出去，他们通常不会回来。

Now, it is extremely common (and promoted by university officials) for faculty as well as students to gain permission to pursue research or advanced degree work abroad. Others are granted opportunities for educational exchanges, one-year study programs at universities or summer study (work) programs in the United States or within many countries around the world especially in Australia and Great Britain. Most of them return to continue their own career path in China.

现在教师和学生被允许出国做研究或攻读学位是很普通的事情，还会得到校领导的支持，也会有很多人有机会去美国或世界各地——如澳大利亚和英国——做交换学者或交换学生，通常为一年的短期项目或暑期项目。他们中大多数人会回来继续他们在中国的事业。

In addition to the university level, increased numbers of younger students are participating in a wide variety of international experiences. One vibrant example among many of these productive exchanges was with students and teachers of the Fu Xiao Elementary School directly affiliated with ShiDa.

除了大学一级的国际交往外，越来越多的中小学生正在参与到各种各样的此类活动中来。陕西师大附小学生和老师参加的交换活动就是它们中的一个范例。

2004，西安．美国公园路小学学生非常希望与师大附小的新朋友们交流
Parkway Elementary students are eager to communicate with their new friends from the Fu Xiao School, Xi'an, 2004

Fu Xiao and Parkway students exchange ideas
附小和公园路小学学生的思想交流

The Principal of the Fu Xiao Elementary School, Gao Hongjian, spoke with me in 2000 about the idea of establishing a sister school with an elementary school in the United States. They had already established a total English immersion program in a cooperative effort with Canada and were interested in providing even more international exposure for their students.

2000年，陕西师大附小校长高红健对我提起与一所美国小学建立姊妹学校的设想。陕西师大附小已经与加拿大合作开展了浸入式英语强化项目，而且有兴趣给学生们提供更多的国际交流机会。

With the enthusiastic support of the American Principal Dr. Sandi Mond and art teacher Margot Bittenbender of the Parkway Elementary School in Greenwich, Connecticut, a sister school relationship was established. Educators on both sides shared a global vision of promoting understanding, beginning with young children.

在康涅狄格州格林威治市公园路小学校长森蒂·蒙德和艺术老师马估·贝特班德的热情支持下，陕西师大附小和公园路小学建立了姊妹学校的关系。双方一致赞同增进两国人民的相互理解应该从孩子做起。

2002，西安，建立姊妹学校的签字仪式，高红健校长和森蒂·蒙德校长签字
Signing of the sister school relationship by Principals Gao Hongjian and Sandi Mond, Xi'an, 2002

Chinese students to America
中国学生在美国

The students, teachers and principals of the Fu Xiao and Parkway Schools engaged in visits to each other's schools and countries. Fu Xiao participants were introduced to new teaching methods while attending classes and later returned to implement certain elements of Parkway's writing program and Parent Teacher Association in their school in China. Both sides shared knowledge about the history and culture of their countries and useful discussions concerning comparative educational practices. Some of the most meaningful learning took place outside the classroom as they shared personal stories and developed lasting friendship. One of the Fu Xiao teachers expressed the impact of the exchange, "It made a difference in the way I interacted in the classroom with my students and with other teachers. It made a difference in my life."

陕西师大附小和公园路小学的学生、老师和校长实现了对对方学校和国家的互访。陕西师大附小的客人们上了公园路小学的课，并了解了新的教学方法。他们也了解了那里的写作课和父母-教师协会，并在回国后吸收了其中的某些元素。在这次交流活动中，双方都学到了对方国家的历史和文化，也就双方的教育实践作了有意义的讨论。他们互相交流并发展起长久的友谊，而这些极有价值的东西是在教室里无法学到的。一位陕西师大附小老师道出了这种交流的影响："它改变了我与学生和其他老师的互动方式，也改变了我的生活。"

2004，康涅狄格州麦迪逊，中国师生访问美国，包括刘建君校长、张晓侠老师和森蒂·蒙德校长在雪莲家
Chinese students and teachers visiting America, including Principal Liu Jianjun, Teacher Zhang Xiaoxia and Principal Sandi Mond at Sharon Crain's house, Madison Connecticut, 2004

American students to China
美国学生在中国

2007，户县农民欢迎美国学生
Local peasants playing traditional Shaanxi provincial music to welcome American students, Huxian, 2007

After years of fruitful exchanges between the two elementary schools the relationship expanded to the high school level. Two hundred members of the Greenwich Connecticut High School Band and fifty parents traveled to China and were warmly embraced by Fu Xiao students. The American students performed on the Great Wall in Beijing, the Concert Hall in Xi'an and the Fu Xiao School before proceeding to the high school in the rural area of Huxian where they were welcomed by local peasants playing traditional Shaanxi provincial music.

多年富有成果的交流之后，小学间的交流关系又扩展到高中层次。康涅狄格州格林威治高中管乐团的200名成员和50位父母访问了陕西师大附小，受到了学生们的热烈欢迎。这批美国学生曾在北京长城、西安音乐厅和陕西师大附小作了演奏，最后还去了户县的一所中学。在那里，本地农民用陕西地方音乐欢迎他们。

2007，美国中学乐队在户县演出
American high school band member performing in Huxian, 2007

2007，户县，中美观众观看室外演出
Americans and Chinese watching the outdoor performance, Huxian, 2007

When a sudden sand storm swirled in and threatened to ruin their performance and blow their sheet music to the wind, the Chinese students spontaneously rushed to hold the music of their new American friends. It was a special moment that brought them closer together. One 16-year-old American band member said, "Playing on the Great Wall was exhilarating but nothing in my life can ever surpass the welcome we felt from the local people."

演出期间突然大风骤起，尘土飞扬，乐谱被吹向空中，此时中国学生赶忙过来为刚从美国来的朋友抓住了乐谱。在这个时刻，他们彼此变得更为亲近。管乐团一位16岁的成员说："在长城演奏是令人非常愉快的，但没有什么能超过我们在农村演奏时受到的欢迎。"

How to communicate without words
超越语言的交流

Extensive international exchanges have taken place between students, government officials, sister-city leaders, university scholars, scientists and businessmen with official documents and unofficial agreements. However, the words of one ten-year old boy are especially poignant on how to communicate without words.

中美两国间的交流是多层次、全方位的，不但在两国学生之间，也在两国政府官员间、姊妹城市的市长间，以及大学的学者、科学家和商人们之间广泛地进行。有的是官方的正式访问，有的只是非官方的友好互动。不过，一位10岁男孩在说到怎样进行无言交流的时候特别一针见血。

When Chris Kontes from Parkway Elementary School in Connecticut returned from an exchange visit to the Fu Xiao sister school in Xi'an he said:

公园路小学的克里斯·孔德从附小访问回来时这样写道：

"When we first arrived I was overwhelmed by 2,300 cheering students welcoming us. They seemed pleased that we had traveled halfway around the world. I thought it might be difficult to communicate with the students because I don't speak Chinese. I didn't know that what I was about to experience would be one of the greatest moments of my life. By the end of our visit I realized I could communicate with them by showing respect and kindness as they showed me."

"当我们刚刚步入校园，就听到2300名孩子们欢呼起来。他们似乎为我们飞越半个地球来看他们而感到开心。我曾想，要想与那里的学生交流大概很困难，因为我不会说汉语。我真的没有想到接下来发生的事情是我这辈子经历的最棒的时刻！在离开那里的时候，我知道我们可以交流，只要我们都对彼此表现出尊敬和友善。"

Years later when a group of adults were being very critical and complaining about problems with China, Chris spoke up and said, " I think you would feel differently if you got to know some of the people personally." At age ten Chris expressed the essence of international exchange and people to people relations, regardless of age or nationality.

一些年后，当一些成年人对于中国问题采取尖锐批评和抱怨的态度时，克里斯站出来说："我认为如果你们亲自和一些中国人接触，你们就会有不同的看法。"10岁的克里斯就发现了国际交流和人民之间关系的实质，做到这一点无关年龄和民族。

Balancing the changes while moving forward
发展与变化的平衡

The far-reaching effects of the bold educational reforms on the current generation matriculating through the process are not yet to be seen but merit close observation as they have the potential for a profound impact on China's future. Primary and secondary schools as well as universities are encouraged to set their sights on academic excellence to prepare students to become innovators and leaders of the 21st century. Government officials and local leaders express concerns that they have a long Way to go.Many in remote areas are still waiting.

对亲历改革进程的这代人来说，这场有魄力的教育改革影响深远。虽然这种影响目前尚未全部看到，但却值得仔细观察，因为这代人对中国的未来具有施加深刻影响的潜力。从国家的角度看，所有的学校都应该树立长远目标，提高他们的教育品质，培养21世纪的创新者和领导人。中央和地方的领导人都知道他们还有很长的路要走。那些地处偏远的人们仍然在等待。

Deng Xiaoping led China on a course that pioneered new frontiers in blending elements of Planned economy and Market economy into a mixed economy uniquely referred to as "socialism with Chinese characteristic". Similarly President Hu Jintao and Premier Wen Jiabao are leading the country in a new educational direction blending once again elements from China's own cultural traditions with Western methodology. Both the economic and education reforms follow China's practical approach of controlled experimentation and careful balancing to discover what works for China to move forward.

邓小平领导中国走上了一条探索新途径的道路，即建成一种计划经济和市场经济兼而有之的混合经济，它的独特性被表述为"有中国特色的社会主义"。与之相似，胡锦涛主席和温家宝总理领导中国进行了一场新的教育改革，将中国的教育传统同西方的教育理念结合起来。不论是经济改革还是教育改革，走的都是中国式受控实验型的实际可行的路子，都在矛盾的两者间寻求巧妙的平衡，以发现哪条路更能将中国推向前进。

Witness to Change, after Mao to Now
亲历巨变：改革开放至今

2007，陕西师大，房喻校长参观展览
University President Fang Yu viewing the exhibition, 2007

2007，陕西师大，副校长张建祥站在我与师大工作期间的五任校长的合影前
University Vice President Zhang Jianxiang stands in front of the photos of all five Presidents of ShiDa during my teaching years, ShiDa, 2007

2007，陕西师大，陕西师范大学图书馆馆长傅绍良和黄英（外事处前副处长）在展览会上
Director of the Library Fu Shaoliang and Huang Ying (former Deputy Director of the International Programs Office) at the exhibition, 2007

2007，陕西师大，妇女文化博物馆馆长屈雅君（展览的负责人）和馆长助手马聪敏博士
Qu Yajun (curator for the exhibition and Director of the Women's Culture Museum) with Dr. Ma Congmin, assistant curator, 2007

Looking back on my thirty years of connections with China I decided in 2007 to organize an exhibition to document, with photographs and words, some of the vast changes that had transformed China since the death of Mao Zedong and the opening up by Deng Xiaoping.

回顾我与中国30年的交往,我决定在2007年举办一次展览,用图片和文字记录从毛泽东去世和邓小平的改革开放以来中国社会发生的一些巨大变化。

Under the excellent guidance of the curator Qu Yajun with the support of President Fang Yu and the help of Huang Ying and many others the exhibition opened in October of 2007 at Shaanxi Normal University. Many of the people who had taught me about China for decades came together to share memories and recall the changes we had witnessed together.

在房喻校长的支持下,在妇女文化博物馆馆长屈雅君的出色指导和外事处副处长黄英及其他人的协助下,图片展于2007年10月在陕西师范大学对外展出。许多这些年来帮助我了解中国的人们都赶来和我分享这些回忆,并共同回顾这些我们曾亲眼目睹的变化。

2007,安危和雪莲站在他1985年与海伦·斯诺一起调研的照片前
An Wei stands with Sharon Crain in front of the photo of his visit and research with Helen Snow in 1985, ShiDa, 2007

One person who attended the exhibition said, "When I saw your photos of 1977 I was deeply moved. I was only a young boy then and the most unforgettable experience was that I was starving all day long. My experience indicates the condition of China at that time. Because of the open door policy everything changed."

一个参观了展览的人说："看到1977年的那些照片时，我被深深地感动了。那时我只是个小孩子，最难忘的就是整天挨饿。我的经历可以反映当时中国的境况，然而对外开放的政策改变了一切。"

One of the students said to me, "I was too young to have seen what you saw, but I am proud of how much progress my country has made."

一个学生跟我说："我太年轻，所以没有能够目睹你经历的巨变，但我为我的国家取得这样巨大的成就而自豪。"

After the exhibition, the idea was formulated to expand the photographs and text into a book, keeping the same threefold aim: first, to present an overview of some of the changes that have taken place during the past thirty years, beginning in 1977 with the "reform and opening up" period; second, to illustrate the complexity of balancing the benefits and burdens resulting from those changes, and third to create awareness of the magnitude of current educational reforms as a forecast of future changes in China. That is what I have tried to do within this book (my visual diary) entitled *Witness to Change: After Mao to Now*.

图片展之后，把图片和文字整理成册出书的想法也随之产生。其目的有三个：第一，全面回顾"改革开放"以来30年所发生的一些重大变化；第二，展示由这些变化导致的将问题和成就加以平衡时的复杂性；第三，了解当前进行的教育改革的重要性，并预测中国的未来发展。这些就是我在这本题为《亲历巨变——一位美国女性眼中的当代中国》的书（我的视觉日记）中想做的事。

Reflecting on my own involvement I am reminded of China's rich cultural heritage as the oldest continuous civilization in the world. My journey of thirty or so years is truly just a glimpse into a limited but remarkable period of time. China has changed and so have I in the process. I remain indebted to all who shared their lives with me along the way so that for a brief meaningful moment I could view China through their eyes.

回顾在中国生活工作的这些年，我深深感受到作为世界最古老文明的中国的丰富文化遗产。我这30多年在中国的经历只是对这一重大时期的有限一瞥。在这个进程中，中国改变了，我也改变了。我对那些与我分享他们的故事，从而使我在一个短暂而又重大的历史时刻可以透过他们的眼睛观察中国的人们表示真诚的感谢。

What a wonderful miracle if only we could look through each other's eyes for an instant.

Henry David Thoreau

如果有一瞬间我们可以参透彼此的眼神，那将是多么不可思议的奇迹！

——亨利·戴维·梭罗

Acknowledgments

致谢

First I want to thank my mother and father for instilling in me a love of learning from other people around the world and then thank all of the students, teachers and many friends in China (half way around the world) for sharing their hopes and fears and dreams with me. My understanding of China and indeed my life has been enriched by their stories and their love. My deepest appreciation goes to my husband, C. William Crain who has encouraged me to teach and learn in China and then to record some of that in my visual diary to share with others. My gratitude embraces all of my children and grandchildren whom I often left as I went off to China but carried their support with me.

首先，我要感谢我的父母，是他们从我幼年起就教导我要向世界各国人民学习；我还要感谢所有我在中国的学生、老师和朋友与我分享他们的希望、畏惧和梦想，他们的故事和他们的爱加深了我对中国的了解，同时也丰富了我的生活。我把最深切的谢意送给我的丈夫威廉·柯雷，是他鼓励我到中国任教游学，记录我的影像日记并与他人分享。同时我还要感谢支持我远赴中国而被疏忽的孩子和孙子们。

Two precious friends who have been absolutely invaluable are Professor Vera Schwarcz, who provided the inspiration for encouraging me to write and shares my passion for China and Dr. Barbara Nicholas who was my editor for corrections but also provided immeasurable guidance.

我有两位极为重要的朋友，舒衡哲教授鼓励我写作并与我分享对中国的挚爱之情；本书草稿编校芭芭拉·尼古拉斯博士为我提供了不可估量的指导。

I remain indebted to President Fang Yu of Shaanxi Normal University for allowing me to teach at his university and continue my quest to understand China. I greatly admire his global vision and appreciate his support for the publication of this book. I am grateful for the support and capable assistance of Sun Binghong, director of the President's Office at the University and Li Weidong, director of the Communications Center.

我要衷心感谢陕西师范大学校长房喻先生邀我任教，以实现我深入了解中国的追求，我非常钦佩他的全球视野，感谢他对本书出版的支持。同时，感谢陕西师范大学校办主任孙冰红先生、新闻中心主任李卫东先生对本书出版的支持。

I offer my sincere thanks to Gao Jingwei, manager of the Shaanxi Normal University Press and Lei Yongli, vice manager for their outstanding work. I am especially appreciative to Zeng Xuemin as the excellent and talented editor in chief of the Shaanxi Normal University Press for his expertise in the publication of this book, and to the others who worked with him to make it possible.

衷心感谢陕西师范大学出版社社长高经纬先生和副社长雷永利先生对本书出版的大力支持。同时，我要特别感谢为本书出版提供专业指导、付出辛勤工作和智慧的陕西师范大学出版社出色的编辑曾学民先生，以及和他一起为本书出版工作的同事们。

Also at the very top of the list, deserving of my utmost gratitude is Professor Wu Jin who served as my translator. His careful attention to words, meaning and linguistic nuances allowed me to communicate in Chinese as well as English. I so appreciate all of his work.

此外，我要极力感谢本书的翻译吴进教授。他对文字、词义以及润色的细致，使我不仅能够用英语而且能够用汉语交流，我对他所做的工作十分感激。

From the very beginning of my photo exhibition in Xi'an, 2007 and throughout the entire development of this visual diary I have relied on the cheerful willingness and excellent capabilities of Li Siyuan to carry out innumerable tasks. I could not have done either without his help.

从西安2007年摄影展到《亲历巨变——一位美国女性眼中的当代中国》这本书的出版，李思远做了不可胜数的工作，他任劳任怨，不辞劳苦，展现了他卓越的才干。没有他的帮助我这本书也不可能出版。

I am forever grateful to An Wei and Niu Jianhua for their friendship and for opening doors of understanding for me and for our two countries for many decades.

我会永远珍惜与安危和牛剑华之间的友谊，几十年来是他们开启了我了解中国以及我们两个国家相互了解的大门。

There are many others who have provided valuable guidance, expertise and inspiration along the way to whom I owe my great thanks including Miao Niya, Janet Luongo and Patrick Dowdey curator of my photo exhibition at Wesleyan University's Mansfield Freeman Center for East Asian Studies.

在本书出版的过程中还有许多朋友为我提供了宝贵指导、专业知识和灵感。他们是苗妮娅、珍妮特·罗恩哥和我在美国维斯大学曼斯菲尔德·弗里曼东亚研究中心图片展的策展人潘特立，我要向他们表示诚挚的谢意。

Sharon Crain　雪莲